"I enjoy reading Phil Moore's b[...]
the Christian life with per[...]
– *Nicky* [...]

"In taking us straight to the he[...]
served us magnificently. We so need to get into the Scriptures and let the Scriptures get into us. The fact that Phil writes so relevantly and with such submission to biblical revelation means that we are genuinely helped to be shaped by the Bible's teaching."

**– Terry Virgo**

"Fresh. Solid. Simple. Really good stuff."

**– R. T. Kendall**

"Phil makes the deep truths of Scripture alive and accessible. If you want to grow in your understanding of each book of the Bible, then buy these books and let them change your life!"

**– P. J. Smyth**, GodFirst Church, Johannesburg, South Africa

"Most commentaries are dull. These are alive.
Most commentaries are for scholars. These are for **you**!"

**– Canon Michael Green**

"These notes are amazingly good. Phil's insights are striking, original, and fresh, going straight to the heart of the text and the reader! Substantial yet succinct, they bristle with amazing insights and life applications, compelling us to read more. Bible reading will become enriched and informed with such a scintillating guide. Teachers and preachers will find nuggets of pure gold here!"

**– Greg Haslam**, Westminster Chapel, London, UK

"The Bible is living and dangerous. The ones who teach it best are those who bear that in mind – and let the author do the talking. Phil has written these studies with a sharp mind and a combination of creative application and reverence."

**– Joel Virgo,** Leader of Newday Youth Festival

*"Phil Moore's new commentaries are outstanding: biblical and passionate, clear and well-illustrated, simple and profound. God's Word comes to life as you read them, and the wonder of God shines through every page."*

**– Andrew Wilson**, Author of Incomparable *and* If God Then What?

*"Want to understand the Bible better? Don't have the time or energy to read complicated commentaries? The book you have in your hand could be the answer. Allow Phil Moore to explain and then apply God's message to your life. Think of this book as the Bible's message distilled for everyone."*

**– Adrian Warnock**, *Christian blogger*

*"Phil Moore presents Scripture in a dynamic, accessible and relevant way. The bite-size chunks – set in context and grounded in contemporary life – really make the make the Word become flesh and dwell among us."*

**– Dr David Landrum**, *The Bible Society*

*"Through a relevant, very readable, up to date storying approach, Phil Moore sets the big picture, relates God's Word to today and gives us fresh insights to increase our vision, deepen our worship, know our identity and fire our imagination. Highly recommended!"*

**– Geoff Knott**, *former CEO of Wycliffe Bible Translators UK*

*"What an exciting project Phil has embarked upon! These accessible and insightful books will ignite the hearts of believers, inspire the minds of preachers and help shape a new generation of men and women who are seeking to learn from God's Word."*

**– David Stroud**, *Newfrontiers and ChristChurch London*

For more information about the Straight to the Heart series, please go to **www.philmoorebooks.com**.
You can also receive daily messages from Phil Moore on Twitter by following **@PhilMooreLondon**.

STRAIGHT TO
THE HEART OF

# Hebrews
# and
# James

## 60 BITE-SIZED INSIGHTS

# Phil Moore

MONARCH
BOOKS

Oxford, UK & Grand Rapids, Michigan, USA

Published by Monarch Books
an imprint of
**Lion Hudson plc**
Wilkinson House, Jordan Hill Road,
Oxford OX2 8DR, England
Email: monarch@lionhudson.com
www.lionhudson.com/monarch

ISBN 978 0 85721 668 7
e-ISBN 978 0 85721 682 3

First edition 2015

**Acknowledgments**
Scripture quotations taken from the *Holy Bible, New International Version* Anglicised. Copyright © 1979, 1984, 2011 Biblica, formerly International Bible Society. Used by permission of Hodder & Stoughton Ltd, an Hachette UK company. All rights reserved. "NIV" is a registered trademark of Biblica. UK trademark number 1448790. Both 1984 and 2011 versions are quoted in this commentary.

A catalogue record for this book is available from the British Library.

Printed and bound in the UK, May 2015, LH26

*This book is for any Jew or Gentile*
*who dares to believe the Gospel promise that, in Jesus,*
*something far better has come.*

# CONTENTS

*About the* Straight to the Heart *Series*                9

Introduction: Something Far Better Has Come          11

## PART ONE – JAMES: A BETTER WAY OF LIVING

Synagogue Sermons (1:1)                              16

Better than Solomon (1:2–11)                         21

Soap-on-a-Rope (1:12–18)                             26

Words of Life and Death (1:18–27)                    30

Uncorrupted Religion (1:27)                          34

Brothers and Sisters (2:1–7)                         38

Law-Breakers (2:8–13)                                43

Faith Which Works (2:14–26)                          47

Mightier than the Sword (3:1–12)                     52

Angels and Demons (3:13–4:3)                         57

How to Make God Your Enemy (4:4–17)                  62

Prime the Pump (4:7–10)                              67

Rich Pickings (4:13–5:6)                             71

Oblias (5:7–11)                                       75

Everyday Church (5:12–16)                            79

Camel Knees (5:16–20)                                84

## PART TWO – HEBREWS 1–7: A BETTER GLIMPSE OF GOD

Twenty Years Later (1:1)                             90

Better than Angels (1:1–14)                          94

What Jesus Hates (1:9)                               99

Warning Sirens (2:1–4)                               103

Down and Up (2:5–18)      108

In Our Shoes (2:5–18)      112

Better than Moses (3:1–6)      116

Don't Miss the Point (3:7–19)      120

God's Detonator (4:1–2)      125

Take a Rest (4:1–13)      129

The Ultimate Hero (4:8)      133

A Threat and a Promise (4:12–13)      137

Wartime Letter (4:14–5:10)      142

The Temptation of Christ (4:15)      146

Why Doesn't God Always Heal? (5:7)      150

Third Warning (5:11–6:12)      154

Basic Christianity (6:1–2)      158

Justice (6:10)      162

The Patience of a Saint (6:11–20)      166

The Priest Who Was King (7:1–28)      170

What Is Jesus Doing Now? (7:25)      174

## PART THREE – HEBREWS 8–10: A BETTER WAY TO KNOW GOD

All Change (8:1–13)      180

No More Camping (9:1–12)      184

Men Who Stare at Goats (9:13–28)      188

There Will Be Blood (9:22)      192

The Final Taboo (9:26–28)      196

Blood Donor (10:1–18)      200

Real Worship (10:19–25)      204

Blood Diamond (10:26–39)      208

## PART FOUR – HEBREWS 11–13: BETTER REASONS TO BELIEVE

Better Reasons to Believe (11:1–3)      214

Before the Flood (11:4–7)      218

Faith Without a Home (11:8–22)      222

None Received (11:23–40) 226

Keep on Running (12:1–13) 230

Final Warning (12:14–29) 234

Tragic Figure (12:15–17) 238

Zion Has Not Fallen (12:22–24) 242

Preaching Class (12:26–29) 246

Inside-Out Love (13:1–3) 250

Pure Sex (13:4) 254

The Golden Idol (13:5–6) 258

Jesus Hasn't Changed (13:7–25) 262

Conclusion: Something Far Better Has Come 267

# About the *"Straight to the Heart"* Series

On his eightieth birthday, Sir Winston Churchill dismissed the compliment that he was the "lion" who had defeated Nazi Germany in World War Two. He told the Houses of Parliament that *"It was a nation and race dwelling all around the globe that had the lion's heart. I had the luck to be called upon to give the roar."*

I hope that God speaks to you very powerfully through the "roar" of the books in the *Straight to the Heart* series. I hope they help you to understand the books of the Bible and the message which the Holy Spirit inspired their authors to write. I hope that they help you to hear God's voice challenging you, and that they provide you with a springboard for further journeys into each book of Scripture for yourself.

But when you hear my "roar", I want you to know that it comes from the heart of a much bigger "lion" than me. I have been shaped by a whole host of great Christian thinkers and preachers from around the world, and I want to give due credit to at least some of them here:

Terry Virgo, David Stroud, Dave Holden, John Hosier, Adrian Holloway, Greg Haslam, Lex Loizides and all those who lead the Newfrontiers family of churches; friends and encouragers, such as Stef Liston, Joel Virgo, Stuart Gibbs, Scott Taylor, Nick Sharp, Nick Derbridge, Phil Whittall, and Kevin and Sarah Aires; Tony Collins, Jenny Ward, Simon Cox and Margaret Milton at Monarch Books; Malcolm Kayes and all the elders of The Coign Church,

Woking; my fellow elders and church members here at Everyday Church in London; my great friend Andrew Wilson – without your friendship, encouragement and example, this series would never have happened.

I would like to thank my parents, my brother Jonathan, and my in-laws, Clive and Sue Jackson. Dad – your example birthed in my heart the passion which brought this series into being. I didn't listen to all you said when I was a child, but I couldn't ignore the way you got up at five o' clock every morning to pray, read the Bible and worship, because of your radical love for God and for his Word. I'd like to thank my children – Isaac, Noah, Esther and Ethan – for keeping me sane when publishing deadlines were looming. But most of all, I'm grateful to my incredible wife, Ruth – my friend, encourager, corrector and helper.

You all have the lion's heart, and you have all developed the lion's heart in me. I count it an enormous privilege to be the one who was chosen to sound the lion's roar.

So welcome to the *Straight to the Heart* series. My prayer is that you will let this roar grip your own heart too – for the glory of the great Lion of the Tribe of Judah, the Lord Jesus Christ!

# Introduction: Something Far Better Has Come

*The law is only a shadow of the good things that are coming – not the realities themselves.*

(Hebrews 10:1)

When I first saw it in the museum, I tried to deny it. *Surely there must be some mistake. What can this be doing here?!* I had been enjoying my day at the museum of technology until I came to this final artefact, but this was different. It didn't belong here at all. You see, I still own a ZX Spectrum computer.

I know that the Sinclair ZX Spectrum dates all the way back to 1982, but somehow I have never been able to throw mine away. I spent too many summers as a child writing programs on its rubber keys or playing classic games such as *Manic Miner* and *Gauntlet* to accept that it belonged in a museum. But there's a reason why I am not writing this book on my ZX Spectrum. Even if its 48K memory could cope, it would be incapable of printing a book, emailing a book or saving a book onto an external hard drive. Much as I love it, I have to confess that it is an obsolete computer. Its day has long since passed, and it belongs exactly where I found it, in a museum. It was fun while it lasted, but times have changed. Something far better has now come.

Hold that thought. If you can sense how I felt when I saw my beloved computer in a museum, it will help you as you read the two New Testament letters that were written primarily for Jews.[1] Hebrews and James are not easy letters to understand,

---

[1] Matthew's gospel was also written for a primarily Jewish audience, but all of the New Testament letters except for these two were written for both Jews

but the task gets easier when we grasp something of the conflicting emotions felt by first-century Jews who decided to follow Jesus. They worried that they had betrayed their culture. They missed many of their synagogue and Temple traditions. Some of them even started drifting back to Judaism and away from Jesus. They became nostalgic, just as I was when I saw my ZX Spectrum in a museum, and they needed to be reminded that Jesus had brought in a new covenant that superseded the Jewish Law. They needed to be reminded that *"The law is only a shadow of the good things that are coming – not the realities themselves,"* and that *"By calling this covenant 'new', he has made the first one obsolete; and what is obsolete and outdated will soon disappear."*[2]

James is the oldest New Testament letter. We can tell that he wrote it before 49 AD because Acts 15 tells us he played a crucial role that year in the Council of Jerusalem, and it is inconceivable that he would have written afterwards without mentioning the seismic decisions that the Council made. He therefore wrote the letter in 48 AD, or perhaps slightly earlier, in order to address the concerns of the earliest Jewish Christians. He warned them not to base their lifestyle on their Jewish culture but, instead, to base it on the teachings of the Jewish Messiah.[3] The format of the letter deliberately mimics the format of the Old Testament book of Proverbs, as James urges his readers not to cling to a ZX Spectrum lifestyle. In Jesus, something far better has come.

James addresses his letter to *"the twelve tribes scattered among the nations."* He refers to their churches as *synagogues* and to their Lord as *Yahweh Sabaoth*.[4] He refers frequently to the

---

and Gentiles.

[2] Hebrews 8:13; 10:1.

[3] We will see later how much James echoes Jesus' teaching in the Sermon on the Mount in Matthew 5–7.

[4] He calls Christian meetings *synagogues* in 2:2. He refers to God as *kurios sabaōth* in 5:4, a Greek form of the Hebrew name *Yahweh Tsabāōth*, meaning *Lord of Armies* or *Lord Almighty*. It is used throughout the Greek Septuagint

Jewish Law and draws heavily from the Jewish Scriptures, using Old Testament characters to teach a new way of living. He wins over his countrymen as he deals firmly with their nostalgia and their reluctance to embrace the fact that a better day has come.

Hebrews was one of the last New Testament letters to be written. Although we do not know who wrote it, we can tell that they were Jewish and that they wrote it after Paul's final letter in early 67 AD and before the destruction of Jerusalem in 70 AD.[5] Whereas James addressed Jews who believed the Christian Gospel but were tempted to compromise on lifestyle, the writer of Hebrews addresses Jews in a more dangerous position. A wave of fierce persecution has caused many of them to drift away from Christian meetings and back towards the Jewish synagogues. He is appalled and warns them that they are in danger of turning their backs on the Gospel. Having started out with Jesus, they have started to side with the Sanhedrin who crucified him. They are like a person who is duped into exchanging a supercomputer for a Sinclair ZX Spectrum.

**James** assumes that we understand the Gospel. He is very practical, spelling out how Jesus shows us **a better way of living**. Hebrews makes no such assumption. It drills down deep into the Gospel, explaining how Jesus fulfilled the hope of Israel through his death and resurrection.[6] **Hebrews 1–7** explains how Jesus has given us **a better glimpse of God**. **Hebrews 8–10** explains how Jesus has opened up **a better way to know God**. This leads to a call in **Hebrews 11–13** for us to surrender everything and follow him, for he has given us **better reasons to believe**. These two letters are challenging to read if we

---

but only twice in the New Testament – here and in a quote from the Septuagint in Romans 9:29.

[5] We will discuss the date of Hebrews in much more detail later. Paul would have mentioned Timothy's imprisonment (13:23), and the writer of Hebrews would have mentioned the destruction of the Temple.

[6] James never uses the words *cross*, *crucify*, *blood* or *resurrection*. Hebrews uses the words 26 times.

know little about the Old Testament, but their message is even more challenging when we understand the background. Their teaching is not easy. Making radical changes to the way we think and live never is. These two letters made the Jewish Christians struggle far more than I did when I saw my ZX Spectrum in a museum.

If you are Jewish, you badly need to understand the message of these two letters. If you are a Gentile, you badly need to understand their message too. Nobody can fully understand the story of *The Lord of the Rings* trilogy unless they understand the story of *The Hobbit*, which went before. Nobody can fully understand the original *Star Wars* movies unless they understand the three prequels. In the same way, nobody can fully understand the story of Jesus and the Church unless they first see the thirty-nine books of the Old Testament through New Testament eyes. That's why Hebrews has been nicknamed "the fifth gospel": it explains who Jesus is in both the Old and New Testaments. That's also why James has been nicknamed "the Proverbs of the New Testament": it shows us how to walk according to the wisdom of Israel's Messiah.

So ask God to speak to you as we travel together through these two letters, which are essential reading for any Christian, whether Jew or Gentile. Ask God to open your eyes to areas where you are still clinging to ZX Spectrum thinking and to a ZX Spectrum lifestyle. Ask him to help you to consign what is obsolete to a museum. Ask him to help you to grasp that something far better has come.

# Part One:

# A Better Way of Living

## (James)

# Synagogue Sermons (1:1)

*James, a servant of God and of the Lord Jesus
Christ.*

(James 1:1)

Everybody knew who James was. He needed no introduction.
Two of Jesus' twelve disciples were called James, but Peter felt
no need to clarify which James he meant when he told the early
Jewish Christians in Acts 12:17 to *"Tell James and the other
brothers and sisters about this."*[1] James was the half-brother
of Jesus, the son of Joseph and Mary, who became an apostle
and the leading elder of the church in Jerusalem. Acts tells us
that he led the influential church in the Jewish mother city,
and Paul describes him as one of its pillars.[2] James needs no
lengthy introduction at the start of his letter because everybody
knew who he was. He was the man who spoke for Jewish
Christianity.[3]

In the first century, more Jews lived outside the borders
of Israel than lived in Israel itself. Philo of Alexandria tells us
that there were more Jews in his Egyptian city than in the whole
of Judea. These expatriate Jews were known as the *Diaspora
Jews* or *Scattered Jews*, and they would travel back to Jerusalem

[1] He said this in 44 AD, just after the execution of one of the two disciples
named James. Despite the death of this James being headline news, Peter felt
no need to clarify which James he meant. Everybody knew.

[2] See Galatians 1:19; 2:9, 12; Acts 15:13; 21:18; Matthew 13:55; Mark 6:3.
Jude was another half-brother of Jesus, but his full brother was so well known
that he refers to himself as *"a brother of James"* in Jude 1.

[3] Although James led the Jerusalem church through a team of elders (Acts
21:18), he writes in his own name rather than in the name of his team. He was
evidently the major preaching voice in the church.

for major festivals at the Temple.[4] They therefore came into contact with the church that James led in the city and were exposed to some of his preaching. James evidently felt a sense of responsibility towards them because he addresses his letter *"to the twelve tribes scattered among the nations."*[5] He sent them a collection of his sermon highlights, perhaps inspired by the prophecy in Isaiah 2:3: *"The law will go out from Zion, the word of the Lord from Jerusalem."* If his letter feels disjointed, it is because he turned his sermons in the Jewish capital into a letter to the Jewish Christians who were scattered across the world.

That's one of the reasons why this letter is so valuable. The book of Acts does not tell us what was preached in early Christian meetings. Most of the sermons it records were delivered to crowds of unbelievers or as legal defences before judges. The church that James led changed the whole world, so it is an enormous privilege to be invited to feast on the same diet that made it strong. This collection of highlights from James' sermons teaches us how to live in light of the fact that the Jewish Messiah has come.

James saw a clear difference between Christian preaching and the sermons that were delivered in the Jewish synagogues. In Acts 15, he pointed out to the Council of Jerusalem that the pagans had not been converted in large numbers despite the fact that *"The law of Moses has been preached in every city from the earliest times and is read in the synagogues on every Sabbath."* James argued that a different type of preaching was needed, and this letter shows us what type of preaching he had in mind. We

---

[4] Acts 2:5–12; 8:27. James uses the Greek word *diaspora* in 1:1, a word which came from the Greek Septuagint translation of Deuteronomy 28:25 and Psalm 147:2. It was first used to describe the Jews who went into exile in Assyria and Babylon in the eighth and sixth centuries BC.

[5] The name James is our translation of the Greek name for *Jacob*. As a fluent Greek-speaker from *"Galilee of the Gentiles"* (Isaiah 9:1), James acts like a father to the 12 tribes of Israel scattered across the Greek world.

need to study it because much modern preaching is what James would dismiss as a synagogue sermon.

Synagogue sermons preach morality from God's Law. Christian sermons preach Jesus as the fulfilment of God's Law. Synagogue sermons urge people to do good works in order to please God. Christian sermons tell people that God is already pleased with them through Jesus and that he will enable them to do the good works he has prepared for them to do.[6] Synagogue sermons are focused on ourselves. Christian sermons are focused on Jesus. Since this letter is a compressed collection of practical applications from many sermons, James does not use the name of Jesus frequently, but all of his teaching proceeds from his opening statement. James tells us that the Christian lifestyle which he preaches stems from the fact he is *"a servant of God and of the Lord Jesus Christ"* – or, more literally, from the fact he is *"a slave of Jesus the Messiah, God and Lord."*[7]

Those are remarkable words. James used to laugh at his half-brother and to call him mad for telling people that he was Israel's long-awaited Messiah. His mocking scepticism changed in a moment when Jesus appeared to him after his resurrection and confirmed that he truly was the Messiah.[8] All of the practical teaching in this letter was inspired by what he saw. James discarded his old way of thinking like an obsolete ZX Spectrum and began proclaiming that Jesus is the God of the Old Testament and the Messiah of Israel.

James shows us that Christian preaching demands that people undergo a similar revolution in their thinking. He

---

[6] See Ephesians 2:10. Certain scholars seek to emphasize the difference between James' and Paul's teaching, but this is ridiculous. Paul emphasizes in Galatians 2:1–10 that he preaches the exact same Gospel as James.

[7] The Greek word *kurios* was used throughout the Greek Septuagint translation of the Hebrew Scriptures to translate *Yahweh*, or *the Lord*. This was therefore a revolutionary statement in the mouth of any Jew.

[8] Mark 3:21, 31–35; John 7:3–5; 1 Corinthians 15:7; Acts 1:14. The *James* mentioned by Paul cannot be one of the disciples, since Paul already mentioned the Twelve two verses earlier.

reinterprets the entire Old Testament for his Jewish readers in view of the fact that their Messiah has come. In just five chapters, he refers to the Law ten times, quotes directly from the Old Testament at least five times and offers Christian commentary on the lives of Solomon, Cain, Abraham, Rahab, Job and Elijah. Preaching from the Old Testament that could be delivered just as easily in a Jewish synagogue is not Christian. It must always proclaim that something far better has come.

James told the Council of Jerusalem that synagogue sermons are powerless to save anyone. He called Christian leaders to preach a different kind of message in their churches. It is therefore no coincidence that the New Testament contains highlights from his preaching in Jerusalem to show us what he means. In this short letter, James teaches us how to preach so passionately about Jesus that we provoke a change of lifestyle in those who hear. It isn't enough for us to make people nod their heads that Jesus is the Messiah. We need to make them get out of their seats and live in the good of it.

James captures our attention with strange paradoxes, vivid metaphors,[9] rhetorical questions and imaginary conversations.[10] In just 108 verses, he uses almost sixty Greek imperatives to issue strong commands, for his sermons to the church in Jerusalem were not meandering essays, like the synagogue sermons that are described in Matthew 7:28–29. He uses strong language to grab his listeners by the lapels and to plead with them to surrender everything to Jesus while they still can.[11] James shows us that Christian preaching always calls

---

[9] Some startling paradoxes can be found in 1:2, 2:13, 2:19, 2:25, 3:1, 3:8, 4:10, 5:5 and 5:11. Some vivid metaphors can be found in 1:6, 1:11, 1:14, 1:18, 1:23, 1:26, 2:26, 3:3–8, 3:11–12, 3:18, 4:1–2, 4:14, 5:2–3 and 5:7.

[10] Rhetorical questions can be found in 2:4, 2:5, 2:6, 2:7, 2:14–16, 2:20, 2:21, 2:25, 3:11–12, 3:13, 4:1, 4:4, 4:5, 4:12 and 4:15. Imaginary conversations can be found in 2:14, 2:18 and 5:13–14.

[11] James uses surprisingly harsh language to capture his listeners' attention in 2:20, 4:4, 4:8 and 5:1–6.

for a radical decision and for urgent action. If Jesus is truly Lord, boring preaching is a crime against heaven.

James shows us some of the preaching that made the Early Church so strong, but make no mistake, he also wants to call us to urgent action of our own. He wants to convince us that the arrival of the Messiah has changed everything. Jesus has brought a better way of living.

# Better Than Solomon
## (1:2–11)

*If any of you lacks wisdom, you should ask God, who
gives generously.*

(James 1:5)

There had once been a time when people came from every
nation to Jerusalem in order to hear the wisdom of Israel's God.
The Queen of Sheba exclaimed to Solomon, *"How happy your
people must be! How happy your officials, who continually stand
before you and hear your wisdom!"* We are told that *"The whole
world sought audience with Solomon to hear the wisdom God
had put in his heart."*[1] Living as they did in foreign lands, the
Diaspora Jews often longed to recapture those heady days back
in the golden age of Israel.

Nowadays things were very different for them. The
pagans wanted nothing from the Jews except their silence. The
Emperor Tiberius had found their religion so distasteful that
he expelled them from Rome in 19 AD. They returned, but the
Emperor Claudius banned them in 41 AD from holding any
religious meetings, expelling them from Rome for a second time
in 49 AD.[2] It helps if we understand this when James begins
his letter by telling his readers to persevere under trials. He
reassures them that Jesus will grant them an eternal reward for
their suffering and that he will grant them the same wisdom as

---

[1] 1 Kings 4:34; 10:8, 24.

[2] The ban on Jewish meetings in 41 AD is recorded by Cassius Dio in his
*Roman History* (60.6.6). The expulsion of the Jews in 49 AD is recorded in Acts
18:2 and by Suetonius in his *Life of Claudius* (25).

Solomon. During the golden age of Israel, the Queen of Sheba envied Solomon's servants for being able to stand before him and hear his wisdom, but Jesus has begun a better golden age in which we can each receive heaven's wisdom for ourselves.

In verses 2–4, James encourages us to do more than endure trials. He commands us to enjoy them![3] This is surprising until we think back to the life of Solomon. His father David only learned how to rule over Israel by suffering as a forgotten shepherd-boy and as a fugitive outlaw. He only learned how to conquer giants by warding off attacks on his sheep from lions and bears. Solomon only learned how to reign in his place by suffering exile with him during Absalom's rebellion and by needing to deal firmly with his father's enemies in his early days as king.[4] James reminds us that trials exercise our faith, that strengthened faith enables us to persevere and that perseverance produces godly character. He reminds us in verse 12 that our joyful attitude towards suffering is therefore a demonstration of our love for Jesus. We may be surrounded by temporary troubles,[5] but they are earning us an eternal victory crown from the nail-pierced hands of the Saviour for whom we suffer.[6]

In verses 5–8, James encourages us to ask God for the same wisdom that he gave to Solomon. We are told in 1 Kings 3 that Solomon began his reign by offering blood sacrifices at the Tabernacle and by asking the Lord to grant him *"a wise*

---

[3] The Greek word *hēgeomai* in 1:2 is also used for *considering* the true worth of things in Acts 26:2, Philippians 2:3, 2:6 and 3:7–8, and Hebrews 11:11 and 11:26. The Greek word *dokimion* in 1:3 is only used in one other place in the New Testament: in 1 Peter 1:7, which also promises an eternal reward for the *testing* of our faith.

[4] 1 Samuel 16:11, 17:28 and 17:34–37, and 1 Kings 1:1–2:46.

[5] The Greek word *peripiptō* in 1:2 means *to fall and be surrounded*. Trials surround us but so does God's love.

[6] Like most first-century Christian writers, James speaks a lot about the Christian hope of life beyond the grave. The Greek word *stephanos* was used to refer to the *victory crowns* awarded to successful athletes at the Olympic Games. The same word is used in 1 Corinthians 9:25, 2 Timothy 4:8, 1 Peter 5:4 and Revelation 2:10.

*and discerning heart."* The pagans flocked to hear him because his prayer was answered. God responded to his faith by filling him with the Holy Spirit, whom Scripture calls *"the Spirit of Wisdom."*[7] We can expect to receive this Spirit too if we put our faith in a better blood sacrifice than those offered by Solomon. Although these verses do not come from the same sermon as the one about *"lacking anything"* in verses 2–4, James links them together because pressure shows us that we *"lack wisdom."* James therefore makes these opening verses an echo of wisdom's call in Proverbs 1–9. He tells us to believe that the Gospel means that *"Christ Jesus... has become for us wisdom from God."*[8]

Jesus offered a better blood sacrifice than the ones Solomon offered at the Tabernacle. It removed the sin which stood against us and granted us access to the blessings of heaven. The Lord finds no fault in those he has forgiven and never reproaches us for asking him to be generous towards us.[9] If we believe in Jesus without any of the double-minded doubting which almost drowned Peter when he tried to walk on the stormy sea, we will receive the great Old Testament promise: we will be filled with the Spirit of Wisdom.[10] The Lord will grant us the wisdom of Solomon and will convince the unbelievers around us that Jesus brings a far better way of living.[11]

In verses 9–11, James encourages us not to throw away

---

[7] Deuteronomy 34:9; Isaiah 11:2; Acts 6:3; Ephesians 1:17. See also James 3:13–17.

[8] James echoes Proverbs 2:1–6, and Paul echoes James in 1 Corinthians 1:24 and 30, and Colossians 2:2–3.

[9] James calls him literally *"The Giving God"*, because he never taunts us. Jesus never rebuked anyone for asking too much in faith. He told us simply to ask, seek and knock to receive the Spirit of Wisdom (Luke 11:9–13).

[10] Compare 1:6 with Matthew 14:22–33. Although James does not teach much explicitly about how to be filled with the Holy Spirit, he focuses on the importance of our being filled in the opening verses of his letter.

[11] James also warns against double-minded dithering in 4:8. Faith means believing that heavenly facts trump earthly ones. If we give equal weight to both, we cannot expect to receive anything from the Lord.

this gift of wisdom, as Solomon did. The first half of Solomon's reign was a golden age for Israel, but the second half was most definitely not. His riches went to his head and he made marriage alliances with every rich and powerful ruler in the region. He ignored his own advice in Proverbs and married pagan women who drew him away from the Lord and into the arms of their idols. God had offered long life to Solomon if he followed him, but he died aged fifty-eight and his kingdom was quickly torn in two. James therefore tells Christians to rejoice in their poverty. Jesus promises us in the Sermon on the Mount that earthly poverty helps us to cry out to God for heaven's power.[12] Rich Christians must therefore be careful. They must remember the Old Testament warnings that this life only lasts for a moment, like a wild flower which quickly withers in the sun and dies.[13] As Christians, we do not live for fleeting earthly fame and fortune. We live for the riches of heaven as we walk in the footsteps of a poor and humble carpenter.

Many readers struggle with the way James lurches from one subject to another throughout his letter. He does this partly because his letter contains highlights from so many sermons, but he also does it as a deliberate echo of the Old Testament book of Proverbs, which also lurches from one topic to another in order to emphasize that wisdom must govern all of life, and that life never fits into our neat and tidy categories. James wants us to understand that faith in Jesus is the same. It means far more than simply asking for our sins to be forgiven. It means embracing a completely new lifestyle as we follow him.

James wants us to remember Jesus' warning: *"The Queen of the South will rise at the judgment with this generation and condemn it; for she came from the ends of the earth to listen to*

---

[12] See Matthew 5:3. This letter echoes the Sermon on the Mount over 20 times. Compare 1:22, 2:5, 2:14, 3:10–12, 3:18, 5:2–3 and 5:12 with Matthew 7:24–27, 5:3, 7:21–23, 7:15–20, 5:9, 6:19–20 and 5:33–37.

[13] Job 14:2; Psalm 37:1–2, 35–36; 90:5–6; 103:15; Isaiah 40:6–7.

*Solomon's wisdom, and now one greater than Solomon is here."*[14] He wants us to grasp that Jesus has begun a far better golden age for Israel. We are not just called to marvel at the wisdom of Jesus. We are called to ask him to fill us with the Spirit of Wisdom and to teach us a far better way of living than that of Solomon.

---

[14] Matthew 12:42. The "Queen of the South" is the Queen of Sheba.

# Soap-on-a-Rope (1:12–18)

*Don't be deceived, my dear brothers and sisters.*
*Every good and perfect gift is from above.*

(James 1:16–17)

The American comedian Bill Cosby observed that *"Fatherhood is pretending the present you love most is soap-on-a-rope."* If you are a parent, you know that it is true. At Christmas and birthdays, parents pretend to love every present that their little children give them. The courtesy is seldom returned. Children say exactly how they feel, and the Jewish Christians did not hesitate to complain to their heavenly Father about the trials he was giving them. James needed to take them back to the start of their Old Testament Scriptures in order to teach them that God never gives his children soap-on-a-rope.

Adam and Eve had two sons named Cain and Abel. We are told in Genesis 4 that Cain tried to impress God with the works of his hands, just like the pagans who brought offerings to their idols in the cities of the Roman Empire. His younger brother Abel was far godlier. He offered firstborn lambs from his flock as a blood sacrifice to the Lord. Thousands of years before the arrival of the Jewish Messiah, he refused to trust in his own hands to save him and instead put his faith in a prophetic picture of the cross of Jesus. Cain is the villain and Abel is the hero, but the story refuses to play by our rules. There is no happy ending. Cain gets angry and murders his younger brother. Abel becomes the first ever martyr for the Gospel.

The early Christians felt as though they were re-enacting the story of Cain and Abel. One of their leaders, Stephen, embodied the teaching of the first verses of James. He was *"a man full of faith and of the Holy Spirit"* whose enemies *"could not stand up against the wisdom the Spirit gave him as he spoke"*, yet he was brutally murdered by the unbelieving Jews in Jerusalem. Many of the Diaspora Jews were living in pagan lands because they had been forced to flee their homes during the fierce persecution that broke out after his death. One of the apostles who stayed behind was executed by Herod.[1] How could James therefore command them to view their trials as *"nothing but joy"*?[2]

In verse 12, James explains: this life is only part of the story. Abel died but Jesus commended his sacrifice thousands of years later, hailing him as the earliest prophet. The writer of Hebrews tells us that his innocent blood still prophesies today.[3] Loud singing, lengthy prayers and confident boasting are no proof of Christian maturity. This is only proven by the way in which we respond to God in difficult times. If we prove our love for Jesus through our willingness to suffer and die for him, James assures us that we will be rewarded with an eternal crown in the age to come. If we complain about our trials and dismiss God's promises about eternity as mere soap-on-a-rope, we show that we do not truly believe the Christian Gospel. James warns us not to despise any of the trials God sends our way. They are preparing our souls for a glorious eternity.

In verses 13–15, James explains that there is a big difference between God testing us and God tempting us. Since the Hebrew word *bāchan* and the Greek word *peirazō* mean both *to test* and *to tempt*, this had led to a great deal of confusion. Many of the persecuted Jewish Christians were making the same mistake as Cain by getting angry with God instead of learning from him. God puts us through trials in order to test what is in our

---

[1]  Acts 6:3, 5, 8, 10; 8:1–4; 11:19; 12:1–2.

[2]  The Greek phrase *pasa chara* in 1:2 can be translated as *"all joy"*, *"pure joy"* or *"nothing but joy."*

[3]  Luke 11:49–51, and Hebrews 11:4, 12:24.

hearts, revealing our secret sins so that he can purify us from them.[4] He never tempts us to sin, since he can no more tempt us to sin than be tempted by sin. James deliberately echoes the Lord's warning to Cain in Genesis 4:7: *"Sin is crouching at your door; it desires to have you, but you must rule over it."* James likens our sinful desires to a woman seducing us, and he likens succumbing to temptation to the act of conceiving a monster. Embryonic thoughts give birth to sin. Sin conceives a grandchild for our thoughts and it is the slow death of Cain. That's why we ought to embrace trials as friends that reveal the evil desires of our hearts before they can destroy us. We ought to consider trials pure joy because they enable us to walk the path of Abel and not of Cain.

In verses 16–18, James therefore urges us not to be deceived by our sinful desires. God is not our enemy in difficult times. He is our greatest ally. He is the God who made the sun and stars, so we can always trust him to transform our darkest night into glorious dawn.[5] Jesus was tempted for forty days and nights in the desert, refusing to turn against his Father like Cain, so he became the true and better Abel, whose innocent blood cries out for our salvation. Abel offered firstborn lambs from his flock, and James tells us that Jesus has turned us into first-fruit offerings for his Father.[6] Our trials are therefore not like soap-on-a-rope. They are good and perfect gifts, which God sends

---

[4] The Bible uses the words *peirazō* and *bāchan* to teach this explicitly in John 6:6, Hebrews 11:17, Jeremiah 12:3, Zechariah 13:9 and Psalm 17:3, 66:10 and 81:7.

[5] James calls God literally *"The Father of the Lights"*, emphasizing that God has no *variation* or *shadow of turning* like the moon and planets. He can no more fail us than the sun.

[6] Jewish readers knew what *first-fruits* were. They were the early crops brought to the Temple at Pentecost as an expression of faith that many more crops were on their way. Sin's grandchild is death, but faith's grandchild is salvation for many more people who observe the lives of those who have been saved. This Greek word *aparchē* is used to describe Christians in Romans 16:5, 1 Corinthians 16:15 and Revelation 14:4.

from heaven in order to reveal the sin in our hearts and to make us run to Jesus for deliverance. Sin gives birth to death but our trials give birth to life by increasing our faith and reliance upon the Gospel.[7]

James practised what he preached. When the Roman governor of Judea died suddenly in 62 AD, his enemies in the Jewish Sanhedrin took advantage of the temporary power vacuum. They took him to the highest point of the Temple, the place in Matthew 4:5 where Jesus had been tempted, and they commanded him to renounce his faith in the Christian Gospel. When he refused to deny Jesus, they threw him down to his death. When he survived the fall, they encircled him and stoned him to death. As he died, he forgave his murderers with a loud voice, counting it nothing but joy to suffer and die for the name of Jesus. He kept his eyes fixed on the eternal crown which he knew his trials had secured him from the hands of his half-brother and Saviour.[8]

James modelled for us a better way of living. He practised what he preached. He therefore means it when he tells us to view our trials as pure joy in the light of eternity. Let's believe him that this life is brief (verses 10–11) and that eternal life is glorious (verse 12). Let's believe him that our trials are a good gift which prepares us for the age to come (verses 13–18). Let's not treat our trials as unwanted gifts, like soap-on-a-rope. Let's treat them as friends that push us closer to Jesus.

---

[7] The Greek word James uses for *giving birth* in 1:15 and 1:18 is used nowhere else in the New Testament. He is therefore drawing a strong contrast between these two possible outcomes for our lives.

[8] Josephus in *Antiquities of the Jews* (20.9.1) and Eusebius in *Church History* (2.23.1–25). Although Eusebius wrote just after 300 AD, he quotes this from the mid second-century Christian historian Hegesippus.

# Words of Life and Death
## (1:18–27)

*Get rid of all moral filth and the evil that is so prevalent, and humbly accept the word planted in you, which can save you.*

(James 1:21)

The Jewish religion was a religion of words. At the start of its sacred Scriptures, God speaks out, *"Let there be light!"* The constant refrain of the 929 chapters that follow is *"The Lord said."* The Jewish nation had been created through God's verbal promises to the patriarchs and through the words of the Law that he gave to Moses on Mount Sinai. Before Joshua led them into the Promised Land, the Lord warned him to *"Keep this Book of the Law always on your lips; meditate on it day and night, so that you may be careful to do everything written in it. Then you will be prosperous and successful."*[1] The Jewish Christians were therefore not surprised when James emphasized the importance of words. They understood that words mean either life or death to a person's soul.

We can tell that James believed in the power of God's Word. The fact that he sent a collection of sermon highlights to the Diaspora Jews demonstrates his belief in the power of his preaching ministry. In verse 18, he calls the Gospel *"the word of truth"* or *"the true message"*, and he tells us that God uses it to transform sinners into born-again believers. He echoes the teaching of Jesus when he tells us literally in verse 21 that

---

[1] Joshua 1:8. Psalms 19 and 119 express how great a value the Jews placed upon their Scriptures.

the Gospel is *"the implanted word which carries power to save your souls."* Jesus likens the Gospel to seed in Luke 8:11 as part of the Parable of the Sower, and he warns us that we have a responsibility to respond to this seed wholeheartedly. If we are shallow in our acceptance of the implications of the Gospel or if we allow evil weeds to suffocate its power to change our lives, our hearts will become like the bad soil in the parable.

In verses 19–21, James therefore warns us not to let our hearts become like the seed that fell among the weeds. If we are quick to fill the air with empty words, we will discover to our cost that God gave us one mouth and two ears for a reason. We need to use them in proportion: *"Everyone should be quick to listen, slow to speak."* James strongly echoes Solomon's teaching in Proverbs when he warns us that one of the biggest reasons why people fail to grow in godliness is that they talk when they ought to listen.[2]

Empty chatter is not the only weed that prevents the Gospel from flourishing in our lives. Ungodly anger also drives away the righteousness that God desires.[3] So does the profane language that James describes as *"moral filth and the evil that is so prevalent."* What we think shapes our speech, and what we speak shapes our thoughts. The only way to break out of the cycle is to stop talking and to start listening humbly to God's Word. This alone can save us and make us godly in an ungodly generation. We need to close our ears to words of death and we need to open them to words of life.

In verses 22–25, James warns us not to let our hearts become like the seed that fell on rocky soil in the parable. It looked impressive above the surface of the soil, but it had such shallow roots that it withered and died before it could bear any

---

[2] See Proverbs 10:8–10, 19; 13:3; 18:13; 21:23. James returns to the task of taming the tongue in 3:1–12.

[3] Jesus expressed the anger of God in Mark 3:5 and John 2:13–17, but James warns against the *"anger of man"*, which Jesus condemned in Matthew 5:22. Solomon also condemns it in Proverbs 12:16, 14:29, 16:32 and 19:11.

fruit. James laughs at the person who nods their agreement to the Gospel, thinking that their broad smiles are a substitute for digging deep roots down into God's Word. He says that such a person is like a man who looks at his face in a mirror and immediately forgets what he looks like – he might as well not bother looking in the mirror at all. James warns us not to deceive ourselves, like the man who built his house on the sand in the Sermon on the Mount, by thinking that listening to God's Word will bring us any blessing unless we act upon it.[4]

This is very important teaching for us as individuals, but it is also vital teaching as we share God's Word with others. James echoes Jesus' teaching in John 8:31 when he tells us in verse 25 that true disciples of Jesus are not those who nod at his teaching, but those who make his teaching their permanent home.[5] We must therefore learn from his evident commitment to Bible preaching and from his passionate belief that God's Word carries power to set people free.[6] If we want to see unbelievers saved, we need to share with them the only message that can save them. If we want to see Christians mature in the Lord, we need to share with them the only message that can bring them to perfect maturity. If we want our churches to become more like the church that James led in Jerusalem, we need to preach the way James did. Ultimately every church leader ends up leading the kind of church that is produced by their preaching.

In verses 26–27, James pleads with us to make our hearts like the seed that fell on fertile soil in the parable. Having told us that we are merely the first-fruits of the Gospel harvest that God is planning for the world, he now encourages us to bear fruit

---

[4] James echoes the teaching of Jesus in Matthew 7:24–27 and John 13:17.

[5] The Greek word *parameno* in 1:25 means *to remain* or *to continue*. It describes permanency in Hebrews 7:23.

[6] James takes the word *law*, which was so precious to the Jews, and uses it to describe the Gospel's better way of living in 1:25, 2:8 and 2:12. Although sinners resist it for fear that it will restrict their lives, the Gospel offers us the only path towards genuine freedom.

all around us through our devotion to God's powerful Word. He uses a horse-riding metaphor when he tells us to put a bit and bridle on our tongues.[7] He echoes the teaching of Solomon in Proverbs when he tells us that the way we bridle our tongues will either carry people away from the Christian religion or towards it.[8] He also echoes the teaching of Solomon when he tells us that true submission to the Word of God always results in love towards the poor and hatred towards sin. It is easy to tell if you are feeding on words of life. It will start to feed the people around you too.

These verses are challenging. They tell us that the true test of our Christianity is not what we say with our lips but what we do with our lives, not what we pray at the end of a Christian meeting but what we do when we go back out into the world. We must not cling to our old ways of thinking and living, for something far better has come. We need to dig up every weed that crowds the Word of God out of our lives, and we need to dig deep roots into the Bible. We need to devote ourselves to the living seed that God has planted in our hearts. Only then will we experience what Jesus promises at the end of the Parable of the Sower in Luke 8:15: *"The seed on good soil stands for those with a noble and good heart, who hear the word, retain it, and by persevering produce a crop."*

---

[7] James evidently recycled some of his illustrations for more than one sermon. He returns to the idea of putting a bit and bridle on our tongues in 3:2–6.

[8] See Proverbs 10:21; 11:30; 12:6, 13–14, 18; 15:4, 7; 18:21; 21:23.

# Uncorrupted Religion (1:27)

*Religion that God our Father accepts as pure and faultless is this: to look after orphans and widows in their distress.*

(James 1:27)

William Booth came home late one night from visiting a relative in hospital. It was the first time he had seen what happened to the streets of London after everyone had gone to bed. Even though it was the middle of the night, he banged on the door of one of his relatives and hauled him out of bed. When he finished telling him about the homeless people he had seen sleeping on park benches and under bridges, his relative was surprised at his strong reaction: *"Why, did you not know?"* William Booth was even more surprised: *"You mean you knew and didn't do anything?"*[1]

William Booth founded The Salvation Army in response to the teachings of James. People who truly surrender their lives to Jesus always catch something of his passionate love towards the poor. That's one of the easy ways in which we can tell if we have dealt with the weeds and rocky soil that stop God's Word from flourishing within us. If our Christianity is self-centred and does not affect those around us, it is no better than the religion of the Pharisees. James tells us that pure and faultless religion always makes people lay down their lives for other people as Jesus laid down his life for them.

This Greek word *thrēskeia*, or *religion*, is unusual. Paul is

---

[1] This quote and the one at the end of this chapter are taken from Roy Hattersley's *Blood and Fire: William and Catherine Booth and Their Salvation Army* (1999).

the only other New Testament writer to use it, and both times it describes corrupted first-century Judaism.[2] James is therefore speaking specifically to Jews and reminding them that the Gospel is a rediscovery of the uncorrupted faith of Abraham and Moses. The Law of Moses expressed God's love for the poor, but the Israelites tended to skim over those verses. The book of Proverbs reminded them that this was a non-negotiable aspect of our worship, but they tended to skim over those verses too. The Old Testament prophets warned them that God took their sin of omission very seriously.[3] James is therefore assuring the Jewish Christians that faith in Jesus as Messiah does not make them unfaithful to their Jewish culture. It actually brings them back to the heart of the Old Testament and exposes the self-centredness of first-century Judaism. If they serve Jesus by helping the poor, they will demonstrate that something far better has come.

This is exactly what James and the other Christians did at the church in Jerusalem. The book of Acts tells us that *"no one claimed that any of their possessions was their own, but they shared everything they had."* They sold houses and fields in order to provide for poor church members so that *"there was no needy person among them."* When two wealthy church members pretended to care for the poor but didn't, the church leaders confronted them in the strongest of terms. Soon the news had spread all across Jerusalem – Jesus must be the Messiah because his followers loved one another far more than did the followers of the Jewish Law. The book of Acts tells us that the city was so impressed that *"the Lord added to their number daily those who were being saved."*[4]

----

[2] Other than here in 1:26–27, the word is only used in Acts 26:5 and Colossians 2:18.

[3] A few examples can be found in Leviticus 19:9–10 and 25:1–55, Deuteronomy 14:28–29, 15:7–11 and 24:17–22, Proverbs 14:31, 19:17, 21:13, 22:9, 22:22–23, 28:27 and 29:7, and Isaiah 1:15–17 and 58:5–10.

[4] Acts 2:44–47; 4:32–37; 5:1–11, 14. Acts 12:12 clarifies that the Jerusalem Christians still had homes. They bought houses smaller than they might have afforded and sold any second homes.

When the Gospel spread out from Jerusalem, it proved that this same revolution grips any community where Christians demonstrate God's heart towards the poor. The Jews in Judea were convinced that the Messiah must have come when they saw the Christians in Joppa feeding and clothing the poor.[5] The Greeks in Antioch were convinced that Jesus was better than their pagan idols when they saw the church in their city taking up a collection for poor believers many miles away. When Paul took the Gospel to the cities of the Mediterranean, he received important advice from James and the other leaders of the church in Jerusalem: *"All they asked was that we should continue to remember the poor, the very thing I had been eager to do all along."*[6] The last pagan Roman emperor reluctantly identified this as the single biggest reason why his empire had converted to Christianity: *"It is disgraceful that... while the impious Galileans support both their own poor and ours as well, everyone sees that our people lack aid from us!"*[7]

I have never met a Christian who does not want the world to turn to Jesus. I have never met a Christian who does not want to see a Gospel breakthrough like the ones we read about in the book of Acts. But I have never met a Christian without excuses either: it's different now, we need healing miracles and a better contextualization of the Gospel before we will ever see a wave of mass conversions. James doesn't buy into our excuses. He simply tells us that *"Religion that God our Father accepts as pure and faultless is this: to look after orphans and widows in their distress and to keep oneself from being polluted by the world."* He points us back to God's promise in Isaiah 58 to every generation of believers: *"Loose the chains of injustice... Share your food with the hungry... Provide the poor wanderer with shelter... If you*

---

[5] Acts 9:36–42. Christian love for the poor is as much a Holy Spirit miracle as what Peter did for Dorcas.

[6] Acts 11:27–30; Galatians 2:9–10.

[7] Emperor Julian the Apostate wrote this in 362 AD in a letter to Arsacius, pagan high priest of Galatia.

*spend yourselves on behalf of the hungry and satisfy the needs of the oppressed, **then** your light will rise in the darkness, and your night will become like the noonday."*

William Booth proved that the same revolution which gripped the first-century world will still grip any modern city if the Christians in it catch God's heart towards the poor. He attacked the corrupted religion of respectable British society, declaring that *"It will be a happy day for England when Christian ladies transfer their sympathies from poodles and terriers to destitute and starving children."*[8] He pointed out that the churches in his city did not have the poor among them, as Jesus expects in Mark 14:7, because they had lost the pure and faultless religion which Jesus commanded in Matthew 25:31–46 and Luke 12:33–34. He called them back to the uncorrupted religion which James taught the church in Jerusalem. When a former prostitute was asked at his funeral why so many tens of thousands of Londoners had been converted to Jesus through William Booth, she simply replied: *"You see, he cared for the likes of us."*

If you are a Christian, James urges you to prove it by the way in which you care about the poor. If you are a church leader, James urges you to preach this message until your church imitates the pure and faultless religion which was modelled by his own church in Jerusalem.[9] Whoever you are, he urges you to do something straightaway, just as William Booth urged the Christians of Victorian London: *"What are you going to do?... The great test of character is **doing**. God, the Church and the world all estimate men not according to their sayings, feelings or desiring, but according to their doings."*

---

[8] Quoted by Helen K. Hosier in *William and Catherine Booth: Founders of The Salvation Army* (1999).

[9] James uses the Greek verb *episkeptomai* in 1:27 to describe Christians *looking after* the poor. This is the root of the word *episkopos*, meaning *overseer* or *elder*. Responsibility for this begins with church leaders.

# Brothers and Sisters (2:1–7)

*My brothers and sisters, believers in our glorious Lord Jesus Christ must not show favouritism.*

(James 2:1)

James had been very offended by Jesus at the end of 28 AD. Considering his half-brother to be a madman and an embarrassment to his family, he had gone with his mother and brothers and sisters to stop him preaching throughout Galilee. When they arrived at the house where Jesus was teaching, he refused to come out and speak to them. He disowned James and the others by declaring over his followers, *"Here are my mother and my brothers! Whoever does God's will is my brother and sister and mother."* It must have been a very painful moment for James. He certainly never forgot it.[1]

So don't miss the significance of the fact that James repeatedly calls the Christian believers *"my dear brothers and sisters."*[2] Like Jesus, he now views his earthly family as secondary. He does not refer to Jesus as his half-brother in verse 1 but as *"our glorious Lord Jesus Christ"*,[3] the one who founded the Church as God's family on earth.[4] James has embraced

---

[1] Mark 3:20–21, 31–35. Jesus also calls believers his brothers and sisters in Matthew 25:40.

[2] James 1:2, 9, 16, 19; 2:1, 5, 14, 15; 3:1, 10, 12; 4:11; 5:7, 9, 10, 12, 19. The Greek word *adelphoi* means literally *brothers*, but it was also used to address a mixed group of *brothers and sisters*.

[3] The Greek can also be translated *"Jesus the Messiah, our Lord of glory."* This was an amazing turnaround of faith for the man who had once accused his half-brother of being a madman.

[4] Peter and Paul both refer to the Church as the family of God in 1 Peter 4:17 and Galatians 6:10.

the teaching that he once found so offensive. In these sermon clippings he refers to Christians as his brothers and sisters twenty times in only five chapters. If we want to grasp what made the church at Jerusalem so strong and what God wants to do in our churches, we need to slow down and take this language seriously. Any Christian church that is worthy of the name must act like a loving spiritual family.

This is important if you come from a Christian background, and particularly if you react badly to James' description of Christianity as a "religion" in 1:27. The bestselling author Philip Pullman epitomizes our culture's aversion towards organized religion: *"When you look at organised religion of whatever sort – whether it's Christianity in all its variants, or whether it's Islam or some forms of extreme Hinduism – wherever you see organised religion and priesthoods and power, you see cruelty and tyranny and repression. It's almost a universal law."*[5] It is therefore no wonder that many Christians fall over themselves to convince the world that Christianity is not a religion at all, much less an organized religion with leaders and structures and accountability towards one another. James refuses to budge on this, however. He insists firmly that Christianity is a rediscovery of the ancient faith of Israel. We are Abraham's family. We are part of the great assembly of believers that God created through the twelve tribes of Israel. Jesus did not come to earth in order to endorse the individualism of Western culture. He came in order to save us from it.

This is also important if you come from a non-Christian background. It is never easy to be the first person in a family to turn to Jesus. For first-century Jews, it meant expulsion from the synagogue. This was far more than a place for Friday evening worship. It was the focal point of Jewish life, so accepting Jesus as Messiah meant being rejected by the entire community.

---

[5] Philip Pullman said this in an interview with the Christian Aid website *Surefish* in November 2002.

Jesus had warned up front that this would be the price many of his followers would have to pay: *"Do not suppose that I have come to bring peace to the earth. I did not come to bring peace, but a sword. For I have come to turn 'a man against his father, a daughter against her mother, a daughter-in-law against her mother-in-law – a man's enemies will be the members of his own household.'"*[6]

This was hard but, in the Early Church, there was a solution for this. Those who were rejected by one family were welcomed into another. Those who were expelled from one community found a place waiting for them in a better one. A Greek who came into contact with the church in Athens was converted by seeing how much

> *they love one another. They do not despise the widow or grieve the orphan. He that has, distributes liberally to him that has not. If they see a stranger they bring him under their roof, and rejoice over him as if he were their own brother; for they call themselves brothers, not after the flesh, but after the Spirit and in God... If there is among them any man who is poor and needy, and they have not an abundance of necessaries, they fast two or three days so that they may supply the needy with the food they need. And they observe scrupulously the commandments of their Messiah.*[7]

When Muslims and Hindus and militant atheists decide to follow Jesus, they need to find a similar family. Without one, their new-found faith will simply not survive. That's why in verse 2 James describes the church literally as a *synagogue*.[8] We are to be their new community. Our services are to be God's

---

[6] John 9:22; 12:42; 16:2; Matthew 10:34–36.

[7] Aristides of Athens wrote this in c.125 AD in his *Apology* (15).

[8] The word *synagogue* is Greek for *gathering*. We must not despise the importance of our Christian meetings.

family meetings and entry points through which anybody can find their place in a new community. If you are lonely, it is where you will find friends. If you are single, it is where you will find a partner. If you are married, it is where you are called to add many other people into your little household.[9]

James therefore fights very hard for the purity of each expression of the family of God across the Roman Empire. We must not treat newcomers differently depending on whether they are rich or poor, fashionably dressed or in rags, beautiful or ugly, endowed with many social skills or none. Brothers are brothers and sisters are sisters, regardless of their personal situation. Since the Lord does not discriminate by outward appearance, neither must we.[10] Since the rich and powerful have historically been the greatest opponents of the Church, we must not give them preferential treatment over the poor.[11] We must demonstrate to the world that our Gospel is true by treating every unsaved rich man as a spiritual pauper and every saved pauper as a prince of heaven.[12]

Welcome to God's family. If you have been rejected by your own friends and family for following Jesus, step right in.[13] If you have been rejected by the people around you for being too fat, too thin, too ugly, too beautiful, too poor, too rich, too Jewish, too Gentile, or for any other reason, this family is yours through

---

[9] Genesis 28:1–2; Psalm 68:6; Acts 2:46; 16:15; Romans 16:13; 2 Corinthians 6:14–18.

[10] 1 Samuel 16:7; Acts 10:34; Romans 2:11; Ephesians 6:9; Colossians 3:25.

[11] God's love for the poor is a big theme of James (1:9–11, 27; 2:15–16; 5:1–6). This world's wealth can easily stop us from wanting *"to be rich in faith and to inherit the kingdom"* (Matthew 5:3; 19:21–26).

[12] James did not attract crowds of poor people to the church in Jerusalem by promising them earthly prosperity through the Gospel, but by promising them heavenly riches through the poverty of Jesus.

[13] This often happens when we obey Jesus by getting baptized in water. James is probably referring to baptism when he talks literally in 2:7 about *"blaspheming the good name which was invoked over you."*

your faith in Jesus. He welcomes you with the same words that offended James so much in 28 AD:

> *Whoever does God's will is my brother and sister and mother.*

# Law-Breakers (2:8–13)

*Whoever keeps the whole law and yet stumbles at just one point is guilty of breaking all of it.*

(James 2:10)

Luis Suárez was doing so well. He had recovered from a knee operation in time to take his place in the Uruguay football team at the World Cup finals in 2014. He played a perfect first game, scoring both of the goals that knocked England out of the competition. He played a crucial role in the next game, knocking out Italy too, without earning so much as a yellow card. However, when FIFA officials inspected television footage of the match, they spotted a transgression. In a moment of anger, he had sunk his teeth into the shoulder of Italian defender Giorgio Chiellini.

At first, Luis Suárez tried to deny it. *"We were both in the area. He thrust his shoulder into me."* When nobody believed him, he changed his story: *"I lost my balance and that destabilised my body and I fell into my opponent. In the moment, my face came into collision with the player."* FIFA were unconvinced. They fined him heavily, banned him from football for four months and sent him back home in disgrace. Even when he admitted his transgression and apologized, one of his team-mates still complained bitterly about the ruling: *"It's a breach of human rights... This is barbarity."*[1]

James wants us to understand that we are all like Luis Suárez when it comes to obeying God's Law. Biting other players is against the rules, even if it only happens once in a ninety-

---

[1] These excuses were reported in *The Telegraph* newspaper on 25th, 28th and 29th June 2014.

minute game. Ninety minutes of obedience cannot outweigh a single moment of madness. James tells us in verse 10 that *"Whoever keeps the whole law and yet stumbles at just one point is guilty of breaking all of it."*

This was very important to Jewish Christians in the first century. They loved the Jewish Law (that's why James uses the Greek word for *law* ten times in these five chapters), but they were being accused of betraying the Law by the Jewish community which had rejected Jesus.[2] They were accused of Sabbath-breaking for treating Sunday as their new holy day because it was the day of Jesus' resurrection.[3] They were accused of impurity because they accepted Gentiles as their brothers and sisters.[4] They were accused of blasphemy for worshipping Jesus as the God of the Old Testament. The Jewish Christians therefore needed to be reassured that they were honouring the Law of Moses far more than any of their devout Jewish critics.

James points out that a person who breaks any aspect of the Jewish Law is by definition a law-breaker. Anyone who thinks they can impress God with their moral lifestyle is as ridiculous as Luis Suárez and his lame excuses. Biting one player in a ninety-minute game is one bite too many. In the same way, breaking even one command in God's Law is one act of disobedience too many.[5]

---

[2] James boasts to Paul in Acts 21:20 about the Jewish Christians in Jerusalem that *"all of them are zealous for the law."* James therefore quotes three times from the Law of Moses in verses 8 and 11: from Leviticus 19:18, from either Exodus 20:14 or Deuteronomy 5:18, and from either Exodus 20:13 or Deuteronomy 5:17.

[3] They referred to Sunday as *"the Lord's Day"* because it was the day he rose from the dead. See Matthew 28:1; Acts 20:7; 1 Corinthians 16:2; Revelation 1:10.

[4] John 18:28; Acts 10:28; 11:2–3; 22:21–22; Galatians 2:11–16.

[5] James said something similar in Acts 15:19–21. Obedience to the Law of Moses cannot save us. It simply shows us how much we need the Saviour that all of its blood sacrifices point towards (Romans 3:20).

We need to hear this message too. Our culture may not place much value on the Law of Moses, but it gets very self-righteous when Christians suggest that its morality may not come up to God's perfect standard. People fool themselves that there are extenuating circumstances for their wrong actions (the equivalent of "I lost my balance and that destabilised my body and I fell"), or they protest that they only acted wrongly because of other people's prior actions towards them (the equivalent of "He thrust his shoulder into me"). Furthermore, people struggle with the very concept that God judges human sin (the equivalent of complaining that "It's a breach of human rights... This is barbarity"). James warns us that God is firmer than FIFA. He isn't fooled by any of our protestations.

In verses 8–11, James explains that there is no such thing as "major" and "minor" sins. Favouritism, adultery and murder look very different but they are simply different faces of one colossal act of human rebellion against God. Luis Suárez bit one of his opponents, but we have all bitten the hand of the Creator who clothes and feeds us. Jesus summarized the Law of Moses in Mark 12:30–31 in just two Old Testament verses: *"Love the Lord your God with all your heart and with all your soul and with all your mind and with all your strength"* and *"Love your neighbour as yourself."*[6] James quotes the second of these two verses in order to convict us that we are all law-breakers. We rebel against God as much by looking down on a pauper as we do by committing adultery or murder. The question is not which one damages the other person more. They are all equally an expression of a heart that is in rebellion against God.

The church in Jerusalem grew strong because its leaders were not afraid to confront sin, but it also grew strong because they showed those humble enough to confess their sin how they could be forgiven. James refers to Jesus' pithy summary of

---

[6] Deuteronomy 6:4–5 and Leviticus 19:18 are also quoted as a summary of the Law of Moses in Matthew 5:43, 19:19 and 22:37–39, Luke 10:27, Romans 13:8–10, and Galatians 5:14 and 6:2.

the Law of Moses as *"the royal law"* or *"the law of the Kingdom."* He therefore fixes our attention on Jesus and warns us that we cannot receive mercy by comparing ourselves favourably with one another.[7] James does not need to name the cross and blood of Jesus when he shouts out that the Christian Gospel means that *"Mercy has triumphed over judgment!"* We have been granted a share in a far better Passover meal than the one instituted by Moses in the Law. James encourages us to stop our excuses and to confess our sin to Jesus as our Saviour.

James hasn't finished. Repentance means more than saying sorry. It means leaving at the foot of the cross every sinful act which made Jesus suffer for us there.[8] James tells us in verses 12–13 that we are not bound by the Law of Moses. Jesus completely fulfilled it for us when he died on the cross in our place.[9] Instead, we are bound by *"the law that gives freedom"* – the law that the Holy Spirit writes upon our hearts and enables us to fulfil through his own indwelling love and power.[10]

James therefore silences those who believe they will be saved through their moral living, and he also silences those who believe that God's forgiveness gives us licence to live however we want. Rebellion never brings freedom, any more than biting an opponent brings a better game of football. James calls us to stop making ridiculous excuses for our sin and to accept gladly from Jesus the restrictions of his new law of love, which alone brings us true freedom.

---

[7] James 2:13 echoes the warning of Jesus that comparing ourselves to others actually makes us guiltier. See Matthew 5:7; 6:12–15; 7:1–2; 18:23–35; Mark 4:24; Luke 6:38.

[8] Christians will not be judged for their sins because Jesus has already been judged for us. James 2:12 describes our giving an account of how we responded to our salvation by embracing his commands (2 Corinthians 5:10).

[9] Matthew 5:17–20. Jesus says that faith in his act of salvation makes us more law-abiding than any rabbi.

[10] 2 Corinthians 3:1–17; Romans 5:5. James also talked about this *"law of freedom"* in another sermon in 1:25.

# Faith Which Works
## (2:14–26)

*A person is considered righteous by what they do
and not by faith alone.*

(James 2:24)

Martin Luther was unimpressed with the letter James wrote to
the mid first-century Jewish Christians. When he translated the
New Testament into German at the start of the sixteenth century,
he warned his readers to be careful as they read it: *"Paul's letters,
especially Romans, Galatians and Ephesians... are the books that
show you Christ and teach you all that it is necessary and good
for you to know... James' letter is really a letter of straw compared
to them, for it has nothing of the nature of the Gospel about it."*
Luther only included it as an appendix to his translation of the
New Testament, explaining that in his view James *"does violence
to Scripture and thereby contradicts Paul and all Scripture...
Therefore I will not have him in my Bible to be numbered among
the true chief books."*[1]

Many modern scholars follow Martin Luther's lead. They
try to drive a wedge between the Gospel that was preached by
Paul and the one that was preached by James, even though Paul
was at pains to stress the continuity between their preaching in
Galatians 2:1–10.[2] This is both tragic and dangerous. We need

---

[1] *Preface to the New Testament* and *Preface to the Epistles of St James and
St Jude* (1522). Martin Luther also placed Hebrews, Jude and Revelation in this
appendix because he felt they contradicted his own views.

[2] James agrees with Paul that Christians are *"believers"* who need to become
*"rich in faith"* (2:1, 5). He also agrees with Paul that God has chosen and

the words of Paul to understand James, and we need the words of James to understand Paul. Martin Luther was wrong to resist the light that James shed on his conviction from the writings of Paul that God makes people righteous through faith alone – end of story. Paul himself made it clear that this was not the end of the story at all.[3] In verses 14–26, James explains why.

Although these verses were probably taken from a different sermon, James places them here because they expand on his teaching about faith and love and law in 2:5 and 2:8–13. James has just exposed the powerlessness of the Jewish Law or of pagan morality to save anyone. We are saved by faith in Jesus alone. Now he clarifies that saving faith in Jesus can never be alone. It is always expressed by a strong desire to do whatever he says. Somebody who claims to believe in Jesus but merely talks about helping the poor and needy within God's family cannot truly possess saving faith at all. Anyone who truly believes that Jesus laid down his life for them will naturally begin to lay down their life for others. James makes it clear in verses 14–17 that Christian talk is no substitute for Christian walk. He emphasizes this even more strongly in verses 18–19 by pointing out that demons believe in the reality of God more than we do without being saved by their belief in God! Saying that we believe in Jesus cannot save us unless our belief is proven to be more than mere intellectual assent by the way that we behave.

James knows that this will meet with some resistance from his hearers, even as it did with Martin Luther almost fifteen centuries later. In our determination to resist the self-reliance of manmade religion, we can often talk about faith in a way that reduces it to nodding our head to certain theological facts instead of something that stirs our hearts to change the whole direction of our lives. James therefore illustrates the

---

adopted us as his children and heirs through faith (2:5).

[3] Paul emphasizes that true saving faith in Jesus will always result in obedient actions in Acts 26:20, Romans 6:15–18, Ephesians 2:8–10 and Galatians 5:6. So does Peter in 2 Peter 1:10.

link between our faith and our actions by taking us back to the example of two Old Testament characters.

In verses 20–24, James uses the life of Abraham to prove that faith is phoney unless it gives rise to obedient action. Abraham was such a man of faith that Paul uses his example in both Romans and Galatians to teach justification through faith alone. James points out that Abraham's faith was only made visible when he took his son up Mount Moriah to obey God's call to sacrifice him in Genesis 22.[4] *"His faith and his actions were working together, and his faith was made complete by what he did."* God made Abraham righteous through faith alone (James affirms this by quoting the same verse which Paul quotes in Romans and Galatians[5]), but he only commended him as righteous when he expressed that faith by leaving Ur of the Chaldees and travelling to Canaan.[6] *"You see that a person is considered righteous by what they do and not by faith alone."* Obedient actions cannot save us in the absence of faith in Jesus, but obedient actions are never absent from true saving faith in Jesus.

In verses 25–26, James uses the example of another Old Testament character to reinforce this further. Rahab was a prostitute and a liar. She was the perfect picture of a person who could never be saved by her own good works. She was precisely the kind of person that Martin Luther would hold up as proof that the Gospel justifies sinful people by faith in Christ alone. James agrees. She was only saved by placing her faith in the blood-red rope which God's messengers commanded her to hang out of her window. But here's the thing: she had

---

[4] God saved Isaac's life by providing a ram to die in his place, but this is precisely James' point. Abraham's faith in God required him to move his legs to Mount Moriah, the very mountain where Jesus would later die.

[5] Paul would quote from Genesis 15:6 a year later in Galatians 3:6–9 and nine years later in Romans 4:1–25.

[6] When James 2:23 tells us that Abraham was called God's friend, it is referring back to 2 Chronicles 20:7 and Isaiah 41:8. John 15:14–15 says that God has also chosen us to be his friends through this same practical faith.

to express that faith by hiding the two messengers on her roof and then dangling the rope out of her brothel window as the outward proof of her inward faith in Israel's God. If she had simply nodded her agreement without turning heart belief into concrete actions, she would have become just another corpse in the ruins of Jericho.[7] *"As the body without the spirit is dead, so faith without deeds is dead."*

Martin Luther actually knew this. He fought against a merely theoretical faith in many of his own sermons. He warned that

> *Theology consists of action and practice, not of speculation and meditation. Anyone who speculates about their household affairs or about the earthly task of governing without putting it into practice is a lost and useless person. If a tradesman makes a business plan for how much profit he will make in the year but puts nothing into practice, he trades in vain speculations and finds afterwards that his accounts fall far too short. It is the same with speculating theologians, as is seen to this day and as I know by experience.[8]*

So don't be foolish and see a rift where there is none between the Gospel as it was preached by Paul and by James. Paul clarifies what James wrote, and James clarifies what Paul wrote.[9] Together they equip us to preach the same Gospel which Paul describes in Acts 26:20: *"First to those in Damascus, then to those*

---

[7] Joshua 2:1–21; 6:17, 22–25; Hebrews 11:31. By way of contrast, Achan professed to be a believing Hebrew yet his actions earned him a place on the pagan body pile in Joshua 7.

[8] Johannes Mathesius was a friend of Luther's and published many of the things Luther said to him over dinner as a book entitled *Table Talk* in 1566. He records this as Luther's Comment 389.

[9] We still desperately need this clarity. We all know Christians who are theologically impeccable and yet who seem to be devoid of any Christian love towards the people around them.

*in Jerusalem and in all Judea, and then to the Gentiles, I preached that they should repent and turn to God and demonstrate their repentance by their deeds."*

# Mightier Than the Sword
# (3:1–12)

*Not many of you should become teachers, my fellow
believers, because you know that we who teach will
be judged more strictly.*

(James 3:1)

The nineteenth-century author Edward Bulwer-Lytton
triumphantly declared, *"True, this! Beneath the rule of men
entirely great, the pen is mightier than the sword."*[1]

James believed that it was true. He would not have turned
his sermon highlights into a letter had he not believed in the
power of the spoken and written word to change people's lives.
He would not have warned us so strongly about the power of
the human tongue in 1:26, and he would not have returned the
power of the tongue in 3:1–12. Having told us that God's Word
carries power to change both our beliefs and our actions, he now
gives us various snippets from his sermons that emphasize that
what we say demonstrates how much God has truly changed us
on the inside.

In verses 2–8, James tells us that our tongues are far
harder to tame than any animal, bird or fish. A horse can be
tamed and controlled by a tiny bit in its mouth.[2] A large ship
can be steadied and steered through a storm by a tiny rudder.

---

[1] These words are spoken by the title character in his play *Richelieu* (2.2), first
performed in 1839.

[2] The Greek word James uses in 3:2 for *bridling* our body like horse is only
used elsewhere in the New Testament in 1:26. James evidently recycled many
of his illustrations and reused them in other sermons.

In the same way, our little tongues have the power to navigate our destiny, either for good or for ill.[3] Just as a tiny spark can ignite a massive forest fire, our little tongues can set the whole of our lives on fire if they are more influenced by the forces of hell than by the mandates of heaven.[4] James warns us that an untamed tongue is *"a restless evil, full of deadly poison."* But he also encourages us that, if we co-operate with the Holy Spirit to bring our tongues into check, we will find taming every other part of our body relatively easy.

In verses 9–12, James therefore tells us to marshal the power of our tongues towards good instead of towards evil. A spring cannot gush out both fresh water and salt water. We must therefore decide whether we are going to use our tongues to praise the Lord or to curse each other.[5] A tree cannot bear olives and grapes and figs. We must therefore decide what kind of fruit we want to bear with the mighty weapon that the Lord has put into our mouths.

If you are a Christian, this is a very important decision. Jesus has called you to be his witness. Therefore, whatever words you choose to speak with your tongue are either an act of obedience or an act of rebellion. Every Christian testifies about the Lord. The only question is whether the testimony is honourable or evil.

If you have the privilege of teaching other people about the Christian faith – as a preacher, a small group leader, a schools worker, a blogger or an active user of social media –this decision

---

[3] This is also one of the big themes of the book of Proverbs. I address it in more detail in the chapter "The Strongest Muscle" in *Straight to the Heart of Solomon*.

[4] James refers to hell in 3:6 as *Gehenna*, the name of the valley outside Jerusalem where Jewish corpses were piled after its destruction in 586 BC. Jesus uses this name for hell 11 times in the gospels, but this is the only other occurance in the New Testament. James constantly echoes the teaching of Jesus.

[5] When James says that humans are made in God's image, he echoes Genesis 1:26–27, 5:1 and 9:6.

is even more important. James warns us firmly in verse 1 that *"Not many of you should become teachers, my fellow believers, because you know that we who teach will be judged more strictly."* This is therefore a good moment to take a step back and note four big lessons from these sermon clippings of how best to teach people about Jesus.

First, we need to show our listeners that we are deadly serious about what we say. This letter may not be brilliantly structured – Martin Luther complains that *"He throws things together so chaotically that it seems to me he must have been some good, pious man who took a few sayings from the disciples of the apostles and thus threw them off on paper; or perhaps they were written down by somebody else from his preaching"*[6] – but even Luther has to admit that the preacher is extraordinarily passionate about what he has to say. James actually structures this letter very well, echoing the structure of Proverbs, but the impression it leaves on our minds is one of its force rather than its form.[7]

Second, we need to capture the attention of our listeners completely to what it is we have to say. In the TV drama *The West Wing*, the White House Deputy Chief of Staff tells a colleague that *"It's the greatest sin in politics to be bad on television."*[8] Whether or not that is true, few can deny that one of the greatest sins in preaching is to be boring. If we present the greatest message in the world in a boring manner, we are to blame when people ignore what we say. James arrests our attention by using vivid illustrations, mentioning horses and ships and forest fires and sea creatures and snakebites and fountains and farming in these

---

[6] *Preface to the Epistles of St James and St Jude.* Luther's disdain towards James and his letter is bizarre. Galatians 1:19 affirms James as an apostle and Early Church Councils affirmed his letter as Scripture.

[7] James 1:1–8 echoes wisdom's call in Proverbs 1–9. James 1:9–5:20 echoes the miscellany of Proverbs 10–31.

[8] Josh Lyman says this in *The West Wing*, Season 5, Episode 12 – "Slow News Day" (2004).

twelve verses alone.[9] He makes us do a double-take by using very graphic language – for example, warning us that our own tongues are as deadly as a cobra.[10] When our attention flags, he calls us names, recapturing our attention by calling us *"idiots"*, *"double-minded ditherers"*, *"adulterers"* and *"sinners".*[11]

Third, we need to understand the way our listeners think so that we can ram home our message as forcefully as possible. In five short chapters James uses twenty rhetorical questions and imaginary conversations to tease out our biggest questions so that he can give us a reply in its strongest form. Since he is talking to Jewish Christians, he refers ten times to the Law, quotes at least five times from the Old Testament and alludes to over half a dozen of their nation's cultural heroes and villains.

Fourth, we need to call our listeners to make a radical response straightaway. James issues almost sixty direct commands in these 108 verses. Sometimes he seeks to win us tenderly by calling us *"my dear brothers and sisters."* At other times, he uses taunts (2:18), humour (2:19) and threats (5:1–6) to shock us into action. G.K. Chesterton famously observed that *"Humour can get in under the door while seriousness is still fumbling at the handle."*[12] James understood this and he used every weapon in the preacher's arsenal to compel his listeners to surrender every area of their lives to the Lord.

Our tongues are powerful weapons, for good or for evil. They are mightier than the sword. James therefore commands us to tame our tongues and to send them out to war in Jesus'

---

[9] Another great example is in 1:9–11. James does not merely tell rich people that they are about to die. This would be far less memorable than telling them that they are about to wither, fade and die, like wild flowers.

[10] The Greek word *ios* in 3:8 does not simply refer to poison in general. It refers specifically to the *venom* emitted by a snake or spider when they bite. An untamed tongue can therefore bite as badly as a wild cobra.

[11] James 2:20; 4:4, 8. Acts 8:20–23 and 13:9–11 show us that other Early Church leaders spoke as directly too.

[12] Note the way James uses simple humour in 1:23–25 to convince us that our lives need radical change.

name. The church in Jerusalem grew strong because its members were filled with the Holy Spirit, but that is only half the story. It also grew strong because the Holy Spirit helped those believers to train their tongues so that they could call the world around them to a better way of living. Make no mistake. We all get the kind of church our preaching warrants. Ask God to help you to tame and unleash the full power of your tongue.

# Angels and Demons
## (3:13–4:3)

*Such "wisdom" does not come down from heaven
but is earthly, unspiritual, demonic.*

(James 3:15)

When Pope Gregory the Great saw a group of blond and pale-skinned English boys at a slave market in Rome, he asked which race they were. When he was told that they were Angles, he made one of the worst Latin puns in history: *"Non Angli, sed angeli"* – that is, *"Not Angles, but angels."* Pope Gregory looked at their blond hair and white skin and decided that *"They have an angelic face so they must be co-heirs with the angels in heaven."*[1]

The reality was rather different, however. The Anglo-Saxons were brutal warriors who enslaved their enemies and did not hesitate to execute their children if they stole a loaf of bread. Even after Pope Gregory sent missionaries to England, its angel-faced inhabitants continued their constant infighting, vendettas and violent acts of war.

Many people make the same mistake as Pope Gregory when they think about the Early Church. They assume that all of the early Christians were little angels. I find it quite encouraging to read the history books and to discover that the first generation of Christians was just like our one: a mixture of glory and shame, of great purity and great wickedness. If the early Christians were just like us at our worst, it brings hope for

---

[1] Bede records this terrible pun in his *Church History of the English People* (2.1), written in c.731 AD.

us that our generation can also become like the early Christians at their best.

James and his fellow leaders had been forced to root terrible sin out of the church in Jerusalem. There was the couple who lied about their financial dealings to the entire congregation and to God. There were the troublemakers who split the church into different factions and caused infighting between the Jews from Israel and the Jews from Greece. There were the racists who objected very strongly to the idea that uncircumcised pagans should have any share in the Gospel alongside Christian Jews.[2] There must have been times when James held his head in his hands and fell to his knees in desperate prayer about the sinful Christians in Jerusalem. The story was no better when he asked the visitors to Jerusalem about their churches all across the Roman Empire.

That's why James deals firmly with his readers in 3:13 – 4:3. Having taught them to tame their tongues as their first and greatest battle against sin, he now commands them to tame their pride and ambition too. If they do not, those sins will destroy them.

The Jewish Christians who were scattered throughout the Greek-speaking world thought too much of themselves. They had fallen for that great Greek idol, wisdom. They considered themselves to be great thinkers who deserved to be recognized and rewarded with positions of leadership and influence in their churches. They failed to notice how self-centred their prayers were becoming as a result of their so-called wisdom. They were acting more like Kevin Spacey in *House of Cards* than like Jesus in the gospels.[3] James needed to teach them about true heavenly wisdom.

James points out that, while Greek wisdom is about pontificating words, heavenly wisdom is about purity of

---

[2] Acts 5:1–11; 6:1; 11:1–3; 15:1–5.

[3] The Greek word *eritheia* in 3:14 means *selfish ambition, intriguing for office, faction-forming* or *electioneering*.

lifestyle. If our wisdom leads to bitter envy, selfish ambition, infighting and quarrels, it cannot be the wisdom Jesus grants us through his Holy Spirit. Jesus laid down all he had in order to save others and he allowed his enemies to crucify him without his retaliating. The boastful Jewish Christians therefore cannot possess the wisdom that comes from heaven. Their wisdom must be *earthly*: from Greece rather than from God. It must be *unspiritual*: originating in the human soul instead of in God's Spirit. It must be *demonic*: more like the Devil than the Lord, following in Lucifer's footsteps when he lusted for heavenly promotion and was cast down to hell.[4] It must be inspired by evil spirits instead of by the Holy Spirit. It cannot earn them leadership position within the church. It can only earn them an exorcism![5]

James draws a stark contrast between phoney earthly wisdom and the true wisdom that comes down from heaven. If we do as he told us in 1:5–8 and ask God to fill us with his Spirit of Wisdom as he filled Solomon, we will discover the true wisdom which Solomon describes in Proverbs: *"The fear of the Lord is the beginning of wisdom, and knowledge of the Holy One is understanding."*[6] Earthly wisdom inspires us to live for this world's priorities, so it is characterized by self-serving pride. Heavenly wisdom inspires us to live for God's priorities instead, so it is characterized by humility, by purity, by peacefulness, by gentleness, by submission, by mercy, by fruitfulness, by generous faith[7] and by absolute sincerity.[8] Earthly wisdom is

---

[4] Isaiah 14:12–17; Ezekiel 28:11–19; Luke 10:18; Revelation 9:1; 12:3–12.

[5] The Greek word *daimoniōdēs* in 3:15 does not so much mean *like a demon* as *proceeding from a demon*.

[6] Proverbs 1:7; 9:10. Spirit-filled people have always discovered this. See Job 28:28; Psalm 111:10.

[7] The Greek word *adiakritos* in 3:17 can either mean *without favouritism* (as in 2:4) or *without wavering in faith* (as in 1:6). James therefore uses this one word to link back to two earlier passages.

[8] The Greek word *anupokritos* in 3:17 means literally *without any hypocrisy*. Earthly wisdom always leads to subtle scheming. Heavenly wisdom always

big on words and short on godliness. Heavenly wisdom always results in a *"good life"* and in *"deeds done"* by believers. The Message paraphrases verse 13 as *"It's the way you live, not the way you talk, that counts."*

James encourages us to sow heavenly wisdom in our lives and in our churches.[9] He tells us in verse 18 that if we sow heaven's seed, we will reap a harvest of righteousness – in other words, our lives will yield great purity, causing those around us to embrace righteousness through the Gospel of Christ because our lives convince them it is true. Some readers express surprise that James gives no explicit command or instruction about personal evangelism in his letter. There is no call for surprise. Acts 8:1–4 and 11:19–21 tell us that the early Christians were naturally very active in sharing their faith. All that James needed to tell them was that their Christian talk would never win the pagans to Christ unless it was matched by their authentic Christian walk.

James warns us that if we sow earthly wisdom in our lives and churches, it will set us at civil war with one another and at loggerheads with God.[10] We can pray all we want, but he will never answer prayers offered with selfish motives and which seek to indulge our selfish desires.[11] We are called to serve the Lord like angels, not to fight like demons.

So let's not be as foolish as the first-century Jewish Christians who thought that they were wise as they colluded with the enemies of their souls. Let's not turn our churches

---

leads to complete honesty.

[9] This farming metaphor is well-chosen. Our churches can be as fruitful as the Early Church at its best. We simply have to endure the difficult task of learning to be truly wise and humble towards one another.

[10] James uses military terminology when he says in 4:1–2 that our desires are *leading a military expedition* against us in order to fill the church with *fights* and *wars*. The Greek word for *evil desire* is similar in both 1:14–15 and 4:2.

[11] This is a big theme of Proverbs. See Proverbs 15:8, 21:13, 21:27 and 28:9, and Isaiah 1:13–15 and 29:13–14.

into a civil war zone through our own selfish ambition.[12] Let's stop acting like the Early Church at its worst and let's enjoy the rewards of heavenly wisdom which the Early Church enjoyed whenever it was at its best.

[12] The Christians were not actually murdering one another in 4:2. James is echoing Jesus' teaching in the Sermon on the Mount in Matthew 5:21–22. Hating one another is to commit the sin of murder.

# How to Make God Your Enemy (4:4-17)

*God opposes the proud but shows favour to the humble.*

(James 4:6)

Events are easier to interpret when they happen a safe distance away in the pages of the Bible. King Nebuchadnezzar looks out over his city and boasts, *"Is not this the great Babylon I have built as the royal residence, by my mighty power and for the glory of my majesty?"* It is pretty obvious that the tragedy which immediately befalls him is God's judgment on his overweening pride. King Herod encourages the Jewish crowds to chant after one of his speeches, *"This is the voice of a god, not of a man!"* It is pretty easy to link his sudden death to this outrageous act of blasphemy.[1]

But what about events a little closer to home? What about John Sedgwick, a general in the American Civil War who boasted that Confederate sharpshooters could never touch him? He never finished his last sentence: *"They couldn't hit an elephant at this dist..."*[2] Was that also an act of God's judgment against his pride? Or what about the deckhand on the RMS *Titanic* who told a passenger, *"It is unsinkable. God Himself could not sink this ship"*? Was the sinking of that great ocean liner the consequence of a deckhand's pride?[3]

---

[1] Daniel 4:24-37; Acts 12:21-23.

[2] Shelby Foote records this in *The Civil War: A Narrative, Volume III* (1974).

[3] The anonymous deckhand's words were so poignant that they even made it into James Cameron's film.

Let's get even closer to home than that. My wife and I spent the first six months of our married life completely gutting and restoring a dilapidated house. When I came to hammer the very last nail into an upstairs floorboard to complete the job, I turned to my wife and boasted like Nebuchadnezzar: *"Honey, I think we can be proud of the really great job we have done on this house."* The moment I hammered the nail, I heard a terrible sound. I had hit a pipe and water was flooding into the room downstairs. So let me ask you again: Are accidents like that God's judgment against our self-exalting pride?

James helps to answer our question. Having told us in 2:23 that God wants to be our friend, he now warns us that there is an easy way to turn God into our enemy instead. If we exhibit the pride that always flows from earthly wisdom instead of the humility that flows from heavenly wisdom, we declare war on God. James doesn't mention John Sedgwick or the *Titanic* or my flooded downstairs, but he does say this: *"Anyone who chooses to be a friend of the world becomes an enemy of God... That is why Scripture says: 'God opposes the proud but shows favour to the humble.'"*

James is talking about worldliness in general, linking back to 1:27, but he is also talking about the earthly wisdom that lies at the root of all worldly behaviour. He warns us strongly against it by reminding us of three things that the Old Testament teaches us.

In verse 4, he calls us *adulterers* because this is the word used by the prophets to describe the way in which the Israelites jumped into bed with every foreign idol and sinful idea. James says that we become adulterers whenever we break our pledge to follow Jesus by living for the objects of this sinful age instead of for the age to come.

In verse 5, James reminds us of the character of God as it is revealed in the Old Testament. He uses a deliberately ambiguous Greek phrase to summarize the Old Testament in general rather than any one verse in particular. He could be saying that God *"longs jealously for the spirit he has caused to dwell in us"* (since the Old Testament reveals God as a jealous husband who refuses to share his bride with another lover), or it could mean that *"the Spirit he has caused to dwell in us longs jealously"* (since the Old Testament reveals God's passionate desire to save the world by empowering ordinary but obedient people through his Holy Spirit). God so loved the people in the world that he gave his Son to save them out of the world. He expects us to love him back by preferring the Son who saved us to the world which ruined us. Anyone who clings onto this corrupted age has therefore declared war on God. They have decided to turn their greatest friend into their greatest foe.[4]

In verse 6, James reminds us of one of the most important verses in the book of Proverbs: *"God opposes the proud but shows favour to the humble."*[5] When Solomon was filled with God's Spirit of Wisdom, he understood what James teaches us in 3:13 – that true wisdom is humble, confessing freely that God is God and we are not.[6] He grasped that pride is therefore the utmost act of folly. It does not merely forfeit God as our friend. It turns him into our deadliest opponent. God meant it when he declared in Isaiah 42:8, *"I am the Lord; that is my name! I will not yield my glory to another."* Pride seeks to steal a portion of God's glory for ourselves. We should not be surprised when all heaven resists it.

In verses 7–10, James therefore urges us to surrender ourselves to God. Pride prevents us from ever achieving

---

[4] For the humble, James describes the Lord in 1:5 as *"The Giving God"*. For the proud, James describes him in 4:12 as *"The One Who Has Power to Save and to Destroy"*. Choose which way you wish to meet the Lord.

[5] Proverbs 3:34 is worded quite differently from James 4:6 in our English Bibles because he is quoting from the Greek Septuagint translation. The Diaspora Jews used the Greek rather than the Hebrew Old Testament.

[6] Proverbs 1:7; 9:10. See also Psalm 46:10; 111:10. This is so important that Peter also quotes from Proverbs 3:34 and accompanies it with very similar teaching in 1 Peter 5:5–9.

true greatness, in spite of all our clever scheming. Humility alone makes room for God to open doors of opportunity and promotion ahead of us.

In verses 11–12, James tells us that one of the ugly faces of our pride is judging other people.[7] Since God alone is Judge, it is a blasphemous attempt to usurp his throne. The irony of slandering and judging others is that, when we do so, we become far guiltier than they are of breaking God's Law,[8] Pushing ourselves forward will never prosper us. It will only put us in a place where we cannot receive God's favour.[9]

In verses 13–17, James tells us that another ugly face of our pride is making plans as if we were in control of our own destinies. Those who live by heaven's wisdom have learned to walk humbly, concluding their plans with the caveat, *"If it is the Lord's will."*[10] They do not boast about the future because they know the future belongs entirely to the Lord.[11] James warns that living by the maxim, *"I am the master of my fate: I am the captain of my soul,"* makes God our enemy.[12] God is our Master. God is our Captain. Anything other than this is delusional rebellion.

James described this battle for our souls in strong military terms in verses 1–2. He told us that earthly wisdom spawns evil desires which war against us, putting us in dire need of an ally to deliver us from the self-destructive consequences of our

---

[7] *"Neighbour"* in 4:12 contrasts with *"brother or sister"* in 4:11. These are not just instructions on how we are to behave in the Church. They are general instructions on how we are to behave in the world.

[8] James also calls the Lord *the Judge* in 5:9. This links back to his solemn warning in 2:12–13.

[9] James 4:11–12 echoes both 2:8–13 and 3:13–4:3, as well as Jesus' words in Matthew 7:1–5.

[10] Paul uses this phrase in Acts 18:21, and 1 Corinthians 4:19 and 16:5–7. Many generations of Christians have done the same, although having the right attitude matters more than saying the right words.

[11] Solomon also teaches this in Proverbs 16:1, 16:9, 16:33, 19:21 and 21:30–31.

[12] This quotation comes from a poem written by William Ernest Henley in 1875. Entitled *Invictus*, it inspired a movie of the same name.

pride. Therefore don't make God your enemy. You need him as your Friend and Saviour. Humble yourself before the Lord, so that he can lift you up.

# Prime the Pump (4:7–10)

*Humble yourselves before the Lord, and he will lift you up.*

(James 4:10)

There is a famous story about a man who got lost in the desert and was dying of thirst. He stumbled across an old shack with a rusty water pump and, next to it, a little bottle of water with a note. *"The pump is good but it will need priming,"* the note informed him. *"If you pour this small amount of water into the pump, you will displace all the air and be able to pump out all the water that you need."*

The man had a choice. He could survive a few more hours by drinking the small amount of water in the bottle, or he could throw it all away in the belief that it would unlock great unseen reservoirs of water. He took a leap of faith. He poured the water into the pump and began moving the handle. At first his efforts yielded nothing, and he began to fear that he had made the sacrifice for nothing, but then suddenly fresh water began to flow freely. He drank and showered, then filled all of the containers in the shack. They would enable him to find his way out of the desert and back home.

James tells us that we need to follow the example of the man in this story if we want to experience the fullness of God's plan for us. There are four things we need to sacrifice in order to prime the pump of heaven's blessing. None of these four things is easy to discard. Many people refuse and then wonder why their Christian life feels like a desert. If we are willing to throw away these four things in faith, James promises that they will unlock for us a greater walk with Jesus than ever we can imagine.

Verse 7 is all about *submission*. That was just as unpopular a word in the first century as it is today. Most people would rather die than surrender everything to God. As a result, many of them do. James tells us to throw away our independence so that we can be entrusted with the authority of God. *"Submit yourselves, then, to God"* is always the precursor to being told to *"Resist the devil, and he will flee from you."* It is only when we submit our own lives to God's authority that we are able to wield his authority over Satan and his destructive work throughout the world.

The first half of verse 8 is all about *devotion*. James tells us to throw away all of the distractions that keep our hearts from experiencing God's presence every day. James paraphrases a recurring promise in the Old Testament when he tells us to *"Come near to God and he will come near to you."*[1] God wants to be our friend. He wants to fill us with his Holy Spirit. If this is not our daily experience, the problem must therefore be at our end and not at his. There has never been a generation of Christians with greater access to the Bible and greater amounts of leisure time in which to read God's Word and pray. The problem is that there has never been a generation of Christians with a greater number of distractions either. We need to be ruthless and to throw them all away.

The second half of verse 8 and the whole of verse 9 are all about *repentance*. James tells us that we need to turn our backs completely on our former sins if we want to experience the power of God. Like Solomon in Ecclesiastes 7:4, James does not equate cheerfulness with godliness.[2] He tells us to

---

[1] Zechariah 1:3; Malachi 3:7; 2 Chronicles 15:2; Psalm 145:18; Hosea 6:1–3. The passionate language James uses in his letter reveals how strongly he was influenced by the Old Testament prophets.

[2] James 4:9 also strongly echoes Jesus' teaching in Matthew 5:4 and in Luke 6:21–25.

stop smiling and to grieve, mourn and wail over the continued presence of sin in our lives.[3] We are double-minded if we ask Jesus to forgive us for our sins and yet continue to cherish their presence in our lives after we have been forgiven.[4] God wants to fill us with his Holy Spirit to perform great miracles of power, but first he wants us to allow the Holy Spirit to perform in us a great miracle of purity. If we are unwilling say a radical yes to God's Kingdom personally, we cannot expect to be used to advance God's Kingdom in the lives of other people around us.

Verse 10 is all about *humility*. James tells us that we need to throw away our own hopes and ambitions if we want to experience the far better plan which has been prepared for us by God. Joseph woke up one day as a prisoner in a dungeon, but by evening God had made him the prime minister of Egypt.[5] Plotting and scheming our own way to glory is therefore counterproductive. His blessings are only ever given, never stolen. Hanging onto our own plans is simply another ugly face of the pride which turns him into our deadly enemy. Taking up our cross and dying to our own dreams is never easy. Following the crucified Saviour is often painful. But if we embrace the death of Jesus in our own lives, we will also experience the power of his resurrection. James promises us that this is true: *"Humble yourselves before the Lord, and he will lift you up."*

James is not merely talking theory. He has walked this road before us. He has primed the pump of God's blessing by throwing away everything that he once held most dear. When Jesus appeared to him after his resurrection, James threw away his stubborn independence and confessed that the half-brother he had once dismissed as a madman was in fact the Lord and

---

[3] James makes it clear in 4:8 that sinful thinking is just as serious as sinful action. See 2:10.

[4] The only other use of the Greek word for *double-minded* in the New Testament is in 1:8.

[5] Genesis 41:14, 41–45. Conversely, Haman woke up as prime minister of Persia but by evening was hanging from the gallows (Esther 5:10–12; 7:1–10).

King of the universe. He surrendered his own agenda and threw away every distraction that hindered him from making up for lost time by getting to know Jesus better. He became one of the original 120 believers who *"joined together constantly in prayer."* He was rewarded for his devotion when he was filled with the Spirit of Wisdom on the Day of Pentecost.[6]

James turned his back completely on the sinful lifestyle that had once made him so hostile towards his older brother. He accepted that the faith of his mother could not save him and that all of his past trips to the Temple had masked a heart that was in rebellion against God. He repented so thoroughly that he became known to the Early Church as "James the Just" or "James the Righteous". Eusebius tells us that *"his life displayed such an excellent degree of virtue and godliness that everyone held him in esteem as the most just of men."* He died so completely to his own hopes and dreams that he still proclaimed Jesus as Lord, even when he knew that it would cost him his life.[7]

James is therefore not asking us to do anything he has not already done before us. He is simply telling us that we will never experience normal first-century Christianity unless we prime the pump of our walk with God by throwing away the little that we have. Submission, devotion, repentance and humility are the keys that turn weak believers into powerful weapons in God's hands.

---

[6] 1 Corinthians 15:7; Acts 1:14.

[7] Eusebius tells us this in his *Church History* (2.23.2).

# Rich Pickings (4:13–5:6)

*Now listen, you rich people, weep and wail because of the misery that is coming on you.*

(James 5:1)

The first-century Jews were a nation of merchant traders. They had to be. There wasn't really any other option open to them. Scattered into foreign lands, they could not work as landowner farmers. Distrusted by the pagans, they could not work in public office. Determined to guard their own distinctive culture, they could not enlist in the army or in any other trade that might compromise their obedience to the Jewish Law. Instead they used their close-knit network of friends and family across the Roman Empire to become international traders. They became the kind of people James describes in 4:13. They said to one another, *"Today or tomorrow we will go to this or that city, spend a year there, carry on business and make money."*

But there was a price tag to all of this. Growing rich as merchant traders was spiritually costly to the Jews. There is a reason why James devotes more verses to teaching about how to handle money than he does to any other subject save how to tame the tongue. He warns the Jewish Christians that their prosperity presents several subtle dangers to their souls. If they are not careful, their riches will turn them rich pickings for the Devil.

In 4:13–16, James warns us that financial prosperity often leads to self-reliance. As we have already seen, it makes us arrogant and causes us to forget that we are not the masters of our fate or the captains of our soul. We forget that our lives are like the mist in the morning, blown about by the wind and then very quickly gone.[1] There is nothing wrong with our making business plans, just so long as we remember that our business lies in God's hands and not in our own. But if we forget this, our business plans become *"arrogant schemes"* and James warns us that *"all such boasting is evil."*[2]

In 4:17 – 5:3, James warns us that financial prosperity often makes us guiltier before God.[3] We tend to think of sin in terms of doing evil, but Solomon warns us in Proverbs that we also commit sin whenever we fail to do what is good.[4] Having more money grants us greater power (that's why most of us want it), but this greater power carries with it greater responsibility before God for what we fail to do. Basil of Caesarea was right to warn his congregation during the great famine of 368 AD that

> *When someone steals a man's clothes, we call him a thief, so shouldn't we give the same name to one who could clothe the naked and does not? The bread in your cupboard belongs to the hungry, the coat in your wardrobe belongs to the naked, the shoes you let rot belong to the barefoot, the money in your vaults belongs to the poor. You do wrong to all those you could help but do not.*[5]

---

[1] James uses a similarly vivid metaphor when addressing the wealthy in 1:10–11. Arrogant traders soon discover that markets are profoundly unstable and that so is life itself unstable too.

[2] We will see later in Hebrews 13:5–6 that reliance on money cannot co-exist with reliance upon God.

[3] Even though 4:17 probably originated from a different sermon to 4:13–16, it still carries on the same theme. This is why James starts the verse with the Greek word *oun*, meaning *therefore*.

[4] Proverbs 18:9; 21:13. Jesus also teaches this in Luke 10:30–37 and 12:47–48. It is foolish to think that James preached a different Gospel from Paul. He is equally clear that nobody can ever live up to God's Law.

[5] Basil gave this warning in a sermon "On the Rich Fool" from Luke 12:13–21.

First-century Judaism tended to assume that financial prosperity was a sign of God's approval. After all, in the Old Testament God had enriched Abraham, Job, David and Solomon. James addresses this false assumption head on in 5:1, just as he did back in 2:5–7. He tells us that our unused wealth is storing up God's judgment against us. Our mouldy money, our moth-eaten clothes and our toxically corroded gold and silver are proof that we have stored up excess wealth when we ought to have given it away. Our corroded riches will poison us and eat away our flesh when we are judged by God for hoarding money instead of using it to help those who are in need.[6] It is easy to see why the wealthy Christians in Jerusalem sold their houses and fields in response to James' preaching and provided for the poor within the church, but James also preaches these words to you and me. If you are an averagely well-off Westerner, you are in the top 1 per cent of the world's population by income. That carries with it a lot of responsibility. God has entrusted us with riches in order that we might give them away.[7]

In 5:4, James warns us that financial prosperity opens us up to greater temptation. Poor people may have many avenues for sin, but rich people have a great many more. James highlights one single issue: the fact that God holds employers responsible for the way in which they treat their workers. James refers to God as *kurios sabaōth*, the Greek form of the Hebrew name *Yahweh Tsabāōth*, which is frequently used in the Septuagint translation of the Old Testament. The significance of this would not be lost on any first-century Jew. James is reminding them that their own Scriptures are full of commands from the *Lord of*

---

[6] The Greek word *ios* in 5:3 means either *venom* or *rust* and is the same word which James used in 3:8. James knows that gold and silver cannot rust any more than money can go mouldy. He deliberately mixes his metaphors in order to grab hold of our attention.

[7] Although these verses talk more about helping the poor than they do about funding evangelism, there is also a link in Greek between the way our money will *witness* against us on the Last Day (5:3) and our responsibility to *witness* to the world that Jesus is coming back as Lord (Acts 1:8).

*Armies* or the *Lord Almighty* to safeguard the rights of workers, widows, orphans, immigrants and the very poor.

In 5:5–6, James warns us that financial prosperity can foster complacency about the eternal destinies that hang in the balance all around us. It is not easy to live for the age to come when the luxuries and self-indulgent pastimes of this present age crowd our attention. This is one of the reasons why Jesus exclaimed that *"It is easier for a camel to go through the eye of a needle than for someone who is rich to enter the kingdom of God."*[8] It is also one of the reasons why churches tend to be far fuller in the developing world than they are in the wealthy cities of Europe and America. James echoes the Old Testament prophets when he refers to the day of Jesus' return to judge the world as *"the day of slaughter"* and when he warns us that we condemn and murder people if we fail to use our money to feed, clothe and convert them while we still have time.[9]

This was an essential warning for Jewish merchant traders in the first century, but it is also just as essential for us today. Judas Iscariot is not the only would-be disciple of Jesus to sell out his good intentions for a handful of coins. Ananias and Sapphira are not the only church members to sing about their love for Jesus on a Sunday and to deny it through their financial dealings all week long. How we spend our money is a clear sign of whether or not we have truly responded to the Gospel. Jesus commands us in Matthew 6:19–21: *"Do not store up for yourselves treasures on earth, where moths and vermin destroy, and where thieves break in and steal. But store up for yourselves treasures in heaven... For where your treasure is, there your heart will be also."*

---

[8] Mark 10:21–31. See also 1 Timothy 6:9–10 and 17–19.

[9] For example, in Jeremiah 2:13; Ezekiel 3:17–21; 33:1–9. James 5:6 links back to 2:10–11. We can murder people through our lack of positive action just as easily as through our evil actions.

# Oblias (5:7–11)

*Be patient, then, brothers and sisters, until the Lord's coming.*

(James 5:7)

Things were not about to get any easier for the Jewish Christians. Not in the short term, anyway. In the next twenty years before Hebrews was written in around 68 AD, it would become even harder to live as a Jewish Christian in the Roman Empire.

The Emperor Claudius had already banned the Jews in Rome from holding any religious meetings. In 49 AD he would expel them from the imperial capital. This may have simply been an act of general anti-Semitism, but the Roman historian Suetonius suggests that it was particularly provoked by a hatred of Christianity, which at the time was still very Jewish.[1]

That was just the beginning. From 49 AD onwards the Jewish Christians would be increasingly persecuted by their own countrymen too. Paul and Barnabas would travel throughout Cyprus, Asia Minor, Macedonia and Greece, bringing many pagans to faith in Jesus and transforming the largely Jewish church into an international brotherhood of believers. In doing so, they would provoke the Jewish leaders to such jealousy that waves of persecution broke out against them in every city. Eventually, the Jewish leaders would slam the door on the Christian faith altogether, symbolized in Acts by the moment when the people of Jerusalem slam the Temple gates on Paul.

---

[1] Acts 18:2, Cassius Dio, *Roman History* (60.6.6), and Suetonius, *Life of Claudius* (25). Suetonius says that Claudius responded to their trouble-making *"at the instigation of Chrestus"*, probably a reference to *Christ*.

The rift between Judaism and Christianity would grow ever wider for the next 2,000 years.[2]

This would mean the worst of both worlds for the Jewish Christians. They would be persecuted by their fellow Jews for not being Jewish enough, culminating in the illegal execution of James at the hands of the high priest in 62 AD. They would be persecuted by the Romans for being too Jewish after the harsh imperial response to this illegal action provoked the Jewish Revolt in 66 AD. By the time that the first verse of Hebrews was written in around 68 AD, the Jewish nation and its Temple worship would be hurtling along the highway to destruction. If the Jewish Christians found life difficult when James wrote in 48 AD, they needed to know that it was only going to get harder.

That's why James returns to the theme of rejoicing under trials in 5:7–11. He began his letter by talking about how to cope with painful suffering in 1:2–18, and now he ends it in exactly the same way. He compares the Christian life to the long period of waiting which a farmer has to endure between planting seed, receiving rain from heaven and finally harvesting the precious crop into his barns. He warns us that such patient endurance is never easy. We are tempted to grumble against one another and even to give up on the Christian faith altogether. But we mustn't. Our perseverance will yield us a better harvest than any earthly farmer has ever seen. To help us, James gives us three reminders why we can stay cheerful in the midst of any trial.

First, we can persevere because we know *the Lord is coming*. The second coming of Jesus is a constant theme of this letter.[3] It is sobering to know that Jesus is about to return as the Judge of the whole world, but it is also extremely reassuring. People may say that we are traitors to our culture, that we are unwise fools and that we are throwing away our lives for nothing, but a day is coming when the truth will finally be

---

[2] Acts 13:45, 50; 14:1–6, 19; 17:5–7, 13; 18:6, 12; 20:3; 21:27–30.

[3] James 1:12; 2:5, 12–13; 3:1; 4:12; 5:1–6, 7–8, 9, 20.

revealed. Our temporary suffering will feel like nothing on that glorious day when we are vindicated as the beloved children of God and as the wise subjects of Christ's Kingdom.

It is hard not to conclude from this letter that James expected the return of Jesus to happen in his lifetime. He was wrong but, in a sense, he was also right. Jesus told us to expect his return to come suddenly, like a thief in a night, so James was right to live as if the day was just about to arrive.[4] Only a foolish investor would imagine that the past performance of a commodity is a guarantee of its future performance. Only a foolish believer would assume that, because Jesus has not returned for twenty centuries, he will therefore not return in the next twenty years or twenty months or twenty days. In addition to being nicknamed "James the Just", the writer of this letter was also nicknamed "Oblias", which is Aramaic for "Bulwark of the People". The early Christians saw him as an unshakeable bastion of the Christian faith, a solid wall that gave them strength to persevere through any storm. The apostle Paul also hailed him as one of the great pillars of the Church.[5] James therefore wants to strengthen us as he strengthened the believers in Jerusalem. The more we meditate on the second coming of Jesus, the more we will be able to stand up under temporary trials. Expect Jesus to come back any day soon. One day you will be right.

Second, James tells us to persevere because *the Lord knows what he is doing.* His farming metaphor is a reminder that God is always faithful to those who work hard and wait patiently for him. James reminds us that the Old Testament prophets suffered in the same way that we do and that they were eventually vindicated by the Lord. He reminds us of the book of Job in the Old Testament. Job's example shows us that God is able to use

---

[4] Matthew 24:36–25:46. 2 Peter 3:1–14 and Romans 13:11–12 also warn us that it is very dangerous to assume that the return of Jesus is a long way off.

[5] Paul calls James a *pillar* in Galatians 2:9. The second-century Christian historian Hegesippus says his nickname was Oblias, quoted by Eusebius in *Church History* (2.23.7).

even our darkest trials for our good. We need to cling onto the testimony of those who have suffered before us that the Lord is full of wisdom and compassion and mercy.[6]

Third, James tells us to persevere because *the Lord has made us part of a team*. James mentions Job and the prophets in order to remind us that we are not alone. If we reduce Christianity to the private faith of individuals, we will find it hard to stand up under persecution because pieces of string break far more easily on their own than they do when they are woven into a single thick cord. One of the big themes of this letter has been that we are a family which meets together and which draws strength from other members of the same team. The writer of Hebrews says something similar in the face of this persecution: *"Let us consider how we may spur one another on towards love and good deeds, not giving up meeting together, as some are in the habit of doing, but encouraging one another – and all the more as you see the Day approaching."*[7]

We can expect persecution and trials. John 15:20 and 2 Timothy 3:12 warn us that suffering is inevitable for anyone who truly follows Jesus in a world which doesn't. Let's therefore learn from Oblias how our faith can stay rock solid in the midst of trials. Let's remember that the Lord knows what he is doing, that the Lord is coming back and that, in the meantime, the Lord helps us to persevere by making us part of a close-knit team.

---

[6] Romans 8:28. It helps farmers to remember that Jesus is *"Lord of the Harvest"* (Matthew 9:38).

[7] Hebrews 10:24–25. Solomon also teaches this in Ecclesiastes 4:10–12.

# Everyday Church (5:12–16)

*Is anyone among you ill? Let them call the elders of the church to pray over them and anoint them with oil in the name of the Lord.*

(James 5:14)

The church James led in Jerusalem was successful by any standard. Planted by a group of 120 rag-tag believers in May 30 AD, it very quickly grew and began to transform the whole city. It won 3,000 converts through its first public sermon, and new believers were added to the church daily. It won converts among the priestly ruling classes and it won converts among the beggars in the road. Even when it was persecuted and scattered, it survived and planted more churches like itself across the whole of Judea and Samaria.

When most Christians read the book of Acts, they long for their own church to be as successful as the first church in Jerusalem. But our desire needs to be turned into obedient action. That's why it is so helpful to have a record of what the leader of the church preached to his congregation. These verses show us what the church in Jerusalem was really like on the inside. They describe their everyday expectations for church life together. If we are willing to embrace those same priorities, James assures us, our own everyday experience will become like theirs too.

In verse 12, James tells us that the church in Jerusalem was *an authentic church*. They did not wear masks or talk in deceptive language with one another. They were honest about their highs and lows, about their victories and their failures. Yet again James echoes the teaching of Jesus in the Sermon on the Mount when he tells us not to swear oaths like the first-century Jews who rejected Jesus as their Messiah.[1] Our yes should mean yes, and our no should mean no. Churches that thrive under God's hand are churches in which people walk in complete honesty with one another.[2]

In verses 13–16, James tells us that the church in Jerusalem was *a community church*. The believers did not see themselves as private individuals with their own private concerns. Acts 2:44 tells us that *"All the believers were together and had everything in common."* They bore each other's burdens and shared the highs and lows of life with one another. If somebody received some good news, they would celebrate together. If someone was in trouble, they would weep and pray together. If somebody was ill, they would pray for them. If someone sinned, they would help them find forgiveness. If a church has more meetings than it has meetings of heart, it isn't godly. We are not called to put on a Christian performance show. We are called to become a loving community.

In verse 13, James tells us that the church in Jerusalem was *a praying church*. Their natural instinct in every situation was to take things to the Lord in prayer. In good times, they would worship gladly. In more difficult times, they would worship through the tears. They believed the promise of Jesus that *"I will do whatever you ask in my name, so that the Father may be glorified in the Son."*[3] When they took Jesus at his word, they found that their little church made a massive impact. So will we.

In verses 14–16, James tells us that the church in Jerusalem

---

[1] Some Christians take this verse and Matthew 5:33–37 to mean that we should not swear an oath in court. But James is talking about integrity in general, banning the same double-speak as Jesus in Matthew 23:16–22.

[2] Although it probably comes from a different sermon, 5:12 is not a change of subject from 5:7–11. James warned us in 5:9 that we need to guard our tongues in view of Jesus' imminent return as Judge.

[3] John 14:13. Jesus promises seven times to answer our prayers in John 14–16 alone.

was *a faith-filled church*. The Christians did not explain away the healing promises of Jesus. They believed that he had given them authority over sickness and power to chase the Devil's work away. They did not treat healing merely as an evangelistic tool for attracting unbelievers to the Gospel. After all, Jesus had called it *"the children's bread"* in Mark 7:27. They did not treat healing as a spiritual gift granted by God only to the apostles. James expects that every elder and every church member will pray for people to be healed. They did not treat prayer for healing as a long-shot, a last resort which would probably not be answered but which was nevertheless worth a try. James assures us that, when elders pray for those who are ill and anoint them with oil as an expression of their faith in the Holy Spirit, *"the prayer offered in faith **will** make the ill person well; the Lord **will** raise them up."*[4] It is no use fantasizing about what it would be like if our own churches were like the one James led in Jerusalem unless we are willing to take seriously what he says.

It is fairly obvious in the book of Acts that the church in Jerusalem grew rapidly through miraculous healing. Few Christians deny that *"The apostles performed many signs and wonders among the people."* What we tend to forget, however, is that this was not unique to the apostles. Every Christian prayed for God to stretch out his hand to heal through them, and God answered their prayer by healing through many non-apostles such as Stephen, Philip and Ananias.[5] James tells us to expect

---

[4] See Mark 6:13. We are not to anoint people with oil to prepare them for death, but to heal them!

[5] Acts 2:43; 3:1–16; 4:30; 5:12–16; 6:8; 8:6; 9:17–18. It makes no sense when people counter that most of the healings in the book were performed by the apostles. That's because it is called the Acts of the Apostles!

supernatural healing to be normal, everyday Christianity.[6] If we believe him, our churches will become like his.[7]

In verses 15–16, James tells us that the church in Jerusalem was *a humble church*. He expects there to be one team of elders leading a single church in any city, not a plethora of different denominations operating in competition with one another. It may be too late to change the splintered expression of Christianity across our communities, but at the very least James warns us that we need to work in unity with other churches if we want to see our cities impacted like Jerusalem. If we have only one Saviour and only one Lord, we cannot act like many different families of God. On an individual church level, James also expects Christians to be very humble towards their leaders and towards each other.[8] If we learned anything in chapter 4, we should be prepared to confess our sins and deficiencies freely to one another in order to move forward as one united team.

Does the church in Jerusalem sound pretty impressive? Well, it was, yet at the same time it was very ordinary and everyday. In verse 17, James reminds us that *"Elijah was a man just like us."* He tells us that the heroes of ancient Israel were no better than the Christians in Jerusalem and, in doing so, he also tells us that the Christians in Jerusalem were no better than us. They were just a group of everyday believers who behaved as Jesus commanded and who experienced the blessing that always comes to churches that fully embrace his better way of living.

---

[6] James uses the Greek word *sōzō* in 5:15 to refer to healing literally as *saving*, because it is an integral aspect of the Gospel. I explain in more detail how to heal the sick in my commentaries on Matthew, Mark and Acts.

[7] Like Peter in Acts 3:16, James emphasizes the importance of faith in our authority to rebuke illness in Jesus' name. One reason why we see fewer healings than the Christians in Jerusalem is that we expect to.

[8] James is not telling us that we need to make a formal confession in order to be forgiven. He is simply pointing out that sickness is occasionally linked to sin (1 Corinthians 11:29–32 tempered by John 9:2–3), and that we have authority to declare forgiveness over one another after prayer (John 20:23).

If ours is an authentic church, a community church, a praying church, a faith-filled church and a humble church, it will be just like the church in Jerusalem. It will be the everyday kind of church that God always promises to use.

# Camel Knees (5:16–20)

*The prayer of a righteous person is powerful and effective. Elijah was a human being, even as we are.*

(James 5:16–17)

Many people find the way James ends his letter very strange. There are no personal greetings and no goodbyes, just a final sermon clipping and then silence. The final clipping is confusing too, the very opposite of ending on a high. But if we understand the context in which James wrote his letter, we will see that his ending is a work of genius. It is brilliant. It prepares the Jewish Christians to play their part in God's plan to save many from their nation in the difficult years that lie ahead.

James ends his letter by talking about Elijah, a prophet who was sent to the nation of Israel when it turned its back on God. He grew discouraged that so many Israelites rejected God, but the Lord rebuked him: *"I reserve seven thousand in Israel – all whose knees have not bowed down to Baal and whose mouths have not kissed him."*[1] The Jewish Christians must not be discouraged by increased persecution from their countrymen. Nor must we be discouraged by the backslidden nations of Europe or the stubbornly resistant non-Christian people groups of Asia. James ends his letter with a reminder that God knows what he is doing. He is planning to save large numbers of people.

Elijah learned to see his nation God's way. Even though it had been split into a northern kingdom of ten tribes and a

---

[1] The references in this chapter to the life of Elijah come from 1 Kings 17:1, 18:1, 18:30–39, 18:42–46, 19:9–18 and 21:25–29. James adds several details to the account in 1 Kings, presumably from the Jewish oral record.

southern kingdom of two tribes, he rebuilt God's altar using twelve stones in order to express one united hope for the twelve tribes of Israel. Jesus did the same when he appointed twelve apostles as the founders of his Church, and so did James when he emphasized at the start of his letter that the Jewish Christians were still part of *"the twelve tribes scattered among the nations."* James reassures the first-century Jewish Christians that God is planning to save many from their nation through their obedience to him. God wants to save many people in our own nations too.

Elijah changed his nation primarily through prayer. Much of his ministry was unglamorous but very effective. He prayed that God would discipline his nation by stopping it raining for three and a half years. In an agrarian society that was more disastrous than the Great Depression. James warns the Jewish Christians that things may have to get harder for their nation before many Jews are saved. Three and a half years later, the Lord told Elijah that his nation was ready to receive rain. Elijah prayed and the rains suddenly came. James has been calling us to prayer throughout his letter, but this teaching about Elijah brings together his four great principles if we want to see revival.

In 1:6–7, James taught us that *prayer minus faith produces nothing*. He is not calling us to utter endless cries of despair over our nations. Five minutes of prayer that believes in God's promises achieves far more than five weeks of prayerful panicking. *"When you ask, you must believe and not doubt, because the one who doubts is like a wave of the sea, blown and tossed by the wind. That person should not expect to receive anything from the Lord."*

In 4:2, James taught us that *faith minus prayer produces nothing*. Real faith provokes real action, so prayerlessness betrays our lack of genuine faith. Even if we do believe that God will save many people in a nation, our faith is useless unless it drives us to prayer. *"You do not have because you do not ask God,"* James informs us very plainly. Faith without prayer is as useless as prayer without faith.

James is not just talking theory. He was very diligent in playing the role of Elijah for first-century Israel. A second-century historian tells us that *"He was in the habit of entering alone into the temple, and was frequently found upon his knees begging forgiveness for the people. As a result, his knees became hard like those of a camel, because of the way he constantly bent them in his worship of God and in asking forgiveness for the people."*[2] James developed camel knees because he put his teaching into practice. He ends his letter by encouraging us to develop camel knees of our own.

In 4:3, James taught us that *prayer plus faith minus surrender produces nothing.* Even if we believe God's promises and pray them back to him, he will not give us a good gift if he knows we will use that good gift badly. If we are proud and would attribute Gospel breakthrough to ourselves, he will wait until he finds a humble person he can use. If we ask for revival in order to boost our own church numbers, our own denomination or our own reputation, God flatly refuses to answer our prayers. He will not be party to a narcissistic agenda, which seeks to use the Church as a means to glorify ourselves. *"When you ask, you do not receive, because you ask with wrong motives."*

In 5:16–18, therefore, James concludes the teaching about prayer that runs throughout his entire letter. He tells us that *prayer plus faith plus surrender produces breakthrough.* It is the prayer of a righteous person that is powerful and effective – the prayer of anybody who has been justified through the death and resurrection of Jesus and who is truly willing to walk the road of

---

[2] Hegessipus wrote this in a work which has not survived, but this passage survived because Eusebius quoted it in c.300 AD in his *Church History* (2.23.6).

death and resurrection themselves.[3] It is the prayers of people who pray earnestly and persistently which revive nations, symbolized by the way in which Elijah adopted the usual crouching position of a Hebrew woman in labour as he birthed revival through his prayers at the top of Mount Carmel.[4] When Paul arrived in Jerusalem in 57 AD, he found James very excited. His prayers had been answered and he exclaimed to Paul, *"You see, brother, how many tens of thousands of Jews have believed!"*[5] Is it any wonder that the little church in Jerusalem became a mighty megachurch when the Christians devoted themselves so constantly to prayer that, when Peter escaped from prison, he knew exactly where he would find them: at a prayer meeting together?[6] If we behave like old Camel Knees and his friends, our own prayers will be answered too.

In 5:19–20, James therefore ends his letter by warning the Jewish Christians not to see their countrymen as enemies. They have wandered from the truth by rejecting and crucifying their Messiah, but their multitude of sins will be forgiven if the Christians reach out to them as Elijah reached out to Ahab.[7] Incredibly, when wicked Ahab confessed his sin and humbled himself before God, the Lord had mercy upon him. Elijah was a man just like us, and Ahab was a man just like those around us.

James signs off his letter abruptly. He has said all that he needs to say. He has shown us what it truly means to surrender

---

[3] James has already warned us in 3:9–10 that how we use our mouth all day affects its effectiveness in prayer. See also 1 Timothy 2:8; Hebrews 5:7; 1 Peter 3:7; Isaiah 1:15; Proverbs 15:8, 29; 21:13; 28:9.

[4] James actually uses a Hebraism, saying in Greek that *"Elijah prayed with prayer."* James is not so much emphasizing the power of our fervency as he is the power of our prayers.

[5] Acts 21:20. The Greek word *muriades* means literally *tens of thousands*, not just thousands.

[6] Acts 1:14, 24; 2:42; 3:1; 4:24–31; 6:6; 7:59; 12:5, 12. This is the attitude that inspired James 5:13–16.

[7] James 5:20 is not telling us that we can earn forgiveness for ourselves by helping others. The forgiveness we bring about is for them. James is paraphrasing Proverbs 10:12, just like 1 Peter 4:8.

our lives to Jesus as Lord. He has shown us how to turn this message outwards in order to bring salvation to those around us. His letter has finished. It is time for us to surrender our lives to Jesus' better way of living.

# Part Two

# A Better Glimpse of God

## (Hebrews 1–7)

# Twenty Years Later (1:1)

*In the past God spoke to our ancestors through the*
*prophets at many times and in various ways...*

(Hebrews 1:1)

Twenty years is a long time. A lot of things took place between James writing the last verse of his letter in around 48 AD and another Jewish leader writing the first verse of Hebrews in around 68 AD. Nevertheless, the main thing that ought to strike us as we begin the second of the two New Testament letters written primarily to Jewish Christians is not their differences but their similarities. These two letters belong next to one another in the New Testament. They are similar letters, written by similar people and with a very similar message.

Like James, Hebrews emphasizes that the Christian faith is the true fulfilment of Old Testament Judaism. The ancient Jewish faith, which became corrupted by the high priests and the rabbis, has now been restored through the arrival of the long-awaited Messiah. It has been more than restored, because Jesus fulfilled all of the Old Testament prophecies which predicted that God would establish a new and better covenant with his People. The opening words of this second letter emphasize that *"In the past God spoke to our ancestors through the prophets at many times and in various ways, but in these last days he has spoken to us by his Son."* Christianity calls the world back to the religion of Abraham, but it also upgrades it, massively. The Messiah has moved the story on. Something far better has come.

Like James, Hebrews takes the form of a sermon rather than a letter. James begins like a letter but then quickly turns into a series of sermon highlights from the church meetings in Jerusalem. Hebrews ends like a letter, with a few personal greetings and a proper sign-off, but it does not begin like a letter. It dives straight into the meat of the message and is far more like a long and in-depth sermon than any of the other New Testament letters. We do not know whether it consists of highlights taken from several different messages, like James, or whether it was originally one long sermon. All we know is that it reads more like the spoken than the written word, with all the vivid storytelling and threats that James taught us to expect from a first-century Christian preacher.

Like James, Hebrews was written in the midst of persecution. We discover that some Jewish Christians have had their property confiscated as a result of their faith in Jesus. Others have been thrown into prison. Some have even been killed. Since the letter tells us that Timothy has also been imprisoned and Paul says nothing about this in his final letter to Timothy, we can tell that it was written after early 67 AD.[1] We can also tell that the letter was written before the destruction of the Temple in 70 AD because the writer would surely have used that seismic event to prove his message that Temple Judaism was now obsolete and superseded. Since the writer uses the present tense when talking about worship in the Temple, this second letter must have been written between early 67 AD and the middle of 70 AD, with a date of around 68 AD most likely.[2]

This was therefore the period when Jewish Christians were on the receiving end of savage persecution on two separate fronts. The Jewish leaders had illegally executed James in 62 AD. When this led to open revolt against Roman rule in 66 AD, their hostility towards the Christians grew even more savage. At the same time, the Emperor Nero launched his own wave of persecution against the Christians, accusing them of having

---

[1] Hebrews 10:32–34; 13:7, 23.

[2] We find present tenses in 5:1–3, 7:23, 7:27, 8:3–5, 9:6–9, 9:13, 9:25, 10:1, 10:3–4, 10:8, 10:11 and 13:10–11.

started the Great Fire of Rome in 64 AD. During the six years between the fire and the sack of Jerusalem in 70 AD, scores of influential Christians were brutally executed. Peter was crucified. Paul was beheaded. The survivors were terrified but any Jewish Christian had an easy get-out plan. Unlike the Gentile believers, they could secure legal protection by renouncing Jesus as their Messiah and returning to the Jewish synagogues. Old Testament Judaism was officially tolerated by the Roman emperors, so it offered them relative safety. For many Jewish Christians, the lure was irresistibly tempting.

That's why James and Hebrews, for all their similarities, also have some differences too. The writer of Hebrews states much more strongly that first-century Judaism is not a form of Christianity. He warns his readers severely that if they return to the synagogues, they are not choosing safety at all. They are saving their skins at the expense of forfeiting their souls. Whereas James focuses on the practical outworking of the Gospel in order to show Jewish believers that Jesus offers us *a better way of living*, Hebrews focuses on the theological detail of the Gospel in order to teach us that Jesus is our sole source of salvation. He has given us *a better glimpse of God* (chapters 1–7), *a better way to know God* (chapters 8–10) and *better reasons to believe* (chapters 11–13). Old Testament Judaism and Christianity are similar and yet they are also fundamentally different. In Jesus, something far better has come.[3]

This background may also explain why the writer of Hebrews is unknown. Although it is possible that the first few lines of the letter have been lost, it is more likely that the writer failed to state his name because the times were too dangerous. Jerusalem was in revolt against Roman rule, so any letter between the two cities was politically explosive on both sides.[4] Tertullian suggests that the author was Barnabas. Until

---

[3] The words *better*, *greater* and *superior* occur 22 times in Hebrews.

[4] A group of Christians *from* Italy (not *in* Italy) interject their greetings in 13:24. Such an authoritative letter sent to Rome about the Jewish religion was most

the Reformation, most people assumed that it was Paul (which is why Hebrews comes before James in the New Testament even though it was written later), but the style and language is so unlike Paul's that few people believe that now. Some suggest that it was written by Priscilla, although a Greek masculine participle in 11:32 makes such a theory unlikely. Others argue for Apollos. All we can say for certain is that it was written by a Jew with a brilliant command of Greek. It is the only truly anonymous letter in the New Testament.[5]

Knowing who wrote Hebrews is not essential. Knowing what Hebrews teaches is far more important. The Jewish Christians who received the letter evidently knew who wrote it and they trusted his comprehensive explanation of what the Messiah had achieved for God's People.[6] They believed that they needed this letter every bit as much as they needed the gospels to understand the significance of the ministry of Jesus.

They believed that this letter would make them strong to persevere in their faith through the most savage of storms. They believed the writer's message that the arrival of Jesus has changed everything. Something far better has come.

---

likely to have originated in Jerusalem.

[5] Tertullian *On Modesty* (20). The Early Church leader Origen was forced to conclude that *"who wrote the epistle, only God knows"* (quoted by Eusebius in *Church History*, 6.25.11–14).

[6] They knew who he was because he asks them to pray for him in 13:18. If he deliberately omitted to sign the letter, he must have given proof of his authorship to the messenger who delivered it.

# Better Than Angels (1:1–14)

*He became as much superior to the angels as the
name he has inherited is superior to theirs.*

(Hebrews 1:4)

Henry Ford boasted that Americans loved his cars because he knew what they wanted better than they did: *"If I had asked people what they wanted, they would have said faster horses."* Most first-century Jews wanted God to help them but only if he was willing to do it their way. When God sent Jesus as their Messiah, they were offended by his motor-car way of thinking. They rejected Jesus and told God they were happy with their horses.

That's why the writer of Hebrews begins his letter with fourteen verses that celebrate how different Jesus is from the very best that Israel's past has to offer. Hebrews has been nicknamed "the fifth gospel" because it puts the spotlight on Jesus every bit as much as do Matthew, Mark, Luke or John. The words "Jesus" and "Christ" occur four times in James but thirty-four times in Hebrews. James never uses the word "blood" but Hebrews uses it twenty times. James does not explain much about what Jesus has done for us. He focuses more on what it truly means for us to follow him. Hebrews redresses the balance by telling us who Jesus is and what his great sacrifice has achieved for us.

In verses 1–3, the writer tells us that Jesus is far better than all of the Old Testament prophets. This is some of the best Greek in the whole of the New Testament, because the writer crafts these words of worship very carefully.[1] He affirms the ancient Jewish faith by emphasizing that he is as Jewish as his readers (it is the faith of *"our ancestors"*), but he also points out that the Old Testament prophets only received a limited revelation of the Lord. Jesus has opened up a whole new way of knowing God because he is more than just a prophet. He is God's one and only Son.[2]

Muslims are offended when they read these opening verses because they think that "Son of God" implies that God had intercourse with Mary. Of course this is not what the writer is saying at all. Any Jew would instantly recognize it as one of the Messiah's titles in the Old Testament.[3] The true offence in these opening verses is that the writer tells us that there is far more to this title than initially meets the eye. It is much more than an affectionate affirmation of a great human king who has been born to the family of David. It is a statement that the Messiah is the second person of the Trinity.

The writer tells us that Jesus is God's heir.[4] He was with God in the beginning creating the universe.[5] He still sustains the universe today with the powerful sound of his voice.[6] He

[1] It is excellent Greek but it was clearly written by a man who thought like a Jew. He refers literally in 1:3 to *"the word of his power."* That is how a Jew would talk. A native-born Greek would say *"his powerful word."*

[2] The writer tells us in 1:2 that when the Old Testament prophets spoke about *"the last days"* they were prophesying about the whole of AD history. Peter also tells us this in Acts 2:16–17. The last days have begun.

[3] See 2 Samuel 7:14; Psalm 2:7; 89:26; Matthew 16:16; 26:63; John 11:27; 20:31.

[4] He reaffirms this in 1:6, since the Greek word *prōtotokos* does not mean *born first* (Jesus was never created), but *born foremost*. The word is used in the Septuagint for younger sons who became their father's heir (Exodus 4:22; Jeremiah 31:9). Paul also uses it in the same sense in Romans 8:29 and Colossians 1:15.

[5] John 1:1–3; 17:5. Genesis 1:26 hints at this when God says *"Let us make mankind in **our** image, in **our** likeness."*

[6] The voice of Jesus carries world-changing power. That's why it is such a privilege to be permitted to pray and issue commands in his name. Our voices become as powerful as his whenever he backs up our words.

is the perfect image of God the Father and he radiates God's undiluted glory.[7] He is the great Saviour who has fulfilled all the salvation prophecies of the Old Testament so completely that he has now sat down at the right hand of God the Father in heaven. His work is finished. He is sovereign over the entire universe. The first-century Jews might be comfortable referring to the Messiah as the "Son of God", but the writer tells them that this is only because they have not truly understood what it signifies.

In verse 4, the writer spells it out. It means that Jesus is not just superior to any of the prophets. He is also vastly superior to any angel. They are creatures, whereas he is the Creator. More than that, he is the victorious Saviour who has been given a throne and a name (both of these things speak of authority) that are far above those held by any angel, demon or human.[8] False teachers might deny the divinity of Jesus,[9] and some practitioners of Jewish folk religion might encourage people to pray to angels,[10] but this is of secondary importance to the writer of this letter. He is writing against mainstream first-century Judaism, which has become so corrupted by the priests and rabbis that it has rejected its own Messiah. It is stuck in the past, demanding a faster horse from God instead of embracing his motor-car Messiah. The Jewish Christians must not go back to the synagogues in order to escape persecution. The synagogues are preaching a different religion altogether. Christianity proclaims that something far better has come.

The writer emphasizes this by quoting seven times from

---

[7] The Greek word *charaktēr* in 1:3 means *exact likeness*. John 14:9 affirms that to see Jesus is to see God.

[8] We are also told this in Acts 2:36 and Philippians 2:9–11. It is repeated in Hebrews 2:9.

[9] We see this in other books which were written in 62–67 AD: Titus, 1 and 2 Timothy, 1 and 2 Peter, and Jude.

[10] False teachers influenced by Jewish folk religion preached this in Colossians 2:18.

the Old Testament in verses 5–14.[11] These are the first of thirty-five direct quotations in the book of Hebrews, because the writer is determined to prove that the Christian Gospel, and not corrupted synagogue religion, is the true fulfilment of the ancient faith of Israel. A first quotation from Psalm 2:7 and a second from either 2 Samuel 7:14 or 1 Chronicles 17:13 both prove that the title "Son of God" is far more than a term of affection. The Old Testament sometimes refers to the angels as "sons of God", but it never declares any of them to be the "Son of God" in the same way that it does the Messiah.[12]

A third quotation from Deuteronomy 32:43 demonstrates that the Messiah is God (he is worshipped) and yet somehow not God (since it is the Lord who tells the angels to worship him).[13] A fifth quotation from Psalm 45:6–7, which uses Solomon's wedding day to prophesy about the Messiah, does the same, addressing the Messiah as God while proclaiming that God has anointed him King! In between, a fourth quotation from Psalm 104:4 makes a stark contrast between the Messiah and the angels, since the Lord treats angels as servants and not as equals. A sixth quotation from Psalm 102:25–27 reveals that the Messiah is the Creator.[14] A seventh quotation from Psalm 110 reveals the Lord both as Messiah and as the one who invites

---

[11] Some of these quotations seem quite loose because our Old Testaments are translated from the Hebrew text. However, like James, the writer is quoting from the Greek Septuagint because this is what his readers used.

[12] The Septuagint of Deuteronomy 32:43 refers to *"sons of God"*, which the writer changes to *"angels"* in 1:6 in order to remove any ambiguity. He quotes Psalm 2:7 again in 5:5 to reaffirm the uniqueness of God's Son.

[13] This verse does not immediately strike us as having been spoken about the Messiah, but the Holy Spirit inspired the writer to spot what others miss. John 12:41 does the same with a similar passage in Isaiah.

[14] Again, the Holy Spirit revealed to the writer that this psalm talks about Jesus, even though it might not be immediately obvious to all. Although we should look after the environment, this psalm tells us not to panic. As our planet wears out, it prophesies that our Messiah's return is drawing near.

the Messiah to sit at his right hand.[15] This bombardment of Old Testament quotations reaches its excited conclusion in verse 14. The writer wants us to understand that the Jewish Scriptures testify from start to finish that angels are spirits and servants but never saviours. Jesus is unique. In him, something far better has come.[16]

This opening chapter warns us that Hebrews will not be an easy read. It will not allow us to splash around in the shallow end of knowing Jesus. The writer dives into the deep end at the start of his letter and he invites us to dive in with him. The Jews rejected Jesus as their Messiah because they expected a faster horse and not a motor car, yet their own Scriptures had warned them that the Messiah would be far greater than all the prophets and the angels put together. Put aside your own preconceived ideas and dive into the glorious Gospel of God's Son.

---

[15] Jesus quotes this verse to prove his divinity in Matthew 22:41–46, Mark 12:35–37 and Luke 20:41–44.

[16] We see this contrast in 1:3 and 14. He sits; they are sent. He sustains; they serve.

# What Jesus Hates (1:9)

*You have loved righteousness and hated wickedness;*
*therefore God, your God, has set you above your*
*companions by anointing you with the oil of joy.*

(Hebrews 1:9)

You'll have noticed that Hebrews feels very different from the book of James. I don't just mean that the opening chapter contains as many Old Testament quotations as all five chapters of James put together. I mean the way in which the writer drills down deep into the inner workings of the Gospel in order to explain who Jesus is, what Jesus did and why the work of Jesus has changed everything. James assumed that we understood this, so he chose sermon highlights that majored far more on Gospel application than on Gospel explanation. This is not assumed in Hebrews at all, but don't let that make you think that it is therefore a book of abstract teaching. Even as he explains the Gospel, the writer fills every single page with practical challenge and application.

Paul often spends several chapters explaining the Gospel before he applies it. The writer of Hebrews cannot wait that long. He calls us to action even as he teaches profound truth, as is clear from his quotation in verse 9 from Psalm 45:7. Hebrews agrees with James that nobody is saved through professing faith in Jesus unless their faith results in obedient action.

Verse 9 tells us that *Jesus loved righteousness*. Few readers are very surprised by this, since the Old Testament prophesied that he would be the *"King of Righteousness"*, the *"Branch of*

Righteousness" and the "Sun of Righteousness".[1] But the writer isn't simply saying that Jesus was righteous. He is saying that he loved righteousness. That's different. He uses the same Greek word as John 3:16 when it tells us that "God so loved the world that he gave." Saving faith in Jesus means far more than smiling with approval at the idea that God's righteousness is good. It means far more than nodding at the virtues of a Christian lifestyle. It means loving God's righteousness so much that we sacrifice everything in order to lay hold of it. It means responding to Jesus' challenge: "Blessed are those who hunger and thirst for righteousness, for they will be filled."[2] Hebrews reminds us that Jesus was hungry and thirsty for righteousness. The question is, are we?

I have found that one of the easiest ways to answer this question is to put my own name in Paul's description of God's love in 1 Corinthians 13:4–8. Am I as passionate for these words to be true of my life as Jesus was of his?

> I am patient. I am kind. I do not envy. I do not boast. I am not proud. I do not dishonour others. I am not self-seeking. I am not easily angered. I keep no record of wrongs. I do not delight in evil but rejoice with the truth. I always protect, always trust, always hope, always persevere. I never let people down.

Verse 9 also tells us that Jesus hated wickedness. That's interesting, because we tend to talk far more about Jesus' love than we do about his hatred. The writer of Hebrews wants to ensure that we have grasped what the Old Testament teaches us: that loving righteousness and hating wickedness are simply two sides of the same coin. Solomon warns that "To fear the

---

[1] Jeremiah 23:5–6; 33:15–16; Malachi 4:2; Hebrews 7:2.

[2] Matthew 5:6. James kept pointing us back to the Sermon on the Mount. So does Hebrews.

*Lord is to hate evil."*[3] Following Jesus therefore means hating sin as well as loving sinners. Anything less than this is less than true Christian repentance.

Verse 9 tells us that *Jesus succeeded in his mission because he loved righteousness and hated wickedness.* These were not incidental aspects of Jesus' ministry. The word *"therefore"* signifies that these two things were primary factors in God the Father's decision to anoint him with the Holy Spirit. The Greek verb *chriō* means *to anoint* and is the root of the word *Christ*, so we could even translate verse 9 to read that God *Christed* Jesus or *made him his Messiah* because he saw that Jesus loved righteousness and hated sin. This may be the answer to our question, "Why isn't God using my life more?" It is certainly the answer to the question, "Can I become a Christian but still hold onto this one area of sin?" We cannot follow the one who loved righteousness and hated wickedness unless we allow the Lord to change our values so completely that we begin to love righteousness and hate wickedness ourselves. Unless our faith in Jesus unleashes major changes to our lifestyle, it is unlikely to be saving faith in Jesus at all.

Verse 9 tells us that *Jesus was full of the Holy Spirit.* If you were surprised that James says little about our need to be filled with the Holy Spirit, then Hebrews certainly makes up for it.[4] The writer promises us that God will help us make these major lifestyle changes if we allow him to fill our hearts. Jesus did not attempt to live a life of obedience to his Father without being filled with the Holy Spirit, so we must not attempt to follow in his footsteps on our own. We need to know Jesus in the same way as John the Baptist: *"The man on whom you see the Spirit come down and remain is the one who will baptize with the Holy*

---

[3] Proverbs 8:13. See also Job 28:28; Psalm 97:10; 119:104, 128; Amos 5:15; Zechariah 8:17; Romans 12:9; Revelation 2:6.

[4] I personally do not understand why so many people make this complaint. James tells us we need to be filled with the Spirit of Wisdom in 1:5–8 and 3:15–18. He assumes we have been filled with the Spirit in 4:5.

*Spirit."*[5] Anyone can follow Jesus if they allow him to go on filling them with God's Spirit every day.

Verse 9 tells us that *Jesus was full of joy*. Again, that's very interesting. The writer does not tell us that the key sign of our being filled with the Holy Spirit is prophesying or speaking in tongues or healing people. He tells us that the Holy Spirit is *"the oil of joy"*. We can tell who is full of the Holy Spirit by the smiles on their faces, because he grants us an unshakeable gladness that is rooted in God alone. Jesus suffered so horribly that Isaiah 53:3 calls him *"a man of sorrows"*, yet the Holy Spirit made him a man of joy. King David experienced countless trials and afflictions, yet he wrote many joyful psalms through his tears. Paul was the target of bitter persecution, yet he tells us that *"The fruit of the Spirit is joy"* and that *"I rejoice. Yes, and I will continue to rejoice."*[6] That's the power of the Holy Spirit.

So as we enjoy the tremendous insights that the writer of Hebrews gives us into the work of Jesus, let's not miss the equally tremendous insights that he also gives us into the character of Jesus. Gospel explanation must lead to Gospel application. Let's love righteousness and hate wickedness. If we do, God will fill us with the Holy Spirit and give us joy in the midst of our sufferings. He will enable us to follow the one who has been given the name which is above every other name.[7]

We are never more like Jesus than when we hate the sin that lurks in our hearts and lovingly embrace his better way of living.

---

[5] John 1:32–34; 3:34; 7:37–39.

[6] Galatians 5:22; Philippians 1:18. Other verses that link being filled with the Holy Spirit is being joyful include Psalm 46:4, John 15:11, Acts 13:52, Romans 14:17 and 15:13, and 1 Thessalonians 1:6.

[7] Hebrews 1:9 echoes the teaching of James 3:13–4:17. Earthly wisdom cannot promote anybody. A person is only set above their companions if they ask God humbly to fill them with his Holy Spirit.

# Warning Sirens (2:1–4)

*How shall we escape if we ignore so great a salvation?*

(Hebrews 2:3)

The people of Joplin, Missouri, were enjoying their Sunday dinner when a tornado swept through their city. In forty minutes of mayhem on 22nd May 2011, a mile-wide tornado killed or injured over 1,250 people, flattened almost 9,000 homes and businesses, and blew away 18,000 cars. Tragically, many of these deaths could have been avoided had the people of Joplin taken note of the tornado sirens which sounded in plenty of time for them to take cover. They were so used to drills and false alarms that they no longer took the warning sirens seriously. Instead, they were surprised by the storm.

Many people react in the same way to the warning sirens that sound throughout the book of Hebrews. They call them "problem passages", as if the problem were with the passages rather than with themselves. They treat them as problems to be fixed and not as warnings to be obeyed. They forget the call in James 4:11 for us to let Scripture sit in judgment over our thinking, rather than the other way around. We have arrived at the first of the five warning passages in Hebrews, so let's be careful not to dismiss it as a false alarm and so reap the consequences of complacency.[1] The writer of Hebrews sounds this siren for a reason. He believes that we are in real danger.

Let's not fool ourselves that he sounds this siren for

---

[1] The five main warning passages are 2:1–4, 3:7–4:13, 5:11–6:12, 10:19–39 and 12:1–29.

non-Christians. He makes it clear that *"We must pay the most careful attention, therefore, to what we have heard, so that we do not drift away... How shall we escape if we ignore so great a salvation?"* Later on in 6:4–5, he addresses his warnings to *"those who have once been enlightened, who have tasted the heavenly gift, who have shared in the Holy Spirit, who have tasted the goodness of the word of God and the powers of the coming age."* Peter uses similar language in one of his letters when addressing Christians, so let's not filter out the wail of these sirens. It is intended for our ears.

We need to understand these warning passages in their proper context. Jesus assures his followers that they can never lose their salvation: *"I give them eternal life, and they shall never perish; no one will snatch them out of my hand. My Father, who has given them to me, is greater than all; no one can snatch them out of my Father's hand."* Paul, Peter, Jude and John all echo this in their writings.[2] The writer of Hebrews echoes it himself in 7:25 when he assures us that Jesus *"is able to save completely those who come to God through him, because he always lives to intercede for them."* Those whom God saves, nobody can unsave. Not even ourselves.

The writer therefore cannot actually expect his Christian readers to lose their salvation. He cannot be flattering us when he assures us in 10:39 that *"We do not belong to those who shrink back and are destroyed, but to those who have faith and are saved."* His intention in each of these five warning passages is demonstrated by the fact that he ends each of them by reassuring us that God has given us everything we need to persevere as believers. Some of this will only become clear when we reach the other warning passages. For now, a simple picture will suffice.

It is 59 AD. We are in Acts 27. Paul is on his way by ship to

---

[2] John 10:28–29; Romans 8:33–39; Philippians 1:6; 1 Peter 1:5; Jude 24; 1 John 2:19.

Rome. A storm strikes the Mediterranean Sea as suddenly as the tornado that swept through Joplin. Paul gathers his shipmates and assures them that *"Not one of you will be lost; only the ship will be destroyed. Last night an angel of the God to whom I belong and whom I serve stood beside me and said, 'Do not be afraid, Paul... God has graciously given you the lives of all who sail with you.'"* A few days later, when the storm shows no sign of stopping, some of the sailors attempt to lower a lifeboat in order to abandon the ship before it hits some rocks. Paul sees them and warns the rest of his shipmates that *"Unless these men stay with the ship, you cannot be saved."* The shipmates believe him and cut the ropes that hold the lifeboat, allowing it to drift away. Now did God promise to save everyone on board? Yes. Would they have been saved if they had left the ship? No. Was Paul therefore right to issue his stern warning? Most definitely. Was the Lord sovereign over all of this? Of course he was.

I find this a very helpful picture when I read the warning passages in Hebrews. The writer knows that Christians cannot lose their salvation, yet he sees many of the Jewish believers on the brink of making a very foolish decision. They are being persecuted on both sides: by the Jews who think them traitors for abandoning their culture and by the Romans who believe the emperor's propaganda that they deliberately started the Great Fire of Rome.[3] They therefore think that they have found themselves a lifeboat. If they return to the synagogue, the Jews will welcome them back as friends and the Romans will accept them as adherents of a religion that is officially tolerated within the empire. The writer therefore warns them strongly that the synagogue is not a lifeboat but a deathtrap. Unless they stay within the Church, they cannot be saved. Synagogue Judaism is not a different kind of Christianity. It isn't Christianity at all.

---

[3] The Roman historian Tacitus tells us that Nero claimed this in *Annals of Imperial Rome* (15.44).

The writer sounds five warnings in these four verses. The first is the Jewish Law, which is full of examples of people being punished for turning their backs on the Lord.[4] Moses received the Law through angels, whereas we have received the New Covenant through Jesus the Son.[5] Since Jesus is far greater than any angel, the writer therefore asks us, *"How shall we escape if we ignore so great a salvation?"*[6]

The second warning is the fact that the Lord Jesus was crucified by the synagogue leaders whose protection they are seeking. The third warning is the fact that the apostles (*"those who heard him"*) have been flogged and imprisoned and executed by the leaders of first-century Judaism. The fourth warning is the fact that these same things have happened to those converted through the apostles (*"us"*).[7] The fifth warning comes from God himself, since he has performed such great miracles through Jesus, the apostles and their converts that anyone can see that something far better than synagogue Judaism has come.

So don't label these five warning passages as "problem passages". We dare not dismiss them so easily. Knowing that anyone who is truly saved cannot lose their salvation must spur us on to make our salvation sure by rejecting any other lifeboat than the Gospel. Let's cut loose every false lifeboat of compromise and cling to the Church as the only true ship of salvation. Let's deal a death blow to the foolish desire to

---

[4] A few examples are in Genesis 19:26, Exodus 32, Leviticus 10, and Numbers 15:32–36 and 16:1–50.

[5] Although the Jewish Torah never states this explicitly, the writer echoes Acts 7:53 and Galatians 3:19 when he tells us that, unlike the New Covenant, God gave the Law to Moses via angels.

[6] The Greek verb *ameleō* in 2:3 means *to ignore* or *to neglect* or *to act carelessly* towards the Gospel. *"Therefore"* (2:1) and *"For"* (2:2) link this warning to chapter 1's teaching that Jesus is far superior to angels.

[7] The reference to *"us"* is one of the reasons we can be so confident that this letter was not written by one of the Twelve, by one of the 120, or even by Paul who saw and heard Jesus personally on the Road to Damascus.

purchase safety at the cost of our own souls. It's what genuine followers of Jesus always do.

# Down and Up (2:5–18)

*But we do see Jesus, who was made lower than the angels for a little while, now crowned with glory and honour because he suffered death.*

(Hebrews 2:9)

My young children love asking me riddles. Here is their current favourite:

**Question:** *What can go up the chimney down but can't go down the chimney up?*

**Answer:** *An umbrella.*

The writer of Hebrews has a riddle of his own. He asks us, *"What has to go down in order to go up?"* Having read the book of James, we ought to know the answer to the riddle. The answer is you and me. We need to humble ourselves before God and his plan for our lives if we want to open the door to blessing and promotion.

Jesus has modelled this for us. Having quoted seven times from the Old Testament in chapter 1 in order to convince us that Jesus is far greater than the angels, the writer now quotes three times from the Old Testament in order to remind us that Jesus became lower than the angels for a short while too.[1] Jesus personified the lesson that James taught us earlier. He showed us that the only way up is for a person to go down.

The writer quotes from Psalm 8:4–6, that great celebration

---

[1] Hebrews 2:4–18 continues the argument begun in Hebrews 1:5–14. *"Under their feet"* in Psalm 8 follows on from *"a footstool for your feet"* in Psalm 110.

of God's staggering favour towards humanity.[2] David worships God for crowning Adam with glory and honour when he granted him authority to rule over the earth on his behalf.[3] The writer tells us that the psalm was also a prophecy. It was meant to jar in our hearts as we sing it, because anyone can see that the world is not as subject to humankind as David implies.[4] The Devil tempted Adam and Eve to push themselves forward to become like little gods. Their bid for self-promotion failed. It simply pushed them further down. Their sin gave the Devil authority to work his havoc on the earth and to defy the God-given authority of humans. We need help, and the writer tells us that God has provided it. We do not see humans as they are meant to be, *"but we do see Jesus, who was made lower than the angels for a little while."*[5]

A human brought sin into the world by trying to become like God, so God dealt with the sin by becoming a human. Humans lost their authority by trying to pull themselves up, so Jesus regained that authority by stooping down. He became *"a little lower than the angels"* when he was born as a human, and he continued his downward journey. He suffered betrayal and rejection and torture and the public shame of crucifixion, then he descended still further by dying. The author of life became a stone-cold corpse in a lifeless tomb, stooping low enough to

---

[2] The writer's vagueness in 2:6 that *"There is a place where someone has testified"* suggests that these verses were originally part of a spoken sermon. He is more interested in effecting a change in our hearts than he is in giving us the correct reference for our notepads.

[3] Some English translations make the quote from Psalm 8 more inclusive by changing *him* to *them*, but this is quite unhelpful. Although the writer does not mention Adam by name, he is contrasting what *he* lost with what Jesus has won back for us. Paul does the same in Romans 5:12–21 and 1 Corinthians 15:21–49.

[4] Jesus and Paul treat Psalm 8 as a prophecy about the Messiah in Matthew 21:16 and 1 Corinthians 15:25–27.

[5] Some people use 2:8 as proof that God's Kingdom is both "now" and "not yet". This may be true, but 2:6–8 is talking about fallen humans and not about Jesus. Jesus only enters in 2:9 in order to solve the problem.

swallow all the bitter fruit of Adam and Eve's sin. As a result, he can now lead their children upwards in a glorious return journey.

One of the most important Greek words in this passage is *archēgos*, which means *prince* or *pioneer* or *author*. The writer quotes from Psalm 22:22 and from Isaiah 8:17–18 in order to prove that Jesus has become the pioneer of a new human race which can enjoy everything that Adam and Eve lost.[6] Because Jesus was willing to take the downward journey from heaven's throne-room and become a crucified human, he has been crowned by the Father with the glory and authority that sinless humans had in the beginning.[7] The Father has empowered him to share this glory and authority with any human being he makes holy and adopts into God's family as his brother or sister.[8] Because he stooped down, he is able to lead us upwards with him in triumph.

As Jesus travels upwards, the writer explains how we are able to travel with him. The Devil gained authority in the world by tricking Adam and Eve into believing that God was lying when he warned them that if they ate forbidden fruit, they would die. Death therefore became the greatest weapon in the Devil's arsenal, enslaving humans through its power over their lives.[9] When Jesus rose from the dead, he shattered the power of death

---

[6] Psalm 22 prophesies about the Messiah's death. Isaiah 8:17–18 prophesies about his being rejected. Jesus' upward climb in this chapter is a direct result of his willingness to sink down low in order to save us.

[7] Hebrews 2:9 echoes 1:3–4, as well as Acts 2:36 and Philippians 2:9–11, when it tells us that Jesus was promoted because he humbled himself. He embodied the principle that James 3:13–4:17 taught us.

[8] The writer reinforces this by using the same three Greek words *stephanoō* (to crown), *doxa* (glory) and *timē* (honour) in both 2:7 and 9. Since *doxa* and *timē* are also used to describe the high priest Aaron being clothed with *glory* and *honour* in Exodus 28:2 and 40, he may also intend them to prepare us for the amazing message of 2:17.

[9] Genesis 2:17; 3:3; Romans 6:23. *"Fear of death"* in 2:15 means more than fear of dying. It means fear of death as the greatest sign of Satan's authority to rob, kill and destroy.

and consigned the Devil to destruction.[10] He became the Great High Priest for a new human race by paying the penalty for our sin through his own blood.[11]

Chapter 1 made us want to worship Jesus for his greatness as the Son of God. Chapter 2 should make us want to worship him for his humility in becoming a man. But the writer also wants it to do more than that for Jewish Christians. In verse 12, the Greek word he uses for the *assembly* of Israel in his quotation is *ekklēsia*, or *church*. In verse 16, he describes the new family of God as *the seed of Abraham*.[12] In verse 17, he calls it *ho laos*, the same phrase the Greek Septuagint repeatedly uses to refer to *the people* of Israel.[13] He is therefore telling his Jewish readers that the Church, and not the synagogue, is the true continuation of ancient Israel's story. The warning verses at the start of this chapter were not an aside. They were an essential prelude to this teaching.

The writer therefore warns the Jewish Christians that, if they go back to the synagogues to find shelter from persecution, they are leaving Christ's protection to head back out into the Devil's storm. They are siding with sinful Adam instead of with the better Adam who has come. They need to cut away their lifeboats and suffer persecution for Jesus' name.

This is costly. Following a crucified Messiah always is. But it is worth it when we consider his example. When he calls us to sacrifice everything to follow him, he reassures us through his own personal experience that the only way up for us is down.

---

[10] Hebrews 2:14 reads literally, *"so that by his death he might destroy the one who has the power of death – that is, the devil."* In other words, he did not simply destroy the Devil's power. He condemned the Devil himself to destruction!

[11] This first reference to Jesus being our *high priest* will become a major theme of chapters 3–7. The Greek verb *hilaskomai* refers to the *atonement cover* on the Ark of the Covenant, where Aaron put blood on the Day of Atonement in order to take away God's righteous anger towards Israel's sin.

[12] Paul also tells us in Galatians 3:16 and 28–29 that Jesus and his followers are the true *seed of Abraham*.

[13] See Acts 26:17. This was outrageously revolutionary teaching for first-century Jews.

# In Our Shoes (2:5–18)

*For surely it is not angels he helps, but Abraham's descendants. For this reason he had to be made like them, fully human in every way.*

(Hebrews 2:16–17)

Modern science ascribes very little significance to the human race. The American astrophysicist and author Carl Sagan explains:

> *I believe our future depends powerfully on how well we understand this Cosmos in which we float like a mote of dust in the morning sky... We live on an insignificant planet of a hum-drum star lost in a galaxy tucked away in some forgotten corner of a universe in which there are far more galaxies than people... The universe seems neither benign nor hostile, merely indifferent to the concerns of such puny creatures as we are.*[1]

The writer of Hebrews agrees with Carl Sagan that our future depends on how well we understand our place in the universe, but he entirely rejects the rest of his pessimistic view of humanity. One of the reasons why the writer is so excited in this chapter is that he grasps that the Gospel affords extraordinary significance to you and me. There is only one planet in this vast universe to which God has sent his Son. There is only one creature in the universe which Jesus chose to become. We are not an insignificant race of creatures in some forgotten corner

---

[1] Carl Sagan, *Cosmos* (1980).

of the universe. We are the focus of God's love. Jesus proved it when he stepped into our shoes.

Verses 5–9 tell us that David understood this.[2] He celebrated God's undeserved favour towards humanity and prophesied that one day God would become one of us in order to undo the consequences of our sin. The writer tells us that Jesus tasted death for everyone – in other words, he stepped into our shoes so completely that he was able to sacrifice his own life in order to save ours. The only way that people can be saved from death and hell is to believe that Jesus wore their shoes and went there for them.[3]

Verses 10–13 tell us that Jesus is the *archēgos*, or *pioneer*, of a new humanity.[4] As he ascends upwards in victory, he is able to take with him anyone who puts their trust in him. Through his blood sacrifice, he is able to declare sinful men and women to be so holy that he is unashamed to own them as brothers and sisters in God's family. Through his example, he is able to transform their lives and to make them as holy as he declares them to be, since he has suffered the same human temptations as they have. An orange is an orange before it is crushed, but it has to be crushed in order to obtain orange juice. In the same way, Jesus became a perfect man when he was crushed through severe trials and his innocent soul flowed out in practical obedience.[5] Jesus is not like a rabbi or an imam or a self-righteous newspaper reporter, demanding perfection from us but never lifting a finger to help us. He has walked in our shoes. He knows how we feel and he comes alongside us to strengthen

---

[2] The writer emphasizes in 2:5 that he is talking about *"the world to come"*. In other words, he is carrying on from his quotation in 1:13 from Psalm 110. He needs to explain how Jesus won back all that Adam lost.

[3] The writer is not promising that we will never die. He is saying that Jesus has broken the power of death so that, even if we die, we will be raised to live forever with him. See Job 19:25–27 and John 11:25.

[4] Peter uses this word *archēgos* to describe Jesus as the *prince* or *author* in Acts 3:15 and 5:31. Although the word is only used in Hebrews 2:10 and 12:2, it is a major concept behind the entire teaching of the letter.

[5] The writer will explain this more in 5:8–9.

and purify us as we follow him.[6] Verse 18 assures us: *"Because he himself suffered when he was tempted, he is able to help those who are being tempted."* Because he walked in our shoes, he is able to help us to walk in his.

Verses 14–18 tell us that Jesus needed to become a human being in order to save us. The writer tells us that *"**he had to be made like them**, fully human in every way, in order that he might become a merciful and faithful high priest in service to God, and that he might make atonement for the sins of the people."* Only a human being could sacrifice his life for human sin, and only the Son of God could be so sinless that he did not deserve to die. Only a human being could taste death for humanity, and only the Son of God could break the power of death even as he died. Only a human being could act as the Great High Priest for humanity because only the Son of God could be accepted as their holy mediator with his Father. Jesus is the only Saviour of the world because he is the only one who is both God and man.[7] Not Moses and Aaron, who could not even save themselves from dying outside the Promised Land. Not the Buddha, who could not even save himself from dying after eating infected pork. Not Muhammad, who denied that God loves us enough to stoop down and save us, and who told his followers: *"I do not know what will happen to me and to my followers; I am only a plain warner."*[8] Not Carl Sagan and his astrophysicist friends. There is only one Saviour and it is the God-Man Jesus Christ.

With this in mind, let's turn back to the warning verses at the start of this chapter. Suddenly we find them encouraging instead of troubling. The writer assures us in verse 3 that our

---

[6] The quotations from Psalm 22:22 and Isaiah 8:17–18 both emphasize the humanity of Jesus. He enables us to live for God as our Father because he learned to live as a human being for God as his Father too.

[7] The Greek verb *epilambanomai* in 2:16 is deliberately ambiguous. It could mean either that Jesus *helped* humans rather than angels, or that Jesus *took possession* of a human body rather than the body of an angel. Different English translations take a different view because the writer means both.

[8] The Qur'an 46:9.

salvation is very great. It has transformed everything for us. He assures us in verse 4 that God will fill us with the Holy Spirit and give us supernatural gifts to help us live for him and testify about him.[9] When I was a child, I used to watch a TV programme in which the presenter would explain how to make a model by telling the viewer, *"Here is one I finished earlier."* In the same way, the writer tells us that Jesus is the one God finished earlier. He is the pioneer of our salvation who has already walked the path that lies before us. This is amazing news to anyone who is following the spectator-gods of other religions. The writer tells us that God has saved us by becoming one of us.

It is also great news for those who follow the pessimistic dogma of modern science in the same way that other people follow their religion. Carl Sagan's widow explains:

> *When my husband died, because he was so famous and known for not being a believer, many people would come up to me – it still sometimes happens – and ask me if Carl changed at the end and converted to a belief in an afterlife. They also frequently ask me if I think I will see him again... We knew we would never see each other again. I don't ever expect to be reunited with Carl.*[10]

That is tragic. It reminds us that, for all its intelligence, our culture has fundamentally misunderstood the place of humanity in the cosmos. It does not realize that God has become one of us, dealing with the human problem from both sides, both as God and as a human being. It fails to grasp the greatest piece of news ever heard by a mortal human being. God loves us and has made us the centre of his attention in this vast universe. He proved his love for us when he sent his Son to step into our shoes.

---

[9] Hebrews 2:3–4 echoes Acts 1:1 when it says that Jesus began his ministry himself and now continues it through us.

[10] Ann Druyan wrote this in an article for the *Skeptical Enquirer* (November/December 2003 edition).

# Better Than Moses (3:1–6)

*Fix your thoughts on Jesus... Jesus has been found
worthy of greater honour than Moses.*

(Hebrews 3:1, 3)

One of my friends describes himself as an alcoholic. He does
this even though he hasn't had a drink in over fifteen years. He
knows that his weakness towards alcohol has not gone away.
For him, the price of soberness is eternal vigilance. He has been
sober for over fifteen years, but he has never forgotten that
alcohol is his nemesis.

The writer of Hebrews knows that he has a nemesis too.
He belongs to a nation that has a terrible track record of turning
aids to worship into objects of worship. He therefore speaks
as one Jew to many others, warning his readers not to trifle
with synagogue Judaism as if it were merely a harmless form
of Christless Christianity. It would be less dangerous for my
alcoholic friend to spend a lonely evening with an open bottle of
whisky than for them to return to the synagogues. If they do so,
they will end up trading in Jesus for a shabby imitation idol.

This is what the Israelites had done repeatedly. When God
healed them from snakebites in the desert by giving them a
bronze statue of a snake, they named it Nehushtan and offered
incense to it as their new god. When God gave them a golden box
in which to store the Ten Commandments, they turned it into
a talisman, which they believed would guarantee them victory
on the battlefield.[1] When Jesus burst onto the scene and began
to challenge their corrupted religion, the Jewish rabbis warned

---

[1] Numbers 21:4–9; 2 Kings 18:4. Deuteronomy 10:1–5; 1 Samuel 4:3–11.

people who believed in him that *"We are disciples of Moses! We know that God spoke to Moses, but as for this fellow, we don't even know where he comes from."* Jesus responded with a warning of his own. He told the Jewish nation that *"Your accuser is Moses, on whom your hopes are set."*[2]

Unless we know this background, we will fail to understand the book of Hebrews and especially its warning passages. The Jewish Christians were being told that their faith in Jesus made them traitors to the Law of Moses. Stephen had been lynched by men who claimed that *"We have heard Stephen speak blasphemous words against Moses and against God... For we have heard him say that this Jesus of Nazareth will destroy this place and change the customs Moses handed down to us."*[3] Naturally, the Jewish Christians were quick to reassure their countrymen that they were good disciples of Moses – they had simply become followers of Jesus too. The writer therefore warns them not to succumb so easily to the old Jewish nemesis. The synagogues have turned Moses into a new Nehushtan.

In verse 1, the writer encourages them to *"fix your thoughts on Jesus."* Moses was good but Jesus is far better. If Jesus is far greater than the angels who delivered the Old Covenant to Israel, he is certainly greater than the mortal man who received it from them! He alone is the true Apostle (which means *Sent One*), since God sent men like Moses to Egypt from Midian but he sent his Son to earth from heaven.[4] Jesus alone is the true High Priest, since God appointed Moses' brother Aaron to enter the Tabernacle on behalf of Israel but he appointed Jesus to enter the Most Holy Place in heaven on behalf of the entire world.[5]

---

[2] John 5:45; 9:28–29.

[3] Acts 6:11–14.

[4] Church pastors are simply mini-pastors for the great Pastor Jesus (1 Peter 5:1–4). In the same way, therefore, apostles are simply mini-apostles for the great Apostle Jesus.

[5] The writer will expand on what he means by Jesus being our Great High Priest in 4:14–7:28.

Jesus alone gives us a share in the *"heavenly calling"* to become his *"brothers and sisters"* in God's holy family. As James told the Council of Jerusalem, Christianity is not Jesus-Plus-Moses. It is Jesus-Plus-Nothing.[6]

In verses 2–6, the writer backs this up with a quotation from Numbers 12:7. When Aaron and Miriam rebelled against their brother's authority to lead Israel, the Lord rebuked them:

> *When there is a prophet among you, I, the Lord, reveal myself to them in visions, I speak to them in dreams. But this is not true of my servant Moses; he is faithful in all my house. With him I speak face to face, clearly and not in riddles; he sees the form of the Lord. Why then were you not afraid to speak against my servant Moses?*[7]

This was the verse that the synagogue leaders used to browbeat the Jewish Christians into believing that they needed to follow Moses, so the writer uses it to prove that Jesus is far greater than any human leader.

Did the Jews believe that Moses was the greatest religious leader of the Old Testament? That's good. The Lord tells Aaron and Miriam, the high priest and the prophetess of Israel, that their younger brother is far greater than they are. But that is only half the story. If we read Numbers 12:7 slowly, we also see that Moses is not a patch on Jesus. The Lord calls Moses his *servant*, but he calls Jesus his *Son*. The Lord says that Moses is faithful *"in all my house"*, but he says that Jesus is *"the Son over God's house."*[8] Moses taught the members of God's household how to be saved through the Passover and the Red Sea, but he needed to be saved

---

[6] Acts 15:1–5, 13–21.

[7] Numbers 12:6–8. Although the writer paraphrases the Greek Septuagint, he sticks to the text by using the Greek word *therapōn*, meaning *servant*, an unusual word which appears nowhere else in the New Testament.

[8] This is the writer's pithy summary of the ten Old Testament verses he quoted in Hebrews 1–2.

alongside them. Jesus built God's household by becoming the true Passover Lamb when his blood was smeared on the vertical and horizontal frame of a wooden cross and by passing through a better death and burial than the Israelites experienced in the waters of the Red Sea. The synagogue Jews are right: this verse says that Moses is the greatest human religious leader. But they are also wrong: this verse also demonstrates that Jesus is far greater than Moses.

The Jewish nation is not alone in relying too much on religious tokens and too little on God. We therefore need to take this warning to heart. Let's not become so entrenched in our religious views that we act like the clergyman who told William Tyndale to stop translating the Bible into English because it is *"Better to be without God's law than the Pope's."*[9] Let's not become so attached to our human leaders that we act like the Muslim friend who told me that he cannot read the New Testament because his imam tells him that to do so is to dishonour Muhammad. Let's not allow anyone or anything to stand in the way of our following Jesus with all our being. Christianity is not Jesus plus a religious teacher or plus the views of a particular denomination. It is Jesus-Plus-Nothing.

It is a call to fix our eyes on Jesus as the great Apostle and the Great High Priest. It is a call to worship him as the only true Architect of salvation and as the only firstborn Son over God's family. It is a call to worship Jesus as the one who is greater than any angel, greater than any human leader, and greater than you and me. It is a call to surrender everything to him. It is a call to live our lives for Jesus-Plus-Nothing.

[9] Quoted by David Daniell in *William Tyndale: A Biography* (1994).

# Don't Miss the Point
## (3:7–19)

*We have come to share in Christ, if indeed we hold our original conviction firmly to the very end.*

(Hebrews 3:14)

Alan Partridge is a master in missing the point. Steve Coogan's comedy character constantly majors on minors and fails to grasp what really matters. When he interviews a man who was held hostage for two years by Liberian rebels, the traumatized survivor tells him that *"We were just political pawns in a game of cruel chess."* Alan Partridge immediately shoots back a question for clarification: *"So who were the bishops?"*[1]

Sadly, many readers miss the point in the same way when they read Hebrews.[2] They read this second of the five warning passages, stretching all the way from 3:7 to 4:13, and they ask whether the writer believes a person can ever lose their salvation. They fail to grasp the context of the letter, and so they fail to see that the writer did not write these verses in order to address that question. The key to the book of Hebrews is found in its closing verses, where the writer tells us in 13:22 that the letter is *"my word of exhortation."* He did not write it in order to tell us whether or not a Christian can lose their salvation.[3] He

---

[1] This interview took place in *Knowing Me, Knowing You* (episode 3), first broadcast on BBC Radio 4 on 15th December 1992.

[2] This is the second-longest of the five main warning passages (2:1–4, 3:7–4:13, 5:11–6:12, 10:19–39 and 12:1–29).

[3] As we saw earlier, in 7:25 he simply reaffirms the teaching of John 10:28–29, Romans 8:33–39, Philippians 1:6, 1 Peter 1:5, Jude 24 and 1 John 2:19.

wrote it to exhort Jews to prove the reality of their faith in Jesus through their refusal to return to the synagogues in order to escape persecution.

The writer does this by reminding them what happened to the Jews of the Exodus generation. They all professed faith in the blood of the Passover lamb. If they hadn't daubed its blood on the doorframes of their houses, they would not have escaped the slaughter that befell the Egyptians. Yet many among them went on to prove that their profession of faith was a lie. There were many like Achan, whose actions revealed that his heart was more pagan than that of the Canaanite prostitute Rahab. The writer echoes the teaching of James when he warns us that our profession of faith in Jesus is revealed as true or false by the way in which we act after we make it.[4]

This second warning passage is prompted by the writer's statement at the end of verse 6 that professing faith in Jesus will only save us *"if indeed we hold firmly to our confidence and the hope in which we glory."* It revolves around his statement in verse 14 that *"We have come to share in Christ, if indeed we hold our original conviction firmly to the very end."* He has no intention of clarifying which of the Exodus generation were genuinely saved and which were not. He simply wants to point out what is undeniable – that not all of those who painted the blood of the Passover lamb on their doorframes were genuine believers. He wants to warn us that professing faith in Jesus is easy, but that four things show whether our profession of faith is real or a lie.

First, the writer warns us in verse 12 that faith in Jesus always results in separation from the world. He quotes from Psalm 95, the worship song that King David wrote in order to teach his own generation of Israelites not to make the

---

[4] Paul also uses the failure of the Exodus generation to issue a similar warning in 1 Corinthians 10:1–12. There is no inconsistency between these warning passages and the rest of the New Testament.

same mistakes as the Exodus generation.[5] He emphasizes that David's psalm is just as relevant today by telling us in verse 7 that this is not simply what the Holy Spirit said but what *"the Holy Spirit says."* Many of the Hebrews were willing to let God take them out of Egypt but unwilling to let him take Egypt out of them. When he led them to a land that was populated by giants, they chose to focus on the size of the Canaanites instead of on the greatness of God. They voted for an easy life and turned back to Egypt instead of suffering on the battlefield as part of the People of God.[6] This decision proved fatal. It revealed that many of them did not have saving faith in God at all.

Second, the writer warns us in verse 12 that faith in Jesus always results in a passion for God's promises. The goal of the Exodus was not simply freedom from slavery. It was the possession of a land so rich and fertile that the Lord describes it as *"my rest"* in Psalm 95. The hardships of the desert road were not meant to send them running back to Egypt. They were meant to stir a hunger to possess the land that lay ahead of them. In the same way, the goal of the Gospel is never forgiveness. It is the creation of a community of believers in Jesus in every nation of the world. If the believers threw this away and returned to the corrupted religion of the synagogues in order to escape persecution, they would prove that their profession of faith in Jesus was a lie. They would prove they had *"a sinful, unbelieving heart that turns away from the living God."*[7]

Third, the writer warns us in verse 13 that faith in

---

[5] Technically, Psalm 95 is anonymous. We only know that David wrote it because Hebrews 4:7 tells us. The writer quotes from the Greek Septuagint, which tells us that the Israelites rebelled despite seeing miracles for 40 years in the desert. The Hebrew text actually says that they rebelled for 40 years despite seeing miracles in Egypt.

[6] Numbers 14:1–4 tells us that they rejected the Promised Land because they still looked back to Egypt.

[7] The oath described in 3:11 is recorded in Numbers 14:28–35 and in Ezekiel 20:15.

Jesus always results in a desire to gather together with other Christians. This is where having an overview of the entire letter is very helpful, because the fourth warning passage expands on the meaning of this verse in 10:24–25. It urges: *"Let us consider how we may spur one another on towards love and good deeds, not giving up meeting together, as some are in the habit of doing, but encouraging one another – and all the more as you see the Day approaching."*[8] If the Jewish Christians could be satisfied by fellowship with Jews who rejected the Messiah, they ought to question whether they were truly saved at all. If we are so satisfied by friendship with unbelievers that we fail to commit ourselves to regular participation in a local church, we ought to ask ourselves the same question.[9]

Fourth, the writer warns us in verse 14 that faith in Jesus always results in a desire to suffer with Jesus. He reminds us that those who have truly been saved have become *metochoi tou christou* – they have become *partners with Christ* and have received the privilege of sharing in both his blessings and his suffering. If the Jewish Christians bolted for the synagogues in order to avoid being persecuted for their faith in Jesus, it would show they were not truly partners with him. It might sound like an easy option, but in reality it would be fatal. It would show they were as much slaves to *"sin's deceitfulness"* as Achan.

So don't miss the point of this second warning passage. Don't miss what it means to have true saving faith in Jesus. It means choosing a different path from unbelievers because of our passion for the promises of God. It means devoting ourselves to fellowship with other believers because we are partners together in Jesus' blessings and in his suffering, It means holding

---

[8] Hebrews 10:25 does more than shed light on the meaning of 3:13. It reminds us that it will not be "today" forever. "Tomorrow" is coming, and it will be too late to return to Jesus when his Judgment Day arrives.

[9] The Greek word *aphistēmi* in 3:12 can mean *to fall away* from the faith, but it can also mean simply *to withdraw* or *to absent oneself* from the community of believers.

onto the faith we have professed in Jesus, though it costs us all we have. It means standing firm to inherit our share in the true Promised Land.

# God's Detonator (4:1–2)

*The message they heard was of no value to them, because those who heard did not combine it with faith.*

(Hebrews 4:2)

Everybody knows about the atomic bombs the Americans dropped on Hiroshima and Nagasaki, claiming a quarter of a million lives and ending World War Two. But few people know about the atomic bomb they dropped on 24th January 1961 when a bomber broke up in mid-air over Goldsboro, North Carolina. The four-megaton atomic bomb it carried was more powerful than all of the bombs dropped in World War Two put together, including those that were dropped on Hiroshima and Nagasaki. Millions of lives were only spared because a single switch prevented the bomb's detonator from communicating with its nuclear core. The official internal report, which was only made public in 2013, concluded with horror that *"One simple, dynamo-technology, low voltage switch stood between the United States and a major catastrophe."*[1]

The writer of Hebrews believes that the Gospel is far more powerful than any manmade bomb. He began his letter by reminding us that it has come to us through the one who created the universe with his voice and who still sustains it now by his powerful word. He has much, much more to say about the Gospel, but, before he does so, he issues a solemn warning. The power of the Gospel will have no effect in our lives unless

---

[1] Parker Jones, senior nuclear engineer, said this in his report, *Goldsboro Revisited* (1969).

we mix the words we hear with faith. Faith is the detonator that unleashes the power of all God's promises towards us.[2]

The writer is not being anachronistic when he tells us in verse 2 that the Exodus generation had the Gospel message proclaimed to them.[3] They were shown God's holiness by the ease with which his Ten Plagues humiliated the idols of Egypt. They were shown the path to forgiveness for their sins through the blood of the Passover lamb and they were baptized in the waters of the Red Sea. They received greater revelation of God's plan of salvation than anybody else thus far in human history when they received the Law from Moses at Mount Sinai. They were a Gospel people who had more power at their fingertips than was in the atomic bomb that landed on Goldsboro. Yet the writer of Hebrews tells us, shockingly, that *"the message they heard was of no value to them, because those who heard did not combine it with faith."*[4]

The writer wants to clarify what he is saying in this second warning passage. He is not telling us, any more than James, that we are saved through our obedient actions.[5] He is telling us that faith is the essential detonator of the Gospel – without it, to use the words of Humphrey Bogart in the movie *Casablanca*, our obedient actions *"don't amount to a hill of beans in this crazy world."* The Exodus generation had faith to smear blood on the doorframes of their houses: that's why many of them

---

[2] As a gauge of how important faith is to God, note that the word used in 3:10 for God *being angry* with the Exodus generation can just as easily be translated that he *loathed* or *was disgusted with* them. We should not be surprised by this. Unbelief insults God's character as much as faith extols it.

[3] The Greek word in 4:2 is *euangelizō*, from which we get the English word *evangelize*. See also Galatians 3:8.

[4] The Greek text of 4:2 can also be translated *"they did not share the faith of those who obeyed,"* but this is not the most natural reading, nor is it the main way in which the text has been understood for 2,000 years.

[5] Although the Greek word *pistos* can technically refer to our *faithfulness* as well as to our *faith*, the way in which the writer uses the word – supremely in chapter 11 – makes it clear that he is referring to our *faith*.

were forgiven for their sins and why all of them were freed from slavery. The Exodus generation had faith to sing a grateful worship song on the far side of the Red Sea: that's why they started to discover new names for God and to experience his healing and provision and victory in fresh ways as they took the dangerous road to Mount Sinai. But this wasn't enough. Faith is far more than the thing that motivates us to pray a sinner's prayer or to obey the Lord by being baptized in water. Faith is an ongoing lifestyle.

Sometimes people try to draw a distinction between the Gospel that is preached by Paul in his letters to the Gentiles and the Gospel that is preached by James and Hebrews to the Jews. That's unhelpful.[6] Paul's letters explain what the writer of Hebrews means when he tells us that the Gospel is of no value to a person unless they combine it with faith. Romans 1:17 tells us that *"In the gospel the righteousness of God is revealed – a righteousness that is by faith **from first to last**."* How are we cleared of the guilt of our sin? Through faith in what Jesus has done. How are we freed from slavery to sin and transformed in our lifestyle? Also through faith in what Jesus has done. How are we made fruitful in our witness and empowered to back up what we say with miracles? Through faith in what Jesus has done. How do we access the heavenly reward that Jesus has won for us? Through faith in what Jesus has done. At every stage in the Christian life, fresh faith in Jesus is required.[7] Without it, God's powerful promises are like a nuclear bomb without a detonator.

Do you see now why we miss the point if we treat these verses as an essay on whether or not a Christian can ever lose their salvation? The writer sees salvation as far more than the

---

[6] Paul echoes these verses when he tells us in 2 Timothy 3:15 that knowledge of the Scriptures is useless unless we combine our knowledge with faith in Jesus.

[7] Note how Paul describes normal Christianity in 2 Thessalonians 1:3: *"Your faith is growing more and more."*

moment when we receive God's forgiveness for our sins. He sees it as a whole new way of living that requires us to come to God through faith in Jesus every single day. The Israelites who failed to believe in the Gospel for forgiveness went unforgiven. Those who believed in the Gospel for forgiveness but who failed to believe in it for victory over the Canaanite giants failed to detonate the promises that would have given them the land. Their corpses became fodder for wild animals in the desert. *"They were not able to enter, because of their unbelief."*

This is sobering. No wonder the writer warns us in verse 1 to *"be careful"* (or, more literally, to *"be afraid of"*) how we respond to the Gospel.[8] The work of Jesus on our behalf is not something we can acquire and then bury away, like the foolish servant in the Parable of the Talents. It is something we must lay hold of in fresh ways every single day. It isn't simply how we enter into a relationship with God. It is also how we enter into everything else which he has promised to us.

Last week I took my children to what is left of the World War One trenches in north-east France. The tour guide told us a startling fact: 40 per cent of the shells the British fired at the German trenches failed to detonate on landing. Victory only came when they fixed this detonator problem from 1917 onwards. They were only able to advance when their shells could be relied on to explode. We need to fix our own detonator problem.

So how is your walk with Jesus? Do you consistently combine the promises of God with the faith that detonates their life-transforming power? Whether it is faith for forgiveness, faith for changed lifestyle, faith for a miracle or faith to take new ground, don't be like the Exodus generation. The writer warns you soberly: *"The message they heard was of no value to them, because those who heard did not combine it with faith."*

---

[8] The writer makes *phobeō*, or *to fear*, the first word of 4:1 in order to emphasize the sobering message of these two verses. Fear of God can be a very good thing, as the writer reminds us again in 12:28.

# Take a Rest (4:1–11)

*There remains, then, a Sabbath-rest for the people of God; for anyone who enters God's rest also rests from their works.*

(Hebrews 4:9–10)

You may have seen the bumper sticker: *"Jesus is coming back – look busy!"* The writer of Hebrews did not have it on the bumper of his chariot. On the contrary, he insists that busyness can often be the very opposite of Christianity. That ought to challenge us in our stressed-out and caffeine-dependent generation. He insists that the mark of true Christianity is knowing how to take a rest in God.

The writer quotes extensively from Psalm 95 in chapters 3 and 4. He chooses a psalm in which the Lord refers to the Promised Land as *"my rest"* and in which he uses a clever play on words. In Exodus 17, shortly after bringing the Israelites safely across the Red Sea, the Lord led them to a place named Rephidim, which means *resting places* in Hebrew. It was a desert region with no natural water supply, because God wanted to teach them how to rest in his promise that he would provide personally for all of their needs. The lesson did not go well. The Israelites refused to trust him, stressing out that he had let them down and demanding that God get his act together. When he provided them with a miraculous water supply, he renamed the place Massah and Meribah, which means testing and quarrelling in Hebrew. David uses those exact same Hebrew words in Psalm

95:8 when he talks about *testing* and *rebelling* against God.[1] The writer of Hebrews therefore chooses a psalm that speaks clearly about our need to rest in God. He wants to teach us what it truly means to put our faith in Jesus.

In verse 3, he takes us back to the beginning of the Bible: *"God's works have been finished since the creation of the world."* In case we miss this reference to the Sabbath, he quotes in verse 4 from Genesis 2:2: *"On the seventh day God rested from all his works."*[2] God did not rest because he was tired, since the Bible tells us that he never grows tired or sleepy. Jesus explains why God rested when he points out that *"The Sabbath was made for humans."*[3] The seventh day of creation was Adam's first full day of life, so God told him to begin his existence by resting in a garden he had not planted, picking fruit he had not grown and enjoying food he had not cultivated. He taught Adam from the outset that a life of faith means resting in the fact that God is God and we are not. Stress and worry are the symptoms of a world that has forgotten that this is true.

The Lord restated this principle to the Israelites in the desert. Six days a week, he provided them with bread from heaven every morning, but he warned them not to try to gather manna on the Sabbath. He made taking this Sabbath rest the fourth of the Ten Commandments, but the Israelites refused to stop and listen. It's far easier to play at being little gods than it is to stop and take a rest in God.[4]

This principle is so important that the Lord restated it

[1] As usual, the writer quotes from the Greek Septuagint. Although this fails to preserve the double meaning in Hebrew, the writer expects us to know enough about Exodus 17 to fill in the blanks for ourselves.

[2] Strangely, the writer does not tell us from where he is quoting. As in 2:6, he expects that any Christian will know the Old Testament well enough to locate it for themselves. We should find this very challenging.

[3] Psalm 121:4; Isaiah 40:28; Mark 2:27.

[4] Although some English translations of 4:6 and 11 tell us that they failed to enter because of their *unbelief*, the Greek word is actually *apeitheia*, which means *disobedience*. Just like faith, unbelief always leads to action.

again. He made the Promised Land a vivid picture of letting him do the work for us. He promised the Israelites *"a land with large, flourishing cities you did not build, houses filled with all kinds of good things you did not provide, wells you did not dig, and vineyards and olive groves you did not plant."*[5]

The Israelites ought to have understood these prophecies. Nevertheless, they failed to enter into God's rest in the Promised Land. Even when Joshua led their children in successful conquest of the land, the new generation of Israelites still failed to enter into God's rest in all its fullness: *"The promise of entering his rest still stands... If Joshua had given them rest, God would not have spoken later about another day."* The apostle Paul makes this same point when he quotes the words of David and tells us that a Christian is *"the one who does not work but trusts God... the one to whom God credits righteousness apart from works."*[6] Jesus isn't looking for busy people. He is looking for people with faith to take a rest in God.

The writer of Hebrews tells us that Christianity means resting from our own work. Have you got that? Good. Then you are ready for the follow-up. He also tells us in verse 11 that Christianity means working very hard! Resting in the finished work of Jesus means grappling with the daily temptation to rely on our own strength instead of on God's activity in our lives. Even if we manage to place all our trust for forgiveness in the dying cry of Jesus in John 19:30 – *"It is finished!"* – we still face a daily struggle to place all of our trust in that same dying cry for a transformed lifestyle, for power through the Holy Spirit and for evangelistic fruitfulness.[7] The writer warns us that we need to

[5] Deuteronomy 6:10–11. See also Joshua 22:4; 24:13; Nehemiah 9:25; Psalm 105:44.

[6] Romans 4:1–6. Paul's letters never contradict Hebrews. Properly understood, they complement it beautifully, explaining in more detail what the writer of Hebrews means.

[7] This is why sabbatarianism (the strict observance of the Sabbath day) often misses the point. It is even possible to turn Sabbath-observance into a righteous act in which we trust instead of in the finished work of Jesus!

HEBREWS 1–7: A BETTER GLIMPSE OF GOD

"*make every effort to enter that rest.*" Taking a rest in God can be hard work. Resting requires wrestling.

The church I lead in London has some magnificent verses chiselled on its foundation stones. I have lost count of the number of times I have returned to one of them, which was laid by Charles Spurgeon's son. It is a quotation from Psalm 46:10: "*Be still, and know that I am God.*" Every time I face trials and difficulties, I return to that foundation stone and I read the verse again. God is God and I am not. It may take effort to silence my fretful soul long enough to read it, but it is always worth it. This is the essence of Christianity. God does the work so we don't have to. All we need to do is remember the words of Jesus in John 6:29: "*The work of God is this: to believe in the one he has sent.*"

The writer of Hebrews tells us that it is still "Today". He tells us that these are still the words the Holy Spirit says to anyone who wants to follow Jesus. God still invites us to enter into his rest by renouncing our own strength and placing all our faith in the finished work of Jesus. Don't imitate Adam, who ate forbidden fruit in a futile bid to play at God. Don't imitate the Israelites, who became stressed and quarrelled instead of resting at Rephidim, and who failed to trust the Lord to give them the Promised Land. Imitate the Joshua generation who believed and trusted and received.

The writer pleads with us: "*There remains, then, a Sabbath-rest for the people of God; for anyone who enters God's rest also rests from their works... Let us, therefore, make every effort to enter that rest, so that no one will perish by following their example of disobedience.*"[8]

132

---

[8] The Greek word *piptō* actually means *to fall* rather than *to perish*. The writer is not teaching us whether or not a Christian can lose their salvation. He is simply warning us that failure to rest in God spells disaster.

# The Ultimate Hero (4:8)

*For if Joshua had given them rest, God would not have spoken later about another day.*

(Hebrews 4:8)

Every nation has its own cherished heroes. Criticizing them usually gets you into a lot of trouble. If you don't believe me, go into a bar in France and tell people that Napoleon was a megalomaniac whose pathological insecurity caused untold suffering for millions of Europeans. Go to America and tell people that the founding fathers were slave-owners who knew less about the rights of man than the Viet Cong. Go to Saudi Arabia and point out the many inconsistencies in the lifestyle of Muhammad. Write to me and tell me how you got on. I'll be very interested. That is, if you make it home alive.

I'm not looking to offend you if you are French or American or Saudi. I just want to help you to imagine how it must have felt for the Jewish Christians when they received this letter. The writer attacks their sacred national heroes one by one. The Jews believed that the archangel Michael was the protector of their nation, so the writer warns them that Michael and his angels are merely *"ministering spirits sent to serve those who will inherit salvation"* (1:14). The Jews honoured Moses for giving them the Law through which they hoped to gain God's forgiveness, so the writer warns them that *"Jesus has been found worthy of greater honour than Moses"* (3:3). He tells them that *"The message spoken through angels"* to Moses cannot begin to compare with the message that has come to them through Jesus (2:2–3). Their greatest national hero after Moses was Joshua, the mighty conqueror who led their ancestors into the Promised Land. That's why, in talking about faith, the writer also topples Joshua from the pedestal on which the Jews have put him.

Joshua was everything that his unbelieving friends were not. When he and Caleb saw the giants in the Promised Land, they urged the Israelites: *"Do not rebel against the Lord. And do not be afraid of the people of the land, because we will devour them. Their protection is gone, but the Lord is with us. Do not be afraid of them."* As a result of their faith, he and Caleb were the only members of the Exodus generation who survived Israel's forty years in the desert. He spent much of that time in the presence of the Lord in the Tent of Meeting so, when Moses died, the Lord appointed him to be the new leader of Israel. Against all odds, Joshua led the Israelites to conquer the Promised Land.[1]

Joshua was good but he was not the ultimate hero. That's what the writer wants us to understand about every human we admire. Joshua was hoodwinked by the Gibeonites and he was stymied by the Jebusites. He left large tracts of land unconquered, and the Canaanites who lived in them would make life misery for Israel for the next 800 years. He failed to deliver Israel the true rest that God had promised them, which is why their nation descended into the chaos and heartache of the book of Judges after he died. The writer wants to ensure that his readers are not as satisfied with Joshua as the people in the synagogues. If they are, they are as foolish as a person who is satisfied with reading holiday brochures instead of going on a summer holiday.

Joshua's life was a prophecy about a better Joshua to come. His name was actually Hoshea, but Moses renamed him in order to make his life foreshadow that of a far better conqueror.[2] The name Joshua is *Yēshū'a* in Hebrew and *Iēsous* in Greek, and it is normally translated into English as *Jesus*, so when the angel told

---

[1] Exodus 33:11; Numbers 14:6–9, 30; 27:15–23; Deuteronomy 34:9.

[2] Numbers 13:16.

Joseph in Matthew 1:21 to name Mary's baby Jesus, he was not simply telling him to give the child a name meaning *The Lord Saves*. He was telling him to proclaim to Israel that Mary's baby was the true and better Joshua.[3]

The writer wants his Jewish readers to understand this fully. They must not be so foolish as to return to the synagogues and to satisfy themselves with Jewish national heroes. Psalm 95 warns us that Joshua's work was insufficient: *"If Joshua had given them rest, God would not have spoken later about another day."*[4] We need a better Joshua because *"there remains, then, a Sabbath-rest for the people of God."* The writer of Hebrews spends more time on this Old Testament passage than he does on any of the other thirty-four passages that he quotes throughout his letter, because it was so crucial for the land-obsessed Jewish nation. Their nation was about to be destroyed by the Romans and it would disappear from the world atlas for almost 1,900 years. The Jewish Christians must not grieve like the writer of Lamentations when that day arrived. Things had fundamentally changed for Israel. Their new and better Joshua had come.

As I write this chapter, news is breaking that another Christian leader with major international influence has fallen. Christian bloggers are wringing their hands in disappointment over how much his sinful actions have betrayed them: they trusted in him and he let them down. I have been influenced enormously by this man's ministry, but I can't agree. He has not let down the lamenting bloggers. They let themselves down when they made a hero out of a Christian leader and started placing in him trust that belonged only to God. The struggle we read about in Hebrews is not the struggle of another generation.

---

[3] Joshua is spelt *Yēshū'a* in Nehemiah 8:17, although The Hebrew Old Testament normally uses the variant spelling *Yehōshūa'*. He is called *Iēsous* throughout the Greek Old Testament.

[4] Joshua referred to his own work as "God's rest" in Joshua 22:4, but he warned the Israelites in Joshua 23:5 that his work was incomplete. They would need a far better Joshua in the future.

We still live in the "today" about which David prophesies. This is still the day on which God calls his followers to decide. Will we place some of our trust in great Christian men and women or will we place our entire trust in Jesus Christ?

Will we be ruthless with the temptation to make heroes out of one another? Will we refuse point-blank to put our trust in the work of anyone but Jesus? Will we rest from our own work and put our faith in the finished work of Jesus? That's what it means to have faith. That's what it means to take a rest in God. It means renouncing all reliance on our own work and on that of others. It means believing that Jesus is the only real hero.

# A Threat and a Promise
## (4:12–13)

*For the word of God is alive and active. Sharper than any double-edged sword, it penetrates.*

(Hebrews 4:12)

Steven Spielberg does a brilliant job of re-creating the horror of D-Day in the movie *Saving Private Ryan*. The American soldiers become so disorientated by the heavy firepower of the defending Germans that they start to believe that they have been defeated. If you want to understand the message of Hebrews, you need to understand that it was addressed to people who felt the same way.

James had been stoned to death by the Jewish Sanhedrin in 62 AD. The Roman government had begun its first wave of persecution against the Christians in 64 AD. The Roman historian Tacitus describes what happened:

> *Nero... inflicted the most exquisite tortures on a class hated for their abominations, called Christians by the populace. Christ, from whom the name had its origin, had suffered the death-penalty during the reign of Tiberius at the hands of one of our procurators, Pontius Pilate, and a most mischievous superstition, thus checked for the moment, broke out again not only in Judea, where the evil began, but even in Rome... A large number were convicted, not so much for the crime of setting fire to the city as for the fact that people hated them. Mockery of every sort was added to their deaths. Covered with the*

*skins of beasts, they were torn by dogs and perished, or were nailed to crosses, or were doomed to the flames and burnt to serve as nightly illumination when daylight had expired.*[1]

Among those who died were the two leading apostles, Peter and Paul. The Jewish Christians were not tempted to run back to the synagogues because they were weak. They were tempted to do so because the Christian Church looked as if it were about to be defeated.

We need to grasp this context in order to understand what was written to the Hebrews, and nowhere is this more the case than in its five warning passages. We have reached the final two verses of the second warning passage, and this context explains why it ends with a reminder about the power of God's Word. These are not just useful verses to shape our doctrine of Scripture. The context makes them the equivalent of the moment when Tom Hanks turns to the crestfallen officers on the D-Day beaches and commands them: *"Move your men up the beach! Now!"*[2] To stir them into action, the writer gives the Jewish Christians a threat and a promise about God's Word.

The writer threatens the Jewish Christians with the thought that Jesus is the Judge. Although these verses are often quoted to comfort Christians that God's Word is powerful, it's important that we recognize that they are meant to discomfort us too. The writer warns us that God's Word penetrates our souls and that *"it judges the thoughts and attitudes of the heart... Everything is uncovered and laid bare before the eyes of him to whom we must give an account."* Anyone can look obedient until God tells them to do something they do not want to do. Like the Exodus generation on the border of the Promised Land, when God's Word tells us to trust in the finished work of Jesus, it

---

[1] Tacitus reveals his own hatred of the Christians as he records this in his *Annals* (15.44).

[2] *Saving Private Ryan* (Paramount Pictures, 1998).

reveals whether or not our profession of faith in him is genuine. It doesn't matter how loudly we claim to trust in Jesus. Our actions speak louder than our words.

You won't be surprised to hear that Martin Luther did not like this. He consigned Hebrews to the appendix of his German New Testament along with James, complaining that *"This seems to be against all of the Gospel and St. Paul's epistles."*[3] I hope that by now you have understood enough of the message of James and Hebrews to see where Martin Luther went wrong. The writer is not denying that we are saved through faith in Jesus' work alone. He is simply pointing out that faith in Jesus' work will always prompt us to respond with faith-filled actions of our own. If we are unwilling to suffer for the sake of Jesus on the D-Day beaches of Christianity, we are afraid of the wrong thing.[4] Compromise is never the easy road. It buys a brief reprieve from the judgment of men at the expense of far greater judgment later at the hands of God.[5]

The writer follows up this threat with a promise. Although many comfortable Westerners take offence at the thought that God will judge every human sin, those who are being persecuted for their faith always find it extremely comforting. God sees the blood of Christian martyrs and he promises to avenge it. The Jewish Christians could rest assured that the Church was not about to die in 68 AD. The blood of the martyrs was about to seed its magnificent advance.[6] The writer promises the surviving

---

[3] *Preface to the Epistle to the Hebrews* (1522). Martin Luther was much more generous towards Hebrews than James, however, conceding that *"However that may be, it is a marvellously fine epistle."*

[4] Jesus says this in Matthew 16:24–27, Mark 8:34–37 and Luke 9:23–26, warning us that anyone who refuses to follow the way of the cross will suffer a far worse fate when he comes back to judge the world.

[5] The writer uses some extremely strong Greek words in 4:13. He warns us that on Judgment Day everything will be *gumnos* and *trachēlizō* – it will be laid *naked* and will *have its throat exposed* to the executioner.

[6] Tertullian uses this phrase in chapter 50 of his *Apology*, looking back in about 197 AD on the advance of the Church during the 130 years since Hebrews

Christians that *"the word of God is alive and active."*[7] The apostle Paul had been beheaded but his message was *"sharper than any double-edged sword."*[8] The Roman emperor could no more hold back the rising tide of Christianity than the rising tide of the Mediterranean Sea.

For all of his superficial complaints about Hebrews, Martin Luther understood this promise very well. Faced with an angry Pope, with murderous enemies and with hostile armies on the border of his country, he assured his friends that *"When Jesus Christ utters a word, He opens His mouth so wide that it embraces all heaven and earth, even though that word be but in a whisper. The word of the Emperor is powerful, but that of Jesus Christ governs the universe."*[9] Luther was able to look back later on the triumph of his message and to tell those same friends that *"I did no more than pray and preach. The Word did it all... While I sat still and drank beer with Philip and Amsdorf, God dealt the Papacy a mighty blow."*[10]

These two verses therefore complete the faith equation we have already encountered several times in James and Hebrews. We know from Hosea 4:6 that *action minus God's Word equals destruction*. We also know from Hebrews 4:2 that *God's Word minus faith equals destruction*, and from James 2:14–26 that *God's Word plus faith minus action equals destruction*. The two verses therefore complete the equation. They assure us that *God's Word plus faith plus action equals certain victory*.

So don't miss the context of this second warning passage,

---

was written.

[7] This statement ties in with the writer's assurances in 3:7 and 10:15 that Scripture is not simply the record of what God said. It is the record of what he *says*.

[8] This statement echoes the teaching of 1:1–3 that the Word of God carries immense power.

[9] This early comment was preserved as point 230 of his *Table Talk*, published in 1566.

[10] Quoted by Roland H. Bainton in *Here I Stand: A Life of Martin Luther* (1978).

and don't move on until you have embraced what it says. Nothing can stand in the way of God's Word. However dark the situation in which you find yourself and however tempting it may be to choose an easier path, take your rest in Jesus. Regardless of the immediate consequences, you will celebrate God's victory on the Day of Judgment with those from every other generation of believers who have done the same.

# Wartime Letter (4:14–5:10)

*Therefore, since we have a great high priest who has ascended into heaven, Jesus the Son of God, let us hold firmly to the faith we profess.*

(Hebrews 4:14)

Hebrews is a wartime letter. It was written during the Jewish–Roman War, which raged from 66 to 73 AD. One side rallied around the Roman emperor, the other side rallied around the high priest in Jerusalem, and the Jewish Christians were caught in the middle. This letter brought them some very encouraging news in the midst of war.

The Roman emperor claimed to be the *pontifex maximus* – that's Latin for the *greatest bridge-builder* or the *greatest mediator*, so it came to refer to the *greatest priest* in Rome. Julius Caesar saw the immense influence borne by this role, so he acquired it as one of the major stepping stones on his path towards supreme power. Thereafter, every Roman emperor assumed the role of *pontifex maximus*, claiming to be the chief representative of the human race before the pagan gods. Those fighting on the Roman side were very clear who their high priest was: it was the emperor of Rome.

Those fighting on the Jewish side were equally clear. Their high priesthood had been created over 1,300 years before the birth of Julius Caesar. The Lord appointed Moses' brother Aaron at Mount Sinai to serve in the newly constructed Tabernacle as the high priest of Israel. His descendants held the high priesthood until the Jewish exile to Babylon. After the return from exile they became the leaders of the Jewish nation, since there could be no monarchy while Israel remained part of the Persian, Macedonian, Seleucid and Roman empires. The high priest at the Temple in Jerusalem became the natural rallying point for Jewish nationalism. When the future Emperor Titus sacked Jerusalem and its Temple two years after this wartime letter was written, he made sure that he destroyed the office of high priest as one of his major war aims. There has not been a high priest of Israel since the Temple burned in 70 AD.

The writer of Hebrews injects some wonderful news into this wartime situation. The Jewish Christians do not need to take sides, since neither the Roman emperor nor the Temple ruler is the true high priest at all. Jesus is the real *pontifex maximus*. He alone is the Great High Priest.[1] The Christians do not owe allegiance to either of the sides in the Jewish–Roman War. They owe allegiance to Jesus Christ alone.[2]

It's important to note that the writer is not merely saying that Jesus is a better high priest than Aaron. We might have assumed this from the flow of Hebrews so far: Jesus is better than the angels, better than Moses, better than Joshua and now better than Aaron too. But the writer is actually saying something far more radical. The Jewish Christians already knew that Aaron was flawed (he made the golden calf), that his descendants were no better (think of Eli) and that the current high priest in Jerusalem was, in the words of the historian Josephus who knew him, *"a man unworthy of the high priesthood... with the false face of an actor."*[3] The writer is therefore not simply saying that Jesus is better than the high priests of Israel. He is telling

---

[1] The writer has already told us this in 3:1. It will become his major theme in 6:13–10:39.

[2] Since the fall of the Roman Empire, many Popes have assumed the title "*Pontifex Maximus*". In view of this passage, I am convinced they shouldn't. Assuming titles which belong to Jesus alone is never a wise idea.

[3] Writing in c.75 AD, this is how Josephus describes Phannias in his *Wars of the Jews* (4.3.8).

us that Jesus has launched a new and better high priesthood altogether. Something far better has come.

In 4:14–16, the writer tells us that Jesus is a better high priest because *he has entered a better sanctuary*. Aaron and his descendants were the only people authorized to enter the sacred inner room of the Tabernacle and Temple. They were not permitted to bring anybody else inside this Most Holy Place with them. Jesus, on the other hand, has entered the sanctuary of heaven, ascending to the Father's side where he sits enthroned in glory, and he can grant admission through his death and resurrection to anyone who puts their faith in him. He has obtained for God's People far better access to a far better sanctuary than the high priests in Jerusalem. The writer therefore shouts a better battle-cry above the din of the Jewish–Roman War: *"Let us then approach God's throne of grace with confidence, so that we may receive mercy and find grace to help us in our time of need."*

In 5:1–6, the writer tells us that Jesus is a better high priest because *he was chosen by God and not by men*. Julius Caesar bribed his way to being appointed *pontifex maximus* in Rome.[4] Although verse 4 reminds us that this was never to be the way with Aaron's priesthood, the current high priest owed his appointment to *"a cunning contrivance to seize upon the government, derived from those that presumed to appoint governors as they themselves pleased."*[5] In contrast, Jesus was appointed by God himself, just as Aaron was appointed at Mount Sinai. The writer quotes two of David's prophecies about the Messiah – one from Psalm 2:7 and one from Psalm 110:4 – in order to convince his Jewish readers that God always promised to inaugurate a better high priesthood through his Messiah.[6]

---

[4] Suetonius in his *Life of Julius Caesar* (13) and Plutarch in his *Life of Julius Caesar* (7.1–2).

[5] Josephus in his *Wars of the Jews* (4.3.8).

[6] The writer quoted from Psalms 2 and 110 in chapter 1. In chapter 7, he will quote from Psalm 110 again.

They must not go back to the synagogues to become embroiled in the dying struggles of Aaron's superseded order. Jesus is the Great High Priest. The self-appointed pontiffs in Rome and Jerusalem were mere pretenders.

In 5:7–10, the writer tells us that Jesus is a better high priest because *he is perfectly sinless*. He begins to explain that Jesus is more like the high priest Melchizedek in Genesis 14:18–20 than he is like any of the priests of Aaron's order. Although he interrupts himself from 5:11 to 6:12, he will continue this explanation from 6:13 to 7:27. One thing at least is plain from these initial verses. The priests who followed in the footsteps of Aaron were a roguish lot. Aaron died with the unbelieving Israelites in the desert and few of his descendants proved any better, which is why the priests had to offer sacrifices for their own sins as well as for those of the Jewish nation. Jesus, on the other hand, is the Great High Priest of a completely different order. He was tempted in the same way that we are, yet he never sinned. He was perfectly obedient in his reverent submission.[7] As a result, he has become *"the source of eternal salvation for all who obey him."*[8] The high priests in Rome and Jerusalem could keep their feeble titles. Jesus holds the only high priesthood this world can ever need.

Hebrews is a wartime letter, and we still live in a world that is at war. It may not fight over pontiffs and priesthoods, but it still fights over objects that are worthless next to Jesus. So don't take sides with a world that fights for money and power and influence and fame. Fall in behind the Great High Priest who is worth more than all of those things put together. Approach God's throne with confidence that Jesus has made a way for you into God's presence, believing that there you will find everything you need.

---

[7] These statements in 4:15 and 5:8 require further explanation. I have devoted separate chapters to them.

[8] Note that the writer does not simply say *"for all who believe in him."* Like James, he constantly emphasizes to his Jewish readers that true faith always results in obedient action.

# The Temptation of Christ (4:15)

> *We do not have a high priest who is unable to feel sympathy for our weaknesses, but we have one who has been tempted in every way, just as we are – yet he did not sin.*

> (Hebrews 4:15)

Martin Scorsese offended many Christians with his film *The Last Temptation of Christ*. It depicts the Devil tempting Jesus to disobey his Father by lusting after Mary Magdalene, by avoiding the cross and by pursuing his desire to marry her.[1]

Now there are many valid reasons to dislike Martin Scorsese's film. It's completely unhistorical. It ignores the contemporary accounts of the life of Jesus that were written by those who knew him best. It chooses cheap shock and titillation over serious consideration of the real Jesus. But don't reject it because it suggests that Jesus was tempted to doubt his Father, to lust and to disobey. The writer of Hebrews tells us something far more shocking than Martin Scorsese. He tells us that Jesus was *"tempted **in every way**, just as we are – yet he did not sin."*

Reflect for a moment on why that is such good news. If Jesus were a sinful high priest like the one who presided over the Temple in Jerusalem when this letter was written, he would be unable to save us, like a financial advisor who is himself going bankrupt. If Jesus were an inhuman high priest who could not sympathize with sinners, he would be unwilling to help us

---

[1] *The Last Temptation of Christ* (Universal Pictures, 1988).

when we are tempted, a bit like Allah in the Qur'an, making aloof demands of humans from the safety of heaven. The Gospel tells us that Jesus is not a spectator Saviour. He has walked in our shoes and he knows what it is like to be bombarded by a myriad of temptations every day. He has gone ahead of us, remaining sinless through them all, in order to deliver us from temptation.

Jesus has endured far greater sexual temptation than any of us. The writer is not telling us that Jesus was tempted in precisely the same ways that we are – he was not tempted to access internet pornography any more than he was tempted to break the speed limit on the highway – but he was tempted in all of the same categories that we are. If you are tempted to lust after men or women, this is fantastic news. Jesus was constantly surrounded by men and women who hung on his every word, yet he never once succumbed to any of the opportunities this gave him. This is the Gospel for those who are gay or unhappily married or addicted to pornography. Jesus has faced down your strong temptation. He sympathizes with you in your weakness and he promises to grant you victory over these temptations if you let him.

Jesus has endured far greater temptation to despair than any of us. He lived in a culture where almost everybody married and had children, yet there he was: a thirty-something singleton, the Bridget Jones of Galilee. By the time he died, he had only 120 faithful followers, most of whom abandoned him before his crucifixion. Isaiah and David are not exaggerating when they describe the lonely prayers of the Messiah: *"Who has believed our message?"* and *"My God, my God, why have you forsaken me?"*[2]

Jesus has endured far greater temptation towards pride than any of us. We may act as though we are God's gift to the world, but Jesus really was. We may wish that the world revolved

---

[2] Psalm 22:1; Isaiah 53:1; Matthew 27:46.

around us, but it really does revolve around Jesus. The Devil tempted him during his forty days in the desert to put his own interests before those of his Father and those of his followers, but he steadfastly refused. *"Not as I will, but as you will,"* he prayed through gritted teeth in the Garden of Gethsemane. *"The Son of Man did not come to be served, but to serve, and to give his life as a ransom for many."*[3]

Jesus endured far greater temptation towards unforgiveness than any of us. He was far more wronged than anybody else has ever been in human history. His friend Judas sold him for money. His remaining disciples abandoned him to save their own skins. The crowds he had fed and healed cried out for his crucifixion. The Roman soldiers mocked him with false acts of worship. What did he ever do to provoke their hatred but leave the glories of heaven and live in their shabby little empire to save their sinful souls? Nevertheless, in Luke 23:34 he cried out as he died, *"Father, forgive them, for they do not know what they are doing."*

If you are struggling with temptation then, first, remember that temptation is not sin. Jesus never sinned when he was tempted. He *"learned obedience"* when his untested innocence became refusal to succumb to ungodly desires. Let's ask the Lord to *"Lead us not into temptation"* but, if he chooses not to grant our request, let's embrace his refining of our character. The request to be spared from temptation is only half of Matthew 6:13. The second half is a prayer we learn to pray in the midst of temptation: *"Deliver us from the evil one."*

Second, remember that Jesus has freed us from sin's power as well as from sin's penalty. He subjected himself to sin's power on the cross in order to break that power once and for all. In Romans 6, Paul explains how this works in practice for those who believe in Jesus' sacrifice: *"Our old self was crucified with*

---

[3] Matthew 4:1–11; 26:39; Mark 10:45. Adam succumbed to the temptation to act out of self-centred pride in the Garden of Eden. Jesus overcame the same temptation in the Garden of Gethsemane.

him so that the body ruled by sin might be done away with, that we should no longer be slaves to sin." Jesus sympathizes with you right now in your weakness. He is waiting for you to cry out for him to help you.

Third, remember that no temptation can ever be too strong for you to overcome if Jesus is fighting alongside you. He will always provide you with a way out and he will always strengthen you to endure it if you truly hate wickedness as much as he does. As your Great High Priest, he will pull you out of harm's way and into the presence of God. Paul explains in 1 Corinthians 10:13: *"No temptation has overtaken you except what is common to mankind. And God is faithful; he will not let you be tempted beyond what you can bear. But when you are tempted, he will also provide a way out so that you can endure it."*

So don't be offended when the writer of Hebrews tells you that Jesus was subjected to every manner of temptation. This is wonderful news. It means that Jesus has gone before us and has already won our battle with temptation. It means that he sympathizes with our weaknesses and that he comes alongside us to help us overcome temptation through the power of his death and resurrection. He is not a Great High Priest who stands aloof and afar. He stands shoulder-to-shoulder with us and delivers us from every temptation.

# Why Doesn't God Always Heal? (5:7)

*During the days of Jesus' life on earth, he offered up prayers and petitions with fervent cries and tears to the one who could save him from death, and he was heard.*

(Hebrews 5:7)

Later on today I am speaking at my friend's funeral. The last time I saw her was when my fellow church elders and I obeyed the instruction in James 5 by anointing her with oil and praying for her to be healed of cancer. That instruction comes with a promise: *"The prayer offered in faith will make the ill person well."* But she didn't get well. Instead, she died and left behind a young husband and a two-year-old son. Not for the first time, I have had to ask the anguished question: Why doesn't God always heal? I don't just need an answer to that question personally. In a few hours' time I will need to give an answer to an entire congregation. Why do our prayers often seem to go unanswered?

This question is partly answered by a throwaway comment in Hebrews 5:7. Let's not rush over it because, although it initially appears confusing, it is absolutely priceless to anyone who is grieving for a friend who has died unhealed.

This verse describes the prayer life of Jesus. In itself, that's fascinating. Although he was fully God, Jesus demonstrated the importance of a life of constant prayer. He did not just pray occasionally; he prayed on each of the days of his life on earth. He did not pray platitudes but heartfelt *"prayers and petitions"*.

He did not rattle off a dry-eyed prayer list, but brought requests *"with fervent cries and tears"*. He did not shout towards the sky in the vague hope that his wishes might be answered; he lodged petitions with his Father in full confidence that he would be *"heard because of his reverent submission."*[1] This throwaway verse gives us a fly-on-the-wall insight into the intimate prayer life of Jesus.

But note what is strange here. The writer tells us that much of Jesus' praying was directed towards the Father as *"the one who could save him from death."* He tells us that these anguished prayers were answered: *"He was heard because of his reverent submission."* But Jesus wasn't spared from death. He died one of the most brutal deaths imaginable on a cruel cross at Calvary. We cannot sidestep this statement, since the New Testament uses this Greek word to describe prayers which are both heard and answered.[2] So what is the writer trying to tell us here?

We live in a world that is obsessed with the moment. Pleasure can't be deferred. It must be experienced right here, right now. Without realizing it, as Christians, we can import this unhealthy mindset into our relationship with God. But Jesus didn't. He trusted his Father to make the right decisions for his life in the true perspective of eternity. He prayed like Shadrach, Meshach and Abednego when they refused to bow down to a false god in Babylon, telling King Nebuchadnezzar in Daniel 3:17–18 that they were not afraid of being thrown into the fiery furnace: *"If we are thrown into the blazing furnace, the God we serve is able to deliver us from it...* **But even if he does not**, *we want you to know, Your Majesty, that we will not serve your gods."*

Daniel's three friends trusted God to deliver them from

---

[1] Hebrews 5:7 echoes James 5:16 when it tells us that our own submission to God's authority affects our authority in prayer. See also 1 Timothy 2:8; 1 Peter 3:7; Isaiah 1:15; Proverbs 15:8, 29; 21:13; 28:9.

[2] The word *eisakouō* is used to describe God answering prayer in Matthew 6:7, Luke 1:13 and Acts 10:31.

dying (which is precisely what he did), but they also trusted him to be wise enough to decide in the light of eternity whether it was best to deliver them from dying or from death. Jesus did the same in his own prayers, asking to be spared the cross while conceding, *"Yet not my will, but yours be done."*[3] The Greek word the writer uses for Jesus' petitions is *hiketēria*, which means literally the *olive branch* a messenger would extend to a hostile general while pleading for mercy. Jesus therefore had more on his mind while he was praying than the avoidance of personal pain. He was pleading for mercy for you and for me.

Jesus' prayers were answered. He was not delivered from dying on the cross, since this was the only way in which we could be forgiven, but he was delivered from death through the miracle of his resurrection.[4] The Father answered his plea that the prophecy in Psalm 16:8–11 would be fulfilled and that he would not be abandoned to the realm of the dead. It was in this sense that Jesus was able to tell people that he laid down his life and picked it up again. Even though he was a corpse, he had already secured his resurrection through his fervent prayers before he died.[5]

I prayed several times with my friend before she died that she would be healed of her cancer. Whenever I hesitated, pointing out that she had not been healed the previous time, she simply responded, *"You are right, so we had better pray some more."* When my wife tried to prepare her for dying, she replied that *"I believe in God to save me from my cancer and I believe in him to save me from death if he decides not to. I just can't pray for healing and prepare to die at the same time."* In her last few days, when she began to turn her attention towards faith for dying instead of faith for healing, it was not a moment of defeat. She

---

[3] Matthew 26:39; Mark 14:36; Luke 22:42.

[4] A literal translation of the Greek phrase *ek thanatou* is not *from dying*, but *out of death*.

[5] John 2:19–21; 10:17–18. The Son's prayers moved the Father and the Spirit.

expressed the same triumphant faith as Jesus. She believed as firmly in God to save her from death as she had believed for him to save her from dying. Her departure from this cancer-filled world and her entry to paradise was not failure. It was glorious victory.

The great missionary Hudson Taylor stared death in the face during his first voyage to China. When his ship was about to sink, the captain taunted him: *"We cannot live half an hour now: what of your call to labour for the Lord in China?"* Hudson Taylor recalled later, *"It was a great joy to feel and to tell him that I would not for any consideration be in any other position; that I strongly expected to reach China; but that, if otherwise, at any rate the Master would say it was well that I was found seeking to obey His command."*[6]

Like Hudson Taylor, I'm not going to allow this storm to stop me from trusting in the Lord. I am going to keep obeying the instruction in James 5, believing that he will deliver many people from dying, while believing that he is also wise enough to know when instead to save people from death. I am going to give thanks for the people we have seen healed in these past two years, even from cancer, and I am going to keep praying until we see even more. Whatever your own questions, let's be like Hudson Taylor together. Let's be found seeking to obey the Lord's command when he returns.

---

[6] Hudson Taylor recalled this event in his autobiography, *A Retrospect* (1894).

# Third Warning (5:11–6:12)

*Even though we speak like this, dear friends, we are convinced of better things in your case – the things that have to do with salvation.*

(Hebrews 6:9)

In a football match you only get two warnings before you are sent off the pitch in disgrace. You get a yellow card and then a red card. After that, the only thing you get is an early shower. So it says something of the mercy of God that the writer of Hebrews breaks off from his explanation about the priesthood of Melchizedek in order to issue his readers with a third strong warning not to turn away from Jesus. The language is strong because so is the love of God towards the precious people he has saved.

The writer leaves us in no doubt here that he is addressing Christians. He expresses disappointment that they have not yet become Christian teachers (5:12) and he exhorts them towards Christian maturity rather than towards Christian conversion (6:1). He addresses them as enlightened believers who have received the Holy Spirit (6:4) and who have experienced the goodness of God's Word and the power of his coming Kingdom (6:5). He therefore makes it clear that these words are addressed to the same Jewish Christians as the rest of his letter. This warning passage is intended for believers.

The writer also leaves us in no doubt that he is threatening his readers with eternal punishment in hell. The language here is very strong. He talks about *"eternal judgment"* and about the danger of *"being cursed"* and *"burned"* like a worthless field of thorns. His language towards Christians is so shocking that many people struggle to reconcile it with other New Testament passages that reassure us that those whom God saves he also keeps secure in their faith. It therefore requires some slow and careful reading.

In 5:11-14, the writer claims that any difficulty we have in understanding this passage is on our side rather than on his. This may seem like a pretty arrogant assertion, but it is intended as a challenge rather than a boast.[1] He warns us in verse 14 that Christians need to develop their understanding of God through diligent study of the Scriptures. We need to be as diligent in training our minds to think God's way as an athlete is in training his body to run.[2] If we struggle with the spiritual solids contained in this passage, it should challenge us to grow up in our faith and graduate from a diet of spiritual milk.[3] The more we understand the New Testament as a whole, the less we will struggle with passages like this one.

In 6:1-8, the writer lists some of the elements that constitute a basic understanding of Christianity. He makes it clear that he believes his readers are Christians by encouraging them, *"Let us move beyond the elementary teachings about Christ and be taken forward to maturity."* Nevertheless, he begins to warn them solemnly of the dangers of avoiding persecution through returning to the synagogues. It may seem like a little act of compromise, but these are the same synagogues which rejected Jesus and led the persecution against the apostles. Joining them would not be a change of congregation. It would

---

[1] The writer uses a Greek perfect tense in 5:11 to challenge the Jewish Christians literally that *"you have become lazy in your listening."* They had lost the passion for God's Word that had accompanied their conversion.

[2] The Greek word *gumnazō* in 5:14 means *to exercise like an athlete* and it is the root of our English word *gymnasium*. Having gym membership doesn't make us fit if we are too lazy to make use of it.

[3] Paul says something very similar in Romans 12:2. Christians become mature in their understanding of passages like this one by diligently renewing their minds through constant exposure to God's Word.

be a total deviation from the Christian faith.[4] It would mean siding with the enemies of Jesus and crucifying him all over again. It would subject Jesus to public disgrace, because any Jew or Roman who heard the news would automatically assume that he was therefore not the true Messiah.

In 6:1–8, the writer warns that there is no way back to faith in Jesus for anybody who deserts him in this way. Such spiritual turncoats are like a worthless field of thorns and thistles. There remains no repentance for them; only fire. These verses have been abused. For example, at the start of the third century Tertullian seized upon them as a proof text that the apostles offered no forgiveness to Christians who relapsed into sexual sin after their conversion – despite the fact that there are New Testament examples of the apostles doing so![5] It's therefore no wonder that many readers have attempted to soften the message of these verses. Many people argue that, since the writer uses a Greek present participle in verse 6, he is actually telling us that repentance is impossible *while a person is re-crucifying Jesus*. While this statement is undoubtedly true, I have to agree with F.F. Bruce that pointing out that nobody can be brought to repentance while they remain unrepentant *"would be a truism hardly worth putting into words."*[6] We find a better explanation of what the writer means in the final verses of this third warning passage.

In 6:9–12, the writer makes it clear that he does not actually expect any of the Jewish Christians to lose their salvation. He is not flattering them when he tells them that *"even though we speak like this, dear friends, we are convinced of better things in*

---

[4] The Greek word *parapiptō* in 6:6 means *to fall aside* or *to deviate*. The writer is pointing out that synagogue religion is not Christianity-minus-Christ. It is a complete deviation from the Gospel.

[5] Tertullian in chapter 20 of his book *On Modesty*. Contrast this with the example of 1 Corinthians 5:1–5 and its sequel in 2 Corinthians 2:5–11 and 7:8–12.

[6] F.F. Bruce in *The Epistle to the Hebrews* (1963).

*your case – the things that have to do with salvation.*" He does not follow up his warning with a challenge that they are phoney believers who need to surrender to Jesus truly. On the contrary, he urges them not to become lazy in their faith because it will surely be rewarded.[7] So why does he bother issuing such a strong warning at all? Is it all a lot of fuss about nothing?

Not at all. For a start, it is unlikely that in any church in history every single professing believer has been genuinely converted. If Ananias and Sapphira could look like model Christians to everyone except for Peter in Acts 5, then every Christian congregation needs to hear warnings like this one. Our little acts of compromise are never little. They ought to cause us to reflect on whether we have truly surrendered to the Gospel.

Furthermore, strong warnings like this one are the means through which genuine Christians are kept safe from danger. I lecture my children about the dangers of the roads in London, not because I expect them to be run over, but because I trust them to cross the road without me. As we saw earlier, Paul is not contradicting himself when he tells his shipmates that God has said they will all survive the storm (Acts 27:21–26) while warning them that if they leave the ship, they will die (Acts 27:31–32). Nor is he contradicting himself when he promises that God holds onto believers (1 Corinthians 1:8–9) while urging believers to hold onto God (1 Corinthians 6:9–10; 10:1–13).

That is what the writer of Hebrews is doing in this third warning passage. He is warning believers about the dangers of falling away from their faith because that is how God ensures that no true believer will ever fall away from their faith! He warns us that little acts of compromise – our own equivalent of going back to the synagogues – are absolutely deadly. He urges us to hold onto the Saviour who holds firmly onto us. Anything else is simply unthinkable.

---

[7] The writer uses the same Greek word *nōthros* to warn his readers in both 5:11 and 6:12 that they have become spiritually *lazy*. These are the only two uses of the word in the New Testament.

# Basic Christianity (6:1–2)

*Let us move beyond the elementary teachings about
Christ and be taken forward to maturity.*

(Hebrews 6:1)

There are very few passages in the New Testament that
list for us the items that belong on the curriculum of basic
Christianity. Paul goes some way towards it in his two letters
to the Thessalonians, but the clearest list of items occurs here
in Hebrews 6:1–2. While encouraging the Jewish Christians to
graduate from spiritual milk to solids, the writer lists five things
the apostles considered to be the elementary building blocks
of Christianity.[1] We need to read these verses slowly because
the list is absolutely crucial. Does our Christian experience truly
include all five of these things?

The first item on the list is *repentance from dead works*.
This doesn't just mean renouncing the sins which would have
claimed our lives had Jesus not intervened. The Greek phrase
*metanoia apo nekrōn ergōn* refers literally to *repentance from
works that are dead*, not repentance from works that lead to
death. Basic Christianity is more than an admission that we
have sinned against God and need to be forgiven. It is also an
admission that we are powerless to save ourselves. Even our
best actions are dead works. Only when we confess this are we
truly able to trust in the finished work of Jesus.

The Greek word for repentance means far more than

---

[1] The Greek word *stoicheia*, which the writer uses in 5:12 to describe the basic
*principles* of Christianity, is also used to describe the basic natural elements in
2 Peter 3:10 and 12. This list is the A-B-C of Christianity.

saying sorry. *Metanoia* means a *change of mind*, a willingness to embrace God's *new way of thinking*.[2] Think of the Bible passages you find it hardest to submit to. These are the areas where the reality or unreality of your repentance is revealed. Our old way of thinking encourages us to rely on our own strength, on our own resources, on our friends or on our church to bring us to maturity, effectiveness and fruitfulness as Christians. The kings of Israel and Judah were often rebuked for relying on their neighbours instead of on their God. They had to learn that it is a sin to try to *"work salvation for yourself with your own hands."*[3] Basic Christianity means repenting of self-reliance. It means renouncing our own dead works in order to rely on Jesus' work alone.[4]

The second item on the list is *faith in God*. Basic Christianity means accepting what the writer told us in 4:12 – that Scripture is the Word of God, that it is alive and active, and that it is far more relevant and reliable than the hubbub of voices all around us in this unbelieving world. It may sound obvious, but a Christian believer is somebody who believes that what God says is true. There is a place for doubt and questioning in the Christian life, but it needs to lead us towards greater faith in God and not towards treating uncertainty as if it were a Christian virtue. It needs to help us *"taste the goodness of the word of God."* The Lord never lies. He is who he says he is and every verse of the Bible he inspired is completely true. That's not controversial. It's basic Christianity.

The third item on the list is *teaching about baptisms*. Since he is talking to Jewish Christians, the writer uses the Greek word

---

[2] John the Baptist called the religious leaders who came to him a "brood of vipers" for trying to acquire forgiveness from God without submitting to his new way of thinking (Matthew 3:7–8; Luke 3:7–8).

[3] This is a literal translation of David and Abigail's insight in 1 Samuel 25:26 and 33.

[4] Praise God, the writer promises in 9:14 that Jesus is able to free us from our reliance on dead works.

*baptismos*, which refers to the ceremonial cleansing rites that were part and parcel of first-century Judaism.[5] He points out that basic Christianity teaches that such things are no longer needed: the blood of Jesus cleanses us completely.[6] Believers are only commanded to receive two baptisms in order to receive the fullness of his sacrifice: baptism in water, as a public way of identifying with Jesus in his death and resurrection,[7] and baptism in the Holy Spirit.[8]

The fourth item on the list is *the laying on of hands*. The Jewish Christians were used to seeing this take place at ordination services in the synagogues, but basic Christianity teaches that this is also how the Holy Spirit uses anointed believers in ministry. The apostles assumed that every true believer would obey God's command to receive the Holy Spirit (note the way Paul takes it as a given in 1 Corinthians 12:13), and yet they never assumed that being filled with the Holy Spirit was automatic at conversion (note Paul's perceptive question in Acts 19:2, which immediately led to the laying on of hands). The apostles therefore taught their converts that they might need the help of more experienced Christians in order to receive the fullness of the Holy Spirit and of his miraculous gifts.[9] We should be challenged that they simply saw this as basic Christianity. Can you honestly say with the writer in verse 1 that you are carried along by the Holy Spirit, like a sailboat in the wind?[10] Can you honestly say in verse 4 that you *"have tasted*

[5] The word *baptismos* is used in Mark 7:4 and Hebrews 9:10. The Greek word for Christian baptism is *baptisma* in order to emphasize that it is different from Jewish ceremonial washings.

[6] See Matthew 15:1–20; Luke 11:38–41.

[7] Romans 6:1–4; Colossians 2:11–12.

[8] This does not contradict Paul's statement in Ephesians 4:5 that there is only one baptism. In the context he is talking about a single baptism in water. He affirms our need to be baptized with the Holy Spirit in 5:18.

[9] See Acts 6:6–8; 8:17–18; 13:3; 1 Timothy 4:14; 2 Timothy 1:6.

[10] The Greek word *pherō* in 6:1 is used to describe people being *"carried along by the Holy Spirit"* in 2 Peter 1:21.

*the heavenly gift"* which Peter says is elementary Christianity in Acts 2:38?[11] Can you honestly say in verses 4–5 that you *"have shared in the Holy Spirit"* and *"have tasted... the miraculous powers of the coming age"*?[12] If not, there is still a lot of spiritual milk for you to swallow. Find a mature Christian who can lay hands on you today.

The fifth item on the list is *the resurrection of the dead and eternal judgment.* As we can tell from Paul's training curriculum in 1 and 2 Thessalonians, teaching about the age to come is always an essential element of basic Christianity. New converts need to be taught about heaven and hell. They need to believe in both or else their faith will become stunted and deformed. They need to be taught about the new heavens and the new earth which God will re-create when Jesus finally returns.[13]

This list of five items is not meant to be exhaustive. The writer probably chose these because they contrasted Christianity most strongly with the empty rituals practised in the first-century synagogues. Our own list of items may include several items more, but let's be careful that it does not contain anything *less* than these five items. Let's ensure that we experience the entirety of basic Christianity as the writer describes it in these two verses. Then let's move on from this elementary teaching. Let's ask the Holy Spirit to lead us onward and to feed us on the solid food of complete Christian maturity.

---

[11] The Greek word *dōrea* is used in nine other places in the New Testament. In seven of these it refers specifically to the *gift* of the Holy Spirit.

[12] The word *dunamis* in 6:5 is the same word which is used to describe the *miraculous power* of the Holy Spirit in Luke 4:14, 5:17, 6:19, 9:1, 10:13, 19:37 and 24:49, and in Acts 1:8, 2:22, 3:12, 4:33, 6:8, 8:13 and 19:11.

[13] See Isaiah 65:17; Matthew 19:28; Acts 3:21; Romans 8:19–23; Hebrews 2:5; 2 Peter 3:13; Revelation 21–22.

# Justice (6:10)

*God is not unjust; he will not forget your work and
the love you have shown him as you have helped his
people and continue to help them.*

(Hebrews 6:10)

On 13th January 1898, the novelist Émile Zola wrote a front-page article for one of the leading Paris newspapers. Still known by its simple French headline – *"J'accuse…!"* – it attacked those who had played a part in the unjust imprisonment of Albert Dreyfus. It demanded *"the truth… about this appalling miscarriage of justice… this terrible denial of justice from which France is sick… How this miscarriage of justice could be possible!… O justice, what dreadful despair grips the heart!"* As a result of Émile Zola's passionate plea for justice, Dreyfus was given a fair hearing and eventually exonerated of all wrongdoing.

The writer of Hebrews has good news for us. The Lord has no need of an Émile Zola in his heavenly courtroom. He assures us in verse 10 that *"God is not unjust; he will not forget your work."* In other words, he promises us that there is not a single thing we will ever do in our life on earth that the Lord will fail to take into consideration when he comes to judge us at the end of time. God is the paragon of justice, the incorruptible Judge. Are you as excited about this as the writer of Hebrews?

He is telling you that justice demands that God reward every single good thing that you do. This is extremely good news if you have ever felt like the returning Jewish exiles who complained in Malachi 3:14 that *"It is futile to serve God. What do we gain by carrying out his requirements?"* It is also good news if you have ever prayed with Nehemiah, *"Remember me for this, my God, and do not blot out what I have so faithfully done."*[1] The writer tells us that God would be unjust if he forgot to reward any of our obedient actions. He will never forget the ways in which we have expressed our love towards him and the Church which bears his name. We need never accuse the Lord of forgetting justice, like the returning exiles or like Émile Zola. We can trust him to reward us fully for everything we have done.

I became a Christian at university. Like most students, I was always in need of money. Nevertheless, after my conversion I decided to turn down work during the first week of the university holidays in order to feed myself on the spiritual milk I knew I desperately needed from the Bible. I studied the Bible for as many hours each day as I would have worked, praying as I did so that God would perform a miracle to provide me with the money I had turned down in order to do so. At the end of the week, I went to the bank and was told to my surprise that a forgotten investment had skyrocketed, earning the exact sum of money I would have earned had I said yes to my employer. It didn't matter that I had forgotten about the investment, because my bank hadn't. They had been storing it up for me so that God could reveal it at the proper time. Whether you are aware of it or not, that is what the writer says the Lord is doing right now with all of the obedient actions you perform out of your love for Jesus.[2]

But justice works both ways. By definition, the writer is therefore also telling us that justice demands that God punish every single sinful thing we do. Most Westerners resist this. They believe that it is God's job to forgive. In the words of the English poet Alexander Pope, *"To err is human, to forgive divine."*[3] The

---

[1] Nehemiah 5:19; 13:14, 22, 31. He was one of the Jewish leaders in the time of Malachi.

[2] Hebrews 4:13; Matthew 25:34–40; Mark 9:41; Luke 14:12–14; Acts 10:4; Romans 14:10–12; 2 Corinthians 5:10.

[3] He wrote this in his *Essay on Criticism* (1711).

writer of Hebrews corrects this muddled thinking. He tells us that God's job is to judge us fairly. It is to honour the teaching of Proverbs 17:15: *"Acquitting the guilty and condemning the innocent – the Lord detests them both."* That's scary but it is also brilliant news. It means that God's justice will never become corrupted, like the French law courts in the days of Émile Zola. A judge who turns a blind eye to a person's sin is himself a sinner. God's justice demands that he punish every single sin in human history.

Since even our best actions are dead works, this means that we are in grave danger. This verse comes as part of a warning passage for a reason. The writer wants us to understand that it would not be unfair for God to send us to hell. In fact, it would be unfair for him not to do so, were it not for our Great High Priest. Jesus is the only reason why God can be just and at the same time acquit the guilty. Albert Dreyfus was an innocent man imprisoned against his will, but Jesus was an innocent man crucified by his own free will. God's justice was satisfied when Jesus died in your place and in mine.

His crucifixion was the answer to David's prayer in Psalm 25:7: *"Do not remember the sins of my youth and my rebellious ways."* His sacrifice was the only reason God could promise in Isaiah 43:25 that *"I, even I, am he who blots out your transgressions, for my own sake, and remembers your sins no more."* His death alone enabled God to declare in Jeremiah 31:34: *"I will forgive their wickedness and will remember their sins no more."*[4]

If you have placed your faith in Jesus then, when he died on the cross, he bore God's just punishment towards your sin so that your guilt would not be counted against you. As much as it would have been unjust for heaven's courtroom to declare you innocent, it is now unjust for heaven's courtroom to declare you guilty. Sin cannot be punished in two places. It

---

[4] Hebrews 8–10 quotes liberally from Jeremiah 31:31–34 in order to explain what it means for Jesus to be our Great High Priest.

is either punished in the sinner or it is punished in the sinless Saviour who took their place. Jesus was punished for your sin so that you can receive *"his reward... and his recompense."*[5] Jesus stepped into your shoes so that you can stand in his. So don't move on from this warning passage until you have told him that you gladly accept the great exchange which God has made to save your soul.

In his front-page accusation, Émile Zola shared his longing for an *"explosion of truth and justice"*. The writer of Hebrews tells us that this is precisely what God has given us: all that we deserve for our faith-filled response to the Saviour who bore the punishment that we deserve for our sin, and all that he has earned for us through his perfect life, his violent death and his glorious resurrection.

What a holy Judge. What a glorious Gospel. What a Great High Priest we have in heaven.

---

[5] Isaiah 40:10; 62:11; Revelation 22:12. We receive the full reward for his sinless life and reverent submission (Hebrews 4:15; 5:7).

# The Patience of a Saint
## (6:11–20)

*We do not want you to become lazy, but to imitate those who through faith and patience inherit what has been promised.*

(Hebrews 6:12)

It is time for us to leave this third warning passage and to return to the writer's teaching about Jesus being the Great High Priest in the order of Melchizedek. He finds the perfect transition, since he ends these warning verses by confronting the Jewish Christians in verses 11–12 over their laziness and impatience.[1] This enables him to turn the spotlight back onto Abraham, the man who met the mysterious Melchizedek in Genesis 14:18–20. Abraham was the very model of patience in the face of long delay. The writer therefore uses his example to transition us back to his important teaching about Melchizedek.

In verses 13–15, the writer reminds us that Abraham waited patiently to father a son. He quotes from Genesis 22:17, but this is merely one of many promises God gave him about Isaac over the course of several decades.[2] Abraham was a married man in his sixties or seventies when the Lord appeared to him for the first time in his home city of Ur of the Chaldees. He loved his wife, but he could read the signs. She was barren, and he was

---

[1] The Greek word *nōthros*, or *lazy*, is used in both 5:11 and 6:12. It therefore bookends both the beginning and the end of this third warning passage.

[2] This promise actually came after the Lord saved Isaac's life on Mount Moriah. Even after Isaac was finally born, Abraham still needed to persevere with patient faith in order to receive what was promised.

going to die childless. Nevertheless, he believed the Lord when he promised that he would make him the father of a whole new nation. He set out from Ur and headed for the land which the Lord would give to his children as their inheritance.[3]

Abraham settled in Haran, halfway along the road to Canaan, but he did not become a father. Nevertheless, he set out again and arrived in the Promised Land as a childless man of seventy-five. When the Lord appeared to him a second time and promised to give the land of Canaan to his descendants, he did not argue. He believed. It is easy to focus on the way that Abraham occasionally wobbled in his faith, but this was a man with the faith and patience of a saint. Who else would fear that a king eager for an heir might steal away his 65-year-old wife in order to add her to his harem?! When the Lord appeared to him a third time and promised to make his descendants as numerous as the dust of the earth, he did not sneer at the idea. He kept on believing in God.[4]

Time passed by. The Lord appeared a fourth time to Abraham with another promise: his descendants would be as many as the stars in the night sky. Abraham believed him but, frustrated by the delay, he took matters into his own hands and made his wife's slave-girl pregnant instead. This led to the greatest faith test of all. His attempt to receive God's promises through dead works provoked God's silence for the next thirteen years.[5]

Finally, when he was aged ninety-nine and his wife eighty-nine, the Lord appeared to him and promised that his wife would bear him a son within a year. But there was a catch this time. He needed to change his name from Abram,

---

[3] This initial call is described in Genesis 11:31–12:3 and 24:7, as well as in Acts 7:2–3.

[4] These second and third encounters with God took place in Genesis 12:4–9 and 13:14–17.

[5] Genesis 15–16. The time lag between Genesis 16:16 and 17:1 hints at a very difficult period of silence.

meaning *Exalted Father*, to Abraham, which meant *The Father of Many*. You can just imagine the reaction of his friends when they received a card from Abraham, assuming that it was an invitation to his hundredth birthday party. Instead, they found an announcement from a childless nonagenarian that from now on he wanted them to address him as *The Father of Many*. It was humiliating, but then patient faith often is. It is costly but it never goes unrewarded. Sure enough, when Abraham was a hundred and Sarah was ninety, their baby son Isaac was born. The writer of Hebrews encourages us to be patient, therefore, when God's promises seem slow in coming to pass: *"We do not want you to become lazy, but to imitate those who through faith and patience inherit what was promised... After waiting patiently, Abraham received what was promised."*[6]

In verses 16–18, the writer explains how Abraham was able to keep believing throughout the years of disappointment and delay.[7] He believed that the Lord would never lie to him, and God also gave him a second reason to believe by swearing solemnly that his purposes for Abraham's family were already set in stone.[8] Abraham kept his eyes fixed on God's unchangeable character and unchanging purposes. It was not easy, but these two factors were an anchor for his soul. They are still an anchor for you and me today.

In verses 18–20, the writer urges us to imitate the patient faith of Abraham. We have a greater insight into God's unchangeable character, because our focus is not on Isaac but

---

[6] Laziness either makes us give up on God's promises or else dumb them down in order to make our disappointments easier. Abraham is a great example of faith because he refused to do either.

[7] The Greek verb *mesiteuō* in 6:17 means that God *mediated* or *posted bail on behalf* of his oath. Our need for a *mesitēs*, or *mediator*, becomes a major theme from now on in the letter. See 8:6, 9:15 and 12:24.

[8] The Lord set his Will before the creation of the universe (Ephesians 1:9–11) and conforms the whole of history to that Will (Acts 4:27–28). Even when people reject his Will and persecute us (Luke 7:30), we can still trust in God. Nothing can stop his perfect Will from being fulfilled.

on Jesus.[9] We have a greater insight into God's unchanging purposes because we can see what God has done for Abraham's family, all the way down to the birth of Jesus. These two things are still an anchor for our souls whenever they are buffeted by the storms of disappointment and delay. We know that Jesus is our Great High Priest. We know that he has gone on ahead of us[10] into the sanctuary of heaven[11] in order to help us place our faith in the God who is seated on his throne on the other side of the curtain.[12]

The writer has returned to the theme of Melchizedek. He is bursting to explain why Jesus is a better high priest than any of the pretenders in the Temple in Jerusalem. Before he does so, he therefore rounds off the equation we noted earlier: *Action minus God's Word equals destruction* (Hosea 4:6). *God's Word minus faith equals destruction* (Hebrews 4:2). *God's Word plus faith minus action equals destruction* (James 2:14–26). But *God's Word plus faith plus patient action equals certain victory.*

So let's not become lazy like the Jewish Christians who received this letter. Let's not give in to the temptation to compromise our faith for the sake of an easier life. Let's behave like children of Abraham. Let's believe that God's character and God's purposes are unchanging. All we need is the faith and patience to stick to his plan and we will surely inherit everything he has promised us.

---

[9] Although it is not the writer's main point, this passage emphasizes that Jesus is greater than the patriarchs.

[10] The writer calls Jesus our *prodromos* – the *forerunner* or *army scout* who has gone on ahead of us in order to facilitate our advance. The fact that he has already entered heaven on our behalf guarantees our entry with him.

[11] The writer does not feel he has to explain to his readers about the curtain that separated the Most Holy Place from the rest of the Jewish Temple. It will form one of his major themes in chapters 8–10.

[12] The writer is so excited that he completely mixes up his metaphors. An army scout has taken an anchor behind the curtain in the Temple for us. Got that? I'm glad we've cleared that up.

# The Priest Who was King
# (7:1–28)

*This Melchizedek was king of Salem and priest of*
*God Most High.*

(Hebrews 7:1)

Melchizedek is the mystery man of the Old Testament. If David had not sung about him in Psalm 110 and if the writer of Hebrews had not solved the mystery in his letter, we would probably have forgotten all about him. We would have consigned Abraham's brief encounter in Genesis 14:18–20 to the same place in our minds that so many other strange Old Testament verses go. But the writer of Hebrews tells us that those verses are vital. They are an ancient prophecy about the new type of high priesthood God has established through Jesus the Messiah.

In verses 1–3, the writer shows us why Melchizedek was a prophetic picture of Jesus. In Hebrew his name meant the *King of Righteousness* and, since the ancient name for Jerusalem was Salem, he was also the *King of Peace*.[1] He served as both king and priest for the city, something which was never the case for the Hebrew kings who succeeded him in Jerusalem. The throne belonged to David's tribe of Judah but the priesthood belonged to Aaron's tribe of Levi. Melchizedek preceded this Hebrew separation of powers, so he served as a prophetic picture of the Messiah who would be both King of kings and Priest of priests. In addition to all this, Genesis says nothing of his birth or death, hinting that the Messiah would inaugurate an eternal

---

[1] Soon afterwards, the city was renamed Jerusalem, which means the *Foundation of Peace*.

priesthood, which would never end. The writer explains that Melchizedek had far more than a cameo role in Genesis. He was one of the earliest prophetic pictures of the Messiah who was to come.

King David understood this. It was one of the reasons he was so determined to capture Jerusalem at the beginning of his reign. It was why he brought back the Ark of the Covenant, not to Moses' Tabernacle on Mount Gibeon, but to the new Tabernacle which he built for it at the heart of Melchizedek's ancient city. It was also why he did something outrageous when he dedicated this new Tabernacle on Mount Zion. He offered the blood sacrifices personally, forbidding any further blood sacrifices to be offered there in order to prefigure the Messiah's self-sacrifice once and for all.[2] This act was so outrageous that he needed to write Psalm 110 to explain it to his subjects. The writer of Hebrews quoted from the psalm back in chapter 5 and now he returns to the psalm again.

In verses 4–10, he points out that when Abraham received a blessing from Melchizedek he gave him a tenth of all his plunder. The Israelites tithed their income to Aaron and his successors, but this time the tithe worked the other way around. Since Aaron was descended from Abraham's great-grandson Levi, he effectively submitted during this encounter to Melchizedek through his ancestor. Abraham's tithe prophesied that Jesus would become a far greater high priest than anybody in the high priesthood of Aaron.[3]

In verses 11–22, the writer explains that God has therefore

---

[2] It was expressly forbidden for the king to do this (Leviticus 17:8–9; Numbers 18:7; 2 Chronicles 26:16–21), yet David wore the ephod of a high priest and offered all of the blood sacrifices at his new Tabernacle (1 Chronicles 15:27; 16:2). He was conscious that he was prophesying a new covenant through the Messiah.

[3] We may struggle with first-century logic when the writer claims in 7:9–10 that Levi paid a tithe to Melchizedek because he *was still in the body of his ancestor*", but Paul uses similar logic in Romans 5:12–21. The logic may appear unusual but it is sound. My father was at war with Germany on the day

appointed Jesus to be a new type of high priest in the order of Melchizedek.[4] He was born into the royal tribe of Judah, not the priestly tribe of Levi, because he does not owe his appointment to descent from Aaron. He owes it to the fact that he has died and been raised to life forever, fulfilling David's prophecy in Psalm 110:4 that a new high priest would hold the post forever. Jesus was not appointed through political scheming, like the high priest who held the post at the Temple when this letter was written, but through the Lord speaking an even greater oath than the one he spoke when he appointed Aaron at Mount Sinai. This oath links back to what we read about Abraham at the end of chapter 6. God swore this oath so that we might know with absolute certainty that this new high priesthood has been established through God's unchangeable character and as a result of his unchanging purposes.[5]

In verses 11–12 and 22–28, the writer therefore argues that the high priesthood of Jesus is infinitely greater than that of Aaron. It must be greater, or else God would not have declared that the old order of Aaron was now superseded (verses 11–12).[6] It must be greater, because David's Tabernacle on Mount Zion was structured in a way which predicted that a new and better covenant was coming (verse 22).[7] Unlike the Tabernacle of Moses, it had no inner sanctuary in which the Ark was hidden away from the people's gaze, because it foreshadowed a day

---

that he was born, not because of his own actions, but simply because he was born British in 1941.

[4] The Greek word *allos* means *another of the same type* and the Greek word *heteros* means *another of a different type*. The writer therefore uses the word *heteros* in 7:11, 13 and 15 in order to emphasize the difference.

[5] The Greek word for *permanent* in 7:24 is not the same word that is used for *unchangeable* in 6:17–18. Nevertheless, the parallel is deliberate.

[6] The writer is talking specifically here about the laws regarding Aaron's priesthood, but he is also hinting that in his next section he will reveal that the Law of Moses has also been superseded by the Law of Christ.

[7] Jesus is the *enguos*, or *guarantor*, of this new covenant. He has literally staked his life on its promises.

when every worshipper would experience God's presence. It must be greater, because there were over eighty high priests between Aaron and 68 AD. They kept on dying and needing to be replaced, but Jesus is the Great High Priest whose tenure will go on forever (verses 23–25).

The high priesthood of Jesus must also be greater than that of Aaron because he has no need to offer sacrifices for his own sins. He is fully human, but he is also fully sinless (verses 26–28). It must also be greater because the high priests in Jerusalem offered an endless queue of animals every day, whereas Jesus offered his own life as a once-for-all sacrifice which is still effective to this day (verse 27).[8]

We are almost at the end of the second section of this commentary. Whereas James showed that Jesus has brought us a better way of living, Hebrews 1–7 showed that Jesus has given us a better glimpse of God. He is greater than the angels, greater than the patriarchs, greater than Moses, greater than Joshua and greater than the high priesthood of Aaron. Of course, the more we understand the Old Testament the more we appreciate the depth of what this means for us but, however little Old Testament background you understand, this chapter should make you want to stop and worship.

How could the Jewish Christians return to the synagogues in order to avoid persecution? How could they attach themselves to outdated traditions and to an obsolete high priest who was waging a futile war with Rome? How could they fail to see the glory of the Gospel? In Jesus, something far better has come.[9]

---

[8] These Greek words *hapax* and *ephapax*, both meaning *once and for all*, become a major theme in the chapters which follow. See 9:12, 9:26–28, 10:2 and 10:10.

[9] The writer says in 7:18 that certain aspects of the Law are *weak* and *useless*. This was so offensive to first-century Jews that they stoned Stephen to death for saying something far less controversial in Acts 6–7.

# What is Jesus Doing Now? (7:25)

*He is able to save completely those who come to God through him, because he always lives to intercede for them.*

(Hebrews 7:25)

Jesus has been sitting down for almost 2,000 years. Apart from how uncomfortable that sounds, it raises a question. What exactly is Jesus doing right now in heaven? The writer of Hebrews does not treat this as a trivial question. Before he draws this first part of his letter to a close, he gives us a proper answer.

Jesus is reigning over the universe as King. That is one of the major themes of Psalm 110. When Jesus ascended to heaven after his resurrection, the Father greeted him with a coronation promise: *"Sit at my right hand... The Lord will extend your mighty sceptre from Zion, saying, "Rule in the midst of your enemies!"*[1] By quoting from this psalm, the writer therefore echoes the teaching of the rest of the New Testament.[2] Jesus is not simply sitting in a chair. He is sitting on a throne as the invincible ruler of the entire universe.

Jesus is waiting for permission from the Father to return to earth in order to enforce the fullness of his Kingdom rule. There is an urgency to Psalm 110: *"Sit at my right hand until I make your*

---

[1] This is why the quotations from Psalm 110 in Hebrews 1 and 5 are both accompanied by a quotation from the great coronation proclamation which God the Father makes over Jesus the Son in Psalm 2.

[2] Luke 22:69; 1 Corinthians 15:24–25; Ephesians 1:20–22; Hebrews 1:3–4; 1 Peter 3:22.

enemies a footstool for your feet." By quoting from this psalm, the writer therefore reassures us that the pain and suffering of this world will not go on forever. We are speeding towards the moment when God's purposes will be revealed and we will worship him throughout eternity for what he has achieved through history. Acts 3:21 reveals a little of Jesus' eagerness for that Final Day to arrive when it tells us, *"Heaven must receive him until the time comes for God to restore everything, as he promised."*

Jesus is interceding with the Father on your behalf and mine. That's what the writer of Hebrews explains here in verse 25: *"He is able to save completely those who come to God through him, because he always lives to intercede for them."* The Greek word *entungchanō* is the same word which is used to describe Jesus interceding for us at the right hand of the Father in Romans 8:34. It means to go and plead with somebody on behalf of someone else. Jesus is acting as our Great High Priest right now in heaven by doing three things on our behalf. Together, they enable us to experience the fullness of our salvation.

First, verse 25 means that Jesus is praying for you and me right now. There is a beautiful picture in 1 Kings 2:19–20 of King Solomon calling for a throne to be placed at his right hand so that his mother can sit down and make her requests of him. That's what God the Father did for Jesus when he arrived back in heaven. He gave Jesus permission to lodge requests with him on our behalf, presumably the same kind of things he prays in what is known as his "High-Priestly Prayer" in John 17. Intercession means influencing someone's attitude towards another and, although both Romans 11:2 and Acts 25:24 use this Greek word to describe somebody making accusations of guilt, Jesus is constantly interceding positively with the Father for us – both through what he is and what he says. He is constantly reminding him that all our guilt was laid on his shoulders at Calvary so that we are now completely cleansed of our sin.

Second and for this reason, verse 25 means that Jesus is ensuring that our prayers to the Father always get through. Just before his High-Priestly Prayer in John 17, Jesus promises seven times in John 14–16 that our prayers to the Father will always be answered.[3] They will be treated as if he prayed them himself. The English Puritan, Thomas Brooks, comments that

> *God's hearing of our prayers doth not depend upon sanctification, but upon Christ's intercession; not upon what we are in ourselves, but upon what we are in the Lord Jesus; both our persons and our prayers are acceptable in the beloved. When God hears our prayers, it is neither for our own sakes nor yet for our prayers' sake, but it is for his own sake, and his Son's sake, and his glory's sake, and his promise's sake.*[4]

Think of what that means. You have access to the whole of heaven's power right now through Jesus' intercession on your behalf. How could you ever turn your back on your relationship with God?[5] How could you ever forget to ask to be filled with the Holy Spirit every day?[6] Jesus is not just enthroned at the right hand of the Father for his own sake. We are told in Ephesians 1:22 that *"God placed all things under his feet and appointed him to be head over everything **for the church**."* All of heaven's power is therefore at your disposal right now as you seek to follow Jesus. Isn't it about time that you used it?

---

[3] John 14:13, 14; 15:7, 16; 16:23, 24, 26. This is partly what the writer means when he tells us in 7:22 that Jesus is the guarantor of everything which is ours through his better covenant.

[4] Thomas Brooks in *The Privy Key of Heaven* (1665).

[5] The writer clarifies strongly in 7:25 that he is not truly suggesting in his warning passages that a genuine believer can ever lose their salvation. See also John 10:28–29; Romans 8:33–39; Philippians 1:6; Jude 24.

[6] Acts 2:33–36 says that Jesus' authority to fill his followers with the Holy Spirit is closely linked to the coronation promises of Psalm 110, which he received after his ascension.

Third and linked to this, verse 25 means that Jesus bridges the gap between us and the Father so that we can partner together in mission. He is our forerunner who has gone on ahead of us into heaven. We are his emissaries who have gone into all the world to connect heaven's power with earth's need. Mark 16:19–20 reminds us that *"He was taken up into heaven and he sat at the right hand of God. Then the disciples went out and preached everywhere, and the Lord worked with them."* Jesus is so committed to this partnership – the Son interceding with the Father to send the Spirit to fill his Church – that there is only one place in the entire New Testament where he is described as standing instead of sitting after he ascended to heaven. As Stephen witnesses faithfully to the Gospel in the face of death, he sows the seeds of salvation in the heart of a young man named Saul who will go on to lead the apostolic expansion of the Church to the pagan nations of the world. Jesus is so excited about what is happening that Stephen exclaims in Acts 7:56: *"Look! I see heaven open and the Son of Man standing at the right hand of God."*

What a way to end the first section of Hebrews. Jesus didn't just die to forgive us 2,000 years ago. He also lives to intercede for us today. He enables us to partner with the Father for the sake of the world, which is why Psalm 110 promises him that *"Your troops will be willing on your day of battle. Arrayed in holy splendour, your young men will come to you like dew from the morning's womb."*

The only question left is, *will we?* Will we come to Jesus right now and make full use of his intercession for us? Will we experience the fullness of our salvation by taking bold steps of faith through the one who died for us and now always lives to intercede for us?

# Part Three

# A Better Way to Know God

(Hebrews 8–10)

# All Change (8:1–13)

*By calling this covenant "new", he has made the first one obsolete; and what is obsolete and outdated will soon disappear.*

(Hebrews 8:13)

People don't find major change easy. The Jewish Christians who received this letter were no exception. Even though the first part of this letter describes Jesus in such breath-taking terms that it frequently makes you want to put down the letter and worship, the Jewish Christians were filled with conflicting emotions when they read it. They were so attached to their Jewish culture that they struggled when the writer told them that parts of the Law were *"weak and useless"*.[1] Their excitement about the New Covenant was tempered by their continued affection towards the old one.

The English town where I grew up used to be famous for its paper mills. The millworkers were nervous when they heard of the invention of papermaking machines at the start of the nineteenth century and they were appalled when their employers decided to invest in the new technology. Fearing for their jobs, a mob of 200 millworkers gathered in November 1830, broke into the mills and destroyed the machines. Their reaction was unnecessary. Employment increased when the mechanized mills made the town a major printing centre, but

---

[1] If you are not Jewish, you may miss the offensiveness of the writer's words in 7:18 and 22. Find a Jewish friend and read them together. You will quickly get an insight into just how offensive they are!

most of the 200 were not around to enjoy it. They had been transported as convicts to Australia.

That's why the writer of Hebrews devotes three full chapters in this second section of his letter to spelling out exactly what it means for Jesus to be the high priest of a far better order than that of Aaron. He knows that this detail will initially increase the offence to his Jewish readers, but he also knows that in the long run it will reassure them. These three chapters explain why the New Covenant is so much better than the defunct system being practised at the Temple in Jerusalem. The writer curbs their machine-breaking impulses by trying to excite them about the major changes needed in their thinking. He tries to make his readers as glad as he is that something far better than the Old Covenant has come.

In verses 1–6, the writer summarizes his argument so far. Jesus has ascended to the true Most Holy Place in heaven and he sits enthroned at right hand of the Father. Like Melchizedek, he both reigns as King and serves as Great High Priest. He is altogether superior to the high priest who serves at the Temple in Jerusalem.

Jesus is superior because he serves as priest in a superior sanctuary. The Lord gave Moses strict instructions about how to build the Tabernacle because it was *"a copy and shadow of what is in heaven."* That's why the Exodus account constantly reaffirms that Moses was completely faithful to the pattern which God had given him.[2] The Tabernacle would only be effective if he built it God's way but, even built faithfully, it could never rival the real Most Holy Place in heaven.[3] This therefore makes Jesus

---

[2] The quotation in 8:5 is from Exodus 25:40, but the constant refrain of Exodus and Numbers is that the Tabernacle was constructed *"just as the Lord commanded Moses."*

[3] At the dedication for this magnificent Temple, Solomon repeated several times that it was merely a shabby imitation of God's true dwelling-place in heaven (1 Kings 8:27, 30, 32, 34, 36, 39, 43, 45, 49).

a superior high priest, since he *"serves in the sanctuary, the true tabernacle set up by the Lord, not by a mere human being."*

Jesus is also superior because he has offered a superior sacrifice. Verse 3 uses a Greek aorist verb in order to emphasize that the sacrifice Jesus needed to bring was a decisive one-off offering. Verse 2 describes him as a *leitourgos*, the Greek word for a priest or Levite who acted as a *servant* in the sanctuary but who did not offer sacrifices. Unlike the high priests in Jerusalem who were permanently busy with their daily sacrifices, Jesus rests because his sacrifice has been completed. It is finished. The Father requires no further blood sacrifices from him.

Jesus is also superior because he is the mediator of a superior covenant to the one Moses received for Israel on Mount Sinai. In verses 6–13, the writer spells out for the Jewish Christians two reasons why the New Covenant is superior to the Old Covenant.

First, it has been established on far better promises (verse 6). The writer quotes from Jeremiah 31:31–34 and reveals that this prophecy has been fulfilled in Jesus.[4] His New Covenant enables us to be baptized with the Holy Spirit, and it therefore changes everything about the way in which we can worship God.[5] The Spirit makes us want to obey the Lord, fulfilling the promise that *"I will put my laws in their minds and write them on their hearts"* (verse 10). The Spirit enables us to relate more intimately to God, fulfilling the promise that *"They will all know me, from the least of them to the greatest"* (verse 11). The Spirit helps us to respond to the Gospel and to experience the deep work of forgiveness which Jesus has achieved for us. As a result,

---

[4] As with all of the covenants in the Old Testament, 8:8 emphasizes that the New Covenant is made as a unilateral gift by one party. God alone makes the covenant, not any of the people he redeems.

[5] In 8:9–10, the Lord prophesies that the New Covenant will be different from the old one, but then he summarizes it in the same way as he did the old one in Leviticus 26:12! The big, big difference between the two covenants is that under the New Covenant the Holy Spirit helps us from the inside out. No wonder this is included in the summary of basic Christianity in 6:1–2. To ignore this aspect of the Gospel is absolute folly.

the God who pledged never to forget a single human action in 6:10 is able to declare over us, *"I will forgive their wickedness and will remember their sins no more"* (verse 12).[6] In all this, the writer emphasizes that Christianity is not a slightly better version of first-century Judaism. They are as different as a Ferrari from a horse-drawn chariot with a broken wheel.

Second, the Old Covenant did not work. *"If there had been nothing wrong with that first covenant, no place would have been sought for another"* (verse 7). The problem was not with the Law itself, but with the Israelites, who kept rejecting its promises and going after idols.[7] External rules could not change them. They needed to be filled with the Holy Spirit and changed from the inside out by his divine power. The outpouring of the Holy Spirit now renders the Law of Sinai so defunct that the writer prophesies the Temple is about to be destroyed: *"What is obsolete and outdated will soon disappear"* (verse 13).[8]

This was good news for the first-century Jewish Christians. They knew that James had been right to point out to the Council of Jerusalem that the Law of Moses had failed to convert large numbers of Jews, let alone large numbers of pagans. They knew deep down that they needed to change their way of thinking. They could not act like technophobic workers at a paper mill, rejecting this New Covenant and returning to the defunct religious system still being preached in the synagogues. However hard it was to change and however hard the persecution might rage, they had found a far better way of knowing God. They could not turn back from the New Covenant for which the world had long been waiting.

---

[6] This is not the forgetfulness of an absentminded God, but a deliberate decision not to bring our sins to mind.

[7] David delighted in the Law in Psalm 19 because it revealed to him his sinfulness, God's merciful character and the fact that a Saviour was coming. The fault was with the people and not with the Law itself (8:8).

[8] The Greek words *palaioumenos* and *gēraskos* can be literally translated *worn out* and *elderly*. The second of the two words is the root of our English word *geriatric*.

# No More Camping (9:1–12)

*But when Christ came as high priest... he went through the greater and more perfect tabernacle that is not made with human hands.*

(Hebrews 9:11)

Next week I am going camping. It's not something I enjoy. I am speaking at a Bible week of several thousand people so it is worth it, but I know that I will be very glad to get back to my bed in my dry house and to say goodbye to canvas for another year. That's why I'm encouraged by what the writer of Hebrews says next. He says that the New Covenant means that dwelling in tents is now a thing of the past.

As part of the covenant he made with Israel at Mount Sinai, the Lord commanded Moses to build a special tent called the Tabernacle to be his sanctuary. They were to place the Ark of the Covenant inside the inner room of this large tent in the middle of their camp so that the Lord's presence could dwell in seclusion above the Ark. God went camping with Israel, but the writer explains that the big tent prophesied that something far better would one day come.

It may seem strange to you that chapter 9 contrasts the New Covenant with the Tabernacle instead of with the Temple, which was built later as an upgraded sanctuary for the Lord. Since the Roman and Jewish armies were fighting for control of the Temple when this letter was written, the Tabernacle was a far safer illustration, but it was also more than this. The writer wants to contrast the Christian way of worshipping with Judaism at its very best – the faith as it was practised by Moses and Aaron and not as it was corrupted by later generations.[1] He wants to emphasize that the New Covenant is not simply a restoration of what Moses received and Israel managed to lose. It is better than anything that Moses ever tasted.

In verses 1–5, the writer reminds the Jewish Christians how God told Moses to lay out the Tabernacle. The first room in the tent was called the Holy Place and it was accessed by pulling back a thick curtain. It contained the golden lampstand and the golden table on which were placed twelve loaves of bread to represent the twelve tribes of Israel. A second thick curtain barred the way to the inner room of the tent, which was known as the Most Holy Place, and the golden altar of incense stood hard up against this curtain.[2] The Most Holy Place contained the golden Ark of the Covenant, and God's presence dwelt above its lid (known as the atonement cover) and between two golden statues of cherubim angels, which flanked it.[3] The Ark contained three sacred souvenirs from Israel's forty years in the desert: the two tablets on which God had written the Ten Commandments, a golden jar filled with some of the manna God provided for them in the desert and Aaron's staff, which had miraculously budded as a sign from God that he had chosen Aaron's family to serve as the high priests of the Old Covenant.[4]

---

[1] The Ark of the Covenant was not even in the Temple any longer. It had been lost during the sack of Jerusalem by the Babylonians in 586 BC.

[2] Exodus 25:23–40; 30:1–10. Since the altar of incense needed to be tended daily, it was in the outer rather than inner room (30:6). The writer describes it when he talks about the inner room because it stood hard up against the curtain. He assumes in 9:5 that we know Exodus well enough for this simple sketch to suffice.

[3] The literal Hebrew name for this room was the *Holy of Holies*, but this was simply the normal Hebrew way of saying the *Most Holy Place*. The same phrase is used in Exodus 30:10.

[4] Exodus 16:33–34; Numbers 17:1–10; Deuteronomy 10:1–5. 1 Kings 8:9 clarifies that the Greek word *en* in 9:4 means that some of these objects were *by* the Ark, not *in* it. The Ark was only 1.1 metres long – not big enough to contain Aaron's staff.

In verses 6–10, the writer tells the Jewish Christians that God designed the Tabernacle to prophesy clearly that a better covenant was needed. Only one priest was permitted to enter the Holy Place on any given day, so the tent communicated to the Israelites that God was far too holy for their sinful feet to trample his hallway. Only the high priest was permitted to enter the Most Holy Place, and even he was only permitted to enter once a year on the Day of Atonement, communicating even to the priests that God was far too holy for their sinful faces to come into his presence. On the one day that he was permitted to enter, the high priest needed to perform an elaborate series of blood sacrifices – not only for the sins of the people but for his own sins as well. If you have ever given up in despair while reading the long chapters describing such sacrifices in Exodus, Leviticus and Numbers, just imagine how it must have felt to have to offer them.

The writer tells the Jewish Christians that these arduous sacrifices were in fact a prophecy to Israel that a better covenant was needed. *"The Holy Spirit was showing by this that the way into the Most Holy Place had not yet been disclosed."* The Lord was telling the Israelites that *"the gifts and sacrifices being offered were not able to clear the conscience of the worshipper."* The Jewish believers were not betraying their roots by turning their backs on ceremonial washings in favour of Christian baptism or by exchanging Jewish food laws for the bread and wine of the Lord's Supper.[5] They were being far more Jewish than the priests and the synagogue rulers. They were acting in faith that the detail of the Law of Moses was merely a set of *"external regulations applying until the time of the new order"* which God had prophesied to Israel.

In verses 11–12, the writer tells the Jewish Christians that the Tabernacle was therefore only ever intended to serve

---

[5] The word for *ceremonial washings* in 9:10 is the same word as the one used in 6:2. These chapters dovetail together. Just as the phrase used for *dead works* in 9:14 is the same as the one used in 6:1.

as a temporary provision. At this point it helps that he has focused on the Tabernacle rather than on the Temple, because there is something intrinsically temporary about camping in a tent.[6] The day eventually comes (never quite soon enough, in my opinion) when tent-dwelling comes to an end. The time arrives to pack up the tent and to put it away, exchanging it for something better and longer lasting. Solomon dismantled Moses' tent and put it into storage on the day that he dedicated his Temple and, in turn, God was about to use the Romans to dismantle the Temple. Forty years passed between the coming of the New Covenant in 30 AD and the destruction of the Temple in 70 AD. That's the same length of time the Israelites spent in the desert – the length of an entire generation – so it was high time for the Temple to be put away. Something far better had come.

Instead of a tent full of golden furniture which prophesied about a better day, the New Covenant offers us *"the good things that are now already here."*[7] Instead of endless sacrifices of goats and calves, we now have the once-for-all sin sacrifice at Calvary. Instead of a manmade tent built from the fading materials of this created world, we now have the perfect and unfading sanctuary in heaven.

God has finished camping. The Old Covenant is over. When the Temple in Jerusalem was destroyed two years after this letter was written, it did not spell disaster for the Jewish nation. It spelt out loud and clear that God's camping days were over. In Jesus, something far better had come.

---

[6] The Temple was less obviously temporary (Luke 21:5–7), yet it was temporary nonetheless.

[7] This is the most likely reading of 9:11. Some Greek manuscripts appear to have been modified to match 10:1 and therefore read *"the good things that are to come."*

# Men Who Stare at Goats
## (9:13–28)

*The blood of goats and bulls and the ashes of a heifer...*

(Hebrews 9:13)

The Israelites were men who stared at goats. Worshipping at the Tabernacle or Temple involved offering an endless succession of blood sacrifices. Goats, sheep, bulls, heifers, doves – there was a lot of staring and a lot of slaughtering. Some of their worship services resembled a lengthy visit to a busy abattoir.

But those days were about to come to an end with the destruction of the Temple. A better covenant (8:1–13) required a better Tabernacle (9:1–12) and a better sacrifice for sin (9:13–28). The men who stared at goats were in the last days of a superseded order.[1]

In verses 13–14, the writer therefore takes us back to his list of five essential components of basic Christianity. He referred back to 6:1–2 when he talked in verse 10 about outdated *ceremonial washings*, and now he refers back to it again when he talks in verse 14 about the sinfulness of *dead works*. In Numbers 19, the Lord taught the Jewish priests to purify worshippers whenever they became spiritually unclean through touching a dead body. They were to cleanse them from the pollution of touching a corpse by creating another one: a dead goat, a dead bull or the ashes of a dead heifer. Since these were prophetic pictures of the future death of Jesus, sprinkling

---

[1] The Jews have made no Temple sacrifices for almost 2000 years, since the destruction of the Temple in 70 AD.

their blood on worshippers cleansed them, at least on the outside. But now that Jesus has come, his is the only sacrifice we need. Staring at a dead goat or any other animal is now a total waste of time. Worse than that, it is a dead work, since it fools us that we can secure favour with God through our own actions instead of through the finished work of Jesus alone. Unlike the blood of animals, the blood of Jesus can cleanse people on the inside as well as on the outside. The New Covenant calls us to renounce dead works and to trust the living God.

In verse 15, the writer tells us that the blood of Jesus is the only reason why the Old Covenant sacrifices were ever effective. He told us in 6:10 that the Lord would have been unjust not to store up the sins of the Israelites against them in heaven's courtroom, since justice demands that people must be punished for their sins instead of blaming them on innocent animals. These sins became like the *ransom price* which a slave held up in the Roman slave market or which a general demanded from the family of a prisoner of war. Jesus paid this ransom price by becoming the true sacrifice justice demanded, so he was able to *"set them free from the sins committed under the first covenant."*[2] The blood of goats and bulls had not truly satisfied God's justice. It had simply foreshadowed the true and better sacrifice to come. It enabled people who lived before the time of Christ to put their faith in the one who would be fully human and fully God, and who would therefore be the only true mediator between humans and God. Now that Jesus has been revealed, such sacrifices are no longer needed. *"For this reason Christ is the mediator of a new covenant."*[3]

In verses 16–22, the writer explains why Jesus' sacrifice

---

[2] Jesus did not pay the ransom price to Satan. Through his death and resurrection, he condemned Satan to destruction! He paid the ransom price to satisfy God's justice. See Romans 3:26.

[3] This is the second of three important references in Hebrews to Jesus being our *mesitēs*, meaning our *mediator* or *arbitrator*. The other two are in 8:6 and 12:24.

means that the former sacrifices are superseded. In order to understand his logic, we need to know that the Greek word *diathēkē* means a person's last *will* and testament as well as a *covenant*.[4] The writer points out that nobody can claim an inheritance from a person's will until that person has actually died. Moses killed many animals to bring the Old Covenant into effect at Mount Sinai, sprinkling blood over the Israelites, their Torah, their Tabernacle, its golden furniture and all of its worship accessories.[5] Just as the death of those animals brought the Old Covenant into effect, the death of Jesus means that the New Covenant is now in full effect and that the former sacrifices are no longer valid currency in heaven.[6] Relying on the blood of goats and bulls is like trying to go shopping in London today with a handful of Victorian shillings.

In verse 23, the writer tells us something very exciting but you have to read slowly not to miss it. He tells us that Moses purified the earthly sanctuary with the blood of animals but that Jesus has purified the heavenly sanctuary with his own blood. Did you spot it? Heaven did not need to be purified because it was already pure, so the writer must be saying that Jesus has purified *God's People* and made them part of his new sanctuary, since we now live in heaven with him and he now lives in us on earth. The Tabernacle is no longer a worthy home for God's presence, but we are! Jesus has turned us into his New Covenant Temple. The Romans would destroy an outdated building in

---

[4] For this reason, the word *diathēkē* is also used in Greek to refer to the Old and New *Testaments*. When you refer to the two halves of the Bible, you are referring literally to the Old and New Covenants.

[5] The quotation in 9:20 is from Exodus 24:8. Moses used the scarlet wool and hyssop branches as sponges on sticks (see Exodus 12:22; Leviticus 14:4–6; Psalm 51:7; John 19:29).

[6] This is why Jesus talks in Luke 22:20 and 1 Corinthians 11:25 about *"the new covenant in my blood"*.

Jerusalem but they could never destroy the new Temple Jesus has established all over the earth.[7]

That's why the writer includes us in the equation in verses 24–28. Jesus has ascended to heaven for *us*. He has sat down at the Father's right hand for *us*. He has offered his own body as a one-time blood sacrifice which is still effective for *us* today.[8] Jesus did not visit the sanctuary of heaven for a day, like the high priest in Jerusalem on the annual Day of Atonement. He sat down on the throne of heaven to serve as our Great High Priest forever. When he appears a second time, it will not be to die again. It will be to bring fullness of salvation to all those who are faithfully waiting on earth for him. No longer will his sanctuaries in heaven and on earth be separated. He will fuse them together as one eternal sanctuary, as is described in Revelation 21–22.

The opening title card of the George Clooney movie *The Men Who Stare at Goats* confronts the audience with a bold statement: *"More of this is true than you would believe."*[9] Is that true for you in Hebrews 9? If you are Jewish, are you willing to believe that Jesus has brought into effect an infinitely better covenant than the one that saved your ancestors who stared at goats? If you are not Jewish, are you willing to learn enough about Old Testament religion to be stirred by these verses to worship? Are you willing to believe that Jesus has created a new and far better way for people from every nation to worship the God of Israel?

---

[7] For more on this, see 1 Corinthians 3:16–17; 2 Corinthians 6:16; Ephesians 2:21–22; 1 Peter 2:5.

[8] The Greek word *antitupon* in 9:24 means a *prototype*, an *imitation that foreshadows the reality to come*.

[9] *The Men Who Stare at Goats* (Overture Films, 2009).

# There Will Be Blood (9:22)

*Without the shedding of blood there is no*
*forgiveness.*

(Hebrews 9:22)

Some sections of Hebrews can be heavy going if you are not Jewish or if you don't know very much about first-century Judaism. But stick with it. Although this letter is tailored to a specific audience, it contains vital general truth which is highly relevant to you and me. We live in a culture which claims that what a person believes about God doesn't matter, just so long as they are sincere. Nobody really believes this (the sincerity of a violent jihadist does not stop us from throwing them into jail), but it can nevertheless stop Christians from sharing the Gospel with unbelievers. Who are we to tell people that God will not forgive them unless they put their trust in Jesus? It just sounds so arrogant.

The writer of Hebrews is a very logical thinker. He writes the best Greek in the New Testament and he has clearly thought through the implications of the Gospel with the sharp logic of the great Greek philosophers. His logic in dealing with Jewish questions also answers the big question of our multi-faith culture: Isn't it unacceptably arrogant for any one faith group to claim that theirs is the only way to God? His answer in verse 22 is very simple: *"Without the shedding of blood there is no forgiveness."*

When people say that all religions lead to God, it isn't necessarily a mark of their humility. Every culture in history has believed in some sort of god or gods, in some basic moral standard, and in some form of punishment which justice demands the gods impose on those who contravene it. Cultures have disagreed strongly over the detail, but they have at least agreed on these three principles. That's what modern Westerners are contradicting when they argue that it doesn't matter what a person believes, just so long as they are sincere. It is chronological snobbery at its very worst. It declares that we know better than the united view of every other generation that has gone before us. It isn't a mark of humility. It is the opinion of a breathtakingly arrogant generation.

Deep down, everybody knows this. Atheists invoke God's name when they are angry. Secularists rage against the guilt of greedy bankers and express their hope that dying dictators will receive their comeuppance in the afterlife. Most of us are simply too busy or too distracted to think through the logic of our religious views as thoroughly as the writer of Hebrews. That's why we need this letter as much as any first-century Jew. It helps us to test the pithy sound bites of our culture and to arrive at some logical conclusions about God and sin and judgment.

The writer showed us in 6:10 that justice demands that God punish every sin. If God could be persuaded to turn a blind eye to wrongdoing, he would be unjust and therefore himself a sinner. The writer also showed us in 6:1 that not all sincere acts of worship are pleasing to God. If I cannot change the colour of my bedroom wall through sincere faith that yellow is red, nor can I transform dead works into living ones through the sheer force of my sincerity.[1] If God is God, he gets to choose what kind of sacrifice he wants to receive from us.

When the writer tells us that *"without the shedding of blood there is no forgiveness,"* he isn't therefore being arrogant. He is simply reflecting on how God has related to humans throughout human history. Take the life of Adam, as just one example. He

---

[1] This is why the word *blood* is used over five times as often in the New Testament as the word *sincerity*.

lived a life of perfect obedience until the day he committed his first sin. The Lord banished him from paradise for that single sin (proving what the writer taught us in 6:10), but that's not all that happened. Adam knew he needed to find a way to cover up his guilt before God so he attempted to conceal his naked guilt by making himself clothing out of fig leaves. His experiment with dead works was a total failure. Confronted with God's holy presence, Adam hid behind some bushes, confessed his nakedness and looked to God for a proper solution. The Lord killed an animal – the first time that blood was ever shed in paradise – so that Adam's guilt might be covered through the skin of an innocent sacrifice.[2] The writer of Hebrews draws a logical conclusion from Adam's experience: *"Without the shedding of blood there is no forgiveness."*

This is alarming. It means that most Westerners are dangerously complacent. Their unawareness of their sin and their sincere confidence in dead works can never satisfy God's justice. But what of the sincere followers of the world religions that do not centre on Jesus? What does the writer's logic make of their sincerity?

He answers this by tackling Judaism, the world religion that is superficially most similar to Christianity. It believes in thirty-nine of the sixty-six books of the Bible. It attempts to teach the same covenant that saved great Bible characters such as Moses and David. Surely Jewish sincerity will save them? In reply, the writer points out that the blood of goats and bulls only brought the Israelites forgiveness because it pointed forward to the death of Jesus (he explained this to us in 9:9 and 9:15). On this side of the cross, it is therefore only possible to receive forgiveness if we look back in faith to the blood sacrifice of Jesus

---

[2] God warned Adam in Genesis 2:17 that justice would demand death as the penalty for sin. There would be blood. The only question was whose blood it was going to be. See Leviticus 17:11; Romans 6:23.

in the same way that the Israelites looked forward.[3] Suddenly it becomes clear why Stephen, Peter and Paul were willing to risk their lives to preach the Gospel to sincere but Messiah-rejecting Jews. They had to warn them that their Judaism was powerless to save them unless it led them to put their faith in the cross of Jesus.

From here, we can extrapolate the writer's logic to other religions. Buddhists do not rely upon the blood of anyone. It is therefore a religion of dead works. Hindus relying on the blood of Ravana, who amputated parts of his body to appease the god Shiva, are as misguided as those who rely on the blood of goats and bulls. So is any Muslim who closes his eyes to history by denying that Jesus was ever crucified and by hoping to earn forgiveness from Allah through performing dead works such as fasting and making pilgrimages to Mecca. *"Without the shedding of blood there is no forgiveness,"* and the only blood that truly brings forgiveness is the sinless blood of Jesus.[4]

The writer's logic was no more popular in 68 AD than it is today. The Roman Empire was a multi-faith society with as many temples as taverns and as many religions as races. Nevertheless, the early Christians were willing to die for preaching this message to the cities of the ancient world. They declared with the same courage as Peter in Acts 4:10–12, when he spoke to the leaders of the Jewish religion in a city ruled by pagan Rome:

> *It is by the name of Jesus Christ of Nazareth... Salvation is found in no one else, for there is no other name under heaven given to mankind by which we must be saved.*

---

[3] In 9:26, the writer calls Jesus' death *the culmination of the ages* because at that point people stopped using prophetic pictures to look forward to his death for forgiveness and started looking back to it instead.

[4] This is equally true of quasi-Christian groups which seek forgiveness through a re-enactment of Jesus' death. The writer uses the Greek word *hapax* three times in 9:26–28 to stress that his sacrifice was *once and for all*.

# The Final Taboo (9:26–28)

*People are destined to die once, and after that to face judgment.*

(Hebrews 9:27)

There are very few taboo subjects left in our culture. Writers, comedians, artists, filmmakers and singers ensure that no subject, however distasteful, is too far from our ears. But there is one thing still considered very impolite to mention in conversation: the fact that every single one of us is going to die and then face judgment. Having offended his readers by insisting that the only way that we can be forgiven for our sins is through Jesus' blood, the writer of Hebrews now goes a step further. He breaks the final taboo by spelling out what will happen to us if we choose to ignore him.

All of us are going to die. I know that's pretty obvious, but we tend to push it far from our attention. We tend to behave like Groucho Marx when he quipped that *"I intend to live forever, or die trying."* We worship at the shrine of youth, trying to dress and look and act and feel younger than we really are. When we come face to face with death, we laugh it off or try to comfort ourselves with platitudes about harps and clouds or about reincarnation. The writer of Hebrews confronts this head on in verse 27, assuring us that *"People are destined to die once."* It may be an unpleasant thought, but the writer believes that we cannot fully appreciate Jesus' death until we fully appreciate our own.

He does not emphasize that we will only die once in order to silence the preachers of reincarnation. Such an idea was popular in India and among the druids of Gaul and Britannia but it was never embraced by either the Jews or the pagan Romans.[1] The writer emphasizes that we only die once because he knows that most of us spend more time planning where we will spend our two weeks' summer holiday than planning where we will spend eternity. The writer wants to emphasize that this is the biggest question each of us needs to answer in our lifetime and that we only have one lifetime during which to do so.[2]

The writer does not stop there. He breaks the final taboo still further by telling us that we are not merely destined to die. We are destined to die *"and after that to face judgment."*[3] We may fool ourselves in this life that there is no God, that there is no such thing as sin or that we can appease God's justice, but those who fool themselves will be revealed as fools on Judgment Day. Like Adam dressed in fig leaves in the Garden of Eden, our confidence will evaporate in a moment when we experience the presence of God's holy majesty. When a concerned friend broke the final taboo by asking Winston Churchill on the eve of his seventy-fifth birthday whether he was ready to stand before God, he fired back: *"I am prepared to meet my Maker. Whether my Maker is prepared for the great ordeal of meeting me is another matter."* Laughing at Judgment Day may bring us comfort in life, but it will afford us no protection when that day suddenly arrives.

Eternal punishment for those who fail to receive forgiveness through Jesus is a recurring theme in Hebrews. The writer warned us in 4:13 that *"Nothing in all creation is hidden from God's sight. Everything is uncovered and laid bare before the*

---

[1] Plato suggests the possibility in his *Phaedo*, but the idea never gained much traction in Greece or Rome. Julius Caesar highlights it as a very odd view among the druids in his *Gallic War* (6.14).

[2] He also emphasizes that we die once as a parallel to Jesus only appearing and dying once in 9:26 and 28.

[3] Note the immediacy here. The Bible says nothing about Purgatory or any other opportunity to repent after death.

*eyes of him to whom we must give account."* He pleads with us in 10:26–31 to take seriously the *"fearful expectation of judgment and of raging fire that will consume the enemies of God... It is a dreadful thing to fall into the hands of the living God."* We live in a generation where the reality of hell is frequently denied, even among Christians, and where those who believe in hell often claim that it is temporary or that the biblical descriptions of its torment are exaggerated metaphors. The writer of Hebrews has no time for this. He affirms the teaching of the rest of the Bible that hell is real, that hell is hot and that hell is forever.[4] The same Devil who hoodwinked the majority of first-century Jews into missing their Messiah also wants to hoodwink us into missing the plain warnings of Scripture.

But the writer is not just a fire-and-brimstone preacher. He derives no pleasure from breaking the final taboo by threatening us with the reality of hell. The main focus of these final verses is not the horror of judgment and of hell, but the glory of Jesus and of heaven. The writer celebrates the fact that Jesus' death on the cross has marked *"the culmination of the ages"* – the focal point of God's plan of salvation, to which everyone in BC history needed to look forward and to which everyone in AD history needs to look back. He wants us to believe that Jesus stood in the place of judgment for us when he was sentenced to death by crucifixion, enduring the just punishment for our sin when he offered himself as a willing sacrifice. Judgment Day will actually be a day of great joy for all those who are awaiting Jesus' return as the consummation of their salvation.

A few years ago, I spent a day skiing in a remote valley in Switzerland. While I was on the mountain, there was a major avalanche, which blocked the road back to my chalet and my friends. Up until that moment, I had not appreciated the little road which was now buried under many tons of snow, but after

---

[4] For example, in Psalm 9:17; Matthew 5:29–30; 10:28; 13:49–50; 25:41–46; Mark 9:42–48; Jude 7; Revelation 14:10–11; 20:11–15; 21:8.

two days stuck on the mountain I began to fear that I might never make it home. Suddenly a rescue helicopter appeared and I have never seen a more beautiful vehicle in all my life. It's amazing how much more we appreciate the way back home when we have been confronted with the stark alternative.

That's why the writer of Hebrews is willing to break the final taboo. He knows that we will never fully appreciate the way that Jesus has cleared for us through his death and resurrection unless we realize that, without him, there lies only death and judgment and the agonies of hell. Denying or ignoring these unpalatable truths will not make us love God more. It will rob us of an opportunity to grow in our love for Jesus.

If you are not yet a Christian, well done for making it so far into this commentary. You are clearly interested in Jesus. Don't end this chapter without running to Jesus and telling him that you believe he died for you and that you surrender your life completely to him.

If you are already a believer, don't resist the writer's teaching about death and judgment. Look long and hard into the pit of hell. Feel the flames on your face and then look up. Praise Jesus with a new sense of gratitude for all that he has done:

> *Just as people are destined to die once, and after that to face judgment, so Christ was sacrificed once to take away the sins of many.*

# Blood Donor (10:1–18)

*Sacrifice and offering you did not desire, but a body you prepared for me.*

(Hebrews 10:5)

The writer has shown us that Jesus' sacrifice is the only way that anyone can find forgiveness for their sins. He has also shown us the terrible alternative awaiting anyone who refuses to accept this and prefers to brave God's judgment on their own. He can therefore now complete the contrast between the work of Jesus and the Law of Moses. It brings a better covenant (8:1–13), a better Tabernacle (9:1–12) and a better sacrifice (9:13–28 and 10:1–18). It brings a far better way of knowing God.

In verses 1–4, the writer summarizes what he has told us so far. The whole Law of Moses was a prophecy. It foreshadowed a better covenant, which would only come into effect through the arrival of the Messiah. The blood of animal sacrifices had no intrinsic power to forgive anyone. Shifting the blame for our sins onto dumb animals could never truly satisfy God's justice. If it could, the worshippers would not have needed to keep coming back with a never-ending stream of animals to appease their guilty consciences.[1] The overworked priests were meant to serve as a perpetual reminder that, for all their efforts, a better sacrifice was needed.[2] The Law of Moses was not meant to be a

---

[1] The writer uses present tenses to describe these sacrifices in 10:1–4, so this letter was written before 70 AD. Since Paul does not mention Timothy's imprisonment in his letters to him, 13:23 adds that it was written after early 67 AD.

[2] The writer speaks of an *annual* reminder because the high priest was only permitted to enter the Most Holy Place on one day of the year. However, blood

substitute for Jesus. It was meant to prepare the Jews to receive their Messiah by demonstrating to them that *"It is impossible for the blood of bulls and goats to take away sins."*

In verses 5–10, the writer backs up this assertion by quoting the words of David in Psalm 40:6–8. This is more than a recap now. He introduces a fresh Old Testament quotation in order to convince us that those Israelites who delighted most in the Law always understood this. David was under no illusions. He warned worshippers that God took no real pleasure in the slaughter of farm animals at his altar.[3] He only commanded that these sacrifices be offered as a prophetic picture of the one blood sacrifice that would truly please him – the one which 9:26 tells us has now taken place *"at the culmination of the ages."*

David's psalm therefore herds the goats and bulls off the stage in order that the Messiah can step into the empty arena. Both the Hebrew and Greek Septuagint texts prophesy that the Messiah will say to the Father, *"Sacrifice and offering you did not desire, but my **ears** you have opened."* This emphasizes the Father's pleasure in his Son's perfect obedience and the fact that Jesus' sacrifice was truly pleasing to him because of his sinless life.[4] The sacrifice of a dumb animal could never satisfy God's justice, but the sacrifice of a perfectly obedient man could. Here for the first time in history was a human being who deserved no punishment and yet who volunteered to be punished in the place of others.

The writer expects his readers to know Psalm 40 well enough to grasp this and to spot a subtle change which he makes in his quotation. A few variants of the Greek Septuagint

---

sacrifices continued to be offered every single day.

[3] As usual, the writer quotes from the Greek Septuagint but he changes a word in 10:6 to bring it more into line with the original Hebrew text. Instead of not *asking for* animal sacrifices, God is not *pleased with* them.

[4] It emphasizes the same thing as 1 Samuel 15:22, where the Lord tells us that he delights far more in human obedience than he does in the blood of many animal sacrifices.

prophesied that Jesus would say, *"Sacrifice and offering you did not desire, but a **body** you prepared for me."* The writer quotes this variant reading to emphasize that Jesus became a human being in order to be able to shed human blood as the only truly acceptable sacrificial victim in history. He became the blood donor that the human race so badly needed, shedding all of his blood so that all of our guilt could be completely erased. Since the Messiah declares that the scroll of the Jewish Law prophesies about him, this is further proof that the Old Covenant was merely a signpost pointing to the real thing. It has now been superseded by the New Covenant, just as it always promised it would be.

In verses 11–14, the writer uses the golden furniture in the Tabernacle to emphasize this fact still further. The Tabernacle contained a lampstand, a table and an altar of incense, but it did not contain a chair. There was no need for one because the priests were far too busy with their constant slaughter ever to sit down. They had to stand up and keep working but, after offering his own body as a once-for-all sacrifice for sin, Jesus was able to sit down at the right hand of his Father in heaven. It was the first time that an on-duty high priest had ever been able to sit down, and it testified that his work was completed.[5] This is what Psalm 110 meant when it prophesied that the Father would tell the Great High Priest to *"Sit at my right hand until I make your enemies a footstool for your feet."* He never said anything like that to Aaron or his descendants, which is yet another proof that something far better has now come. The high priest who is able to sit must be vastly superior to a high priest who always has to stand.

In verses 15–18, the writer reminds us of the words he quoted in chapter 8 from Jeremiah 31:31–34. He attempts to tie together all of his Old Testament quotations in order to show us

---

[5] In 10:10–14, the writer uses the word *ephapax* once, meaning *once and for all*, and the phrase *eis to diēnekes* twice, meaning *continuously* or *forever*. In doing so, he echoes Jesus' victory cry in John 19:30.

that this one-off blood donation has launched the New Covenant which was promised through Jeremiah. No further sacrifice for sin is necessary now. In fact, as he quotes from the Greek Septuagint, the writer alters the word *wickedness* to *lawlessness* in order to emphasize that any Jewish priest who continues to offer the sacrifices stipulated by the Old Covenant is no longer a law-keeper, but a law-breaker.[6] The destruction of the Temple two years after this letter was written would not be a tragedy. It would simply be the natural outworking of the Gospel.

This deeper understanding of what Jesus has achieved for us through his death on the cross ought to make us want to stop and worship. It should make us want to sing and pray. It should also make us want to worship Jesus by giving him our grateful and unreserved obedience. Perhaps that's why the writer inserts a clever challenge into these verses. He uses the same Greek word in verses 10 and 14 to tell us that we *have been made holy* through Jesus' sacrifice and that we therefore ought to devote ourselves to *being made holy* every day.[7] So let's do it. Let's rise to the challenge Paul lays down in Romans 12:1 when he tells us our only logical response to such great mercy:

> *Therefore, I urge you, brothers and sisters, in view of God's mercy, to offer your bodies as a living sacrifice, holy and pleasing to God – this is your true and proper worship.*

---

[6] Changing the word *adikia* to *anomia* may seem like a small change to us, but to Jews who prided themselves on their Law-keeping it was a deliberate slap in the face.

[7] The Greek verb is *hagiazō*. The first is a perfect passive participle, the second a present passive participle. Both are God's work, but one requires our one-off co-operation and the other a lifetime of co-operation.

# Real Worship (10:19–25)

*Let us draw near to God with a sincere heart and with
the full assurance that faith brings.*

(Hebrews 10:22)

We have a better covenant, a better Tabernacle and a better
sacrifice. So it's hardly surprising that the writer ends this second
section of his letter by spelling out in practical terms what it
means for us to embrace this new and better way of knowing
God.[1] He gives us a list of eight things which must characterize
our relationship with God under this New Covenant. All of them
encourage us to model our walk with God, not on the experience
of Old Testament believers, but on the example of Jesus.

Our walk with God must be characterized by *confidence*
(verse 19). We need to jettison the self-doubt of the priests at
the Tabernacle. Are my robes clean enough? Is this lamb good
enough? Does it have a blemish or a defect or a scab which will
render my worship unacceptable to God?[2] Those regulations
were hoops which the Lord made the priests jump through in
order to teach them that a better sacrifice was needed, but now
that sacrifice has come. There is no longer any need for self-
doubt. Our eyes are not fixed on our own appearance or on our
own flawed actions. They are fixed on Jesus, the perfect sacrifice
for sin. At all times, *"We have confidence."*

Our walk with God must be characterized by *intimacy*
(verses 19–20). We must not sing Psalm 84 in the same way as

---

[1] The Greek word *oun*, or *therefore*, at the start of 10:19 shows us that the
writer sees these instructions as the practical outworking of the teaching which
went before.

[2] Exodus 28:35–43; Leviticus 10:6; 21:10, 18–21; 22:18–22; Malachi 1:8.

the sons of Korah. Our relationship with God is no longer about lingering in Temple courtyards and rejoicing whenever we catch a glimpse of him. It is about dwelling in Jesus at the right hand of God the Father in heaven and allowing the Spirit to dwell in us on earth. It's about non-stop access to God's presence. *"We have confidence to enter the Most Holy Place by the blood of Jesus."*[3] Let's not obsess over the details of the Tabernacle and of the Jewish feasts and food laws. The writer takes one object from the Tabernacle – the curtain that barred the way into the innermost sanctuary – and tells us that this was a picture of Jesus' body, which was torn apart for us so that we can enjoy God's presence permanently.[4] Obsessing over Old Covenant detail does not help us to know God better. It simply reminds us how much we need the New.

Our walk with God must be characterized by *honesty* (verses 21–22). If the psalmists dared to tell God how they really felt, how much more should we, knowing that our Great High Priest is always interceding for us? We need to be honest with the Lord about our feelings and we need to be honest with ourselves about God's promises. Both kinds of honesty are needed. Together they result in *"the full assurance that faith brings."*

Our walk with God must be characterized by *purity* (verse 22). The priests at the Tabernacle continually washed themselves with water from the bronze laver, yet the blood of Jesus purifies us far more deeply – both inside and out. We must not use the scope and scale of our forgiveness under the New Covenant as an excuse to keep on sinning. We must embrace the purity that the Lord wants to work in our hearts through his

---

[3] The Greek word which is translated *new* in 10:20 is *prosphatos*, and it literally means *freshly slaughtered*. The writer is not simply talking about a new path to God, but also about the bloodshed which created it.

[4] This is why, when Jesus died on the cross, the curtain in the Temple was torn in two (Matthew 27:51; Mark 15:38; Luke 23:45). It was torn from top to bottom because it was God's work and not ours.

Holy Spirit. The writer starts with inward change – *"our hearts sprinkled to cleanse us from a guilty conscience"* – because all lasting change begins with our thinking. Only then does he move on to the outward change of godly talk and godly actions – *"our bodies washed with pure water."* This is what Jesus was referring to in Matthew 5:20 when he promised to make his followers far purer in their lifestyle than the very best practitioners of the Old Covenant: *"Unless your righteousness surpasses that of the Pharisees and the teachers of the law, you will certainly not enter the kingdom of heaven."*

Our walk with God must be characterized by *consistency* (verse 23). We must not behave like Old Testament Israel, constantly lurching from devoted prayers of repentance to lives of rank idolatry and rebellion. God's unchangeable character and unchanging purposes act as a double guarantee for our hope in Jesus. Knowing that God is faithful, we must not swerve about like a ploughman looking back over his shoulder. *"Let us hold unswervingly to the hope we profess."*

Our walk with God must be characterized by *active obedience* (verse 24). No one can ever be saved through their love and good deeds, but nor can anyone be saved without it resulting in love and good deeds towards God and one another. Note the way in which the writer underscores the message of James 2:14–26: *"As the body without the spirit is dead, so faith without deeds is dead."*

Our walk with God must be characterized by *worship together* (verses 24–25). There is no such thing as solo Christianity.[5] The Jewish Christians had far more reason than us to neglect meeting together. Their services were under threat, and their enemies would go from house to house seeking to

---

[5] The writer uses the same Greek word *katanoeō* in 10:24 which he used in 3:1 when urging us to *fix our eyes* on Jesus. Those who are truly devoted to Jesus will always be devoted to his Church as well.

arrest whole groups of Christians at a time.[6] Nevertheless, the writer insists that unless we follow Jesus together we will not manage to follow him at all. We need our Sunday services and midweek meetings and Christian friendships in order to *"spur one another on."*[7] Without them, our devotion to Jesus quickly fades. The writer speaks to a generation of Christians with far better reason than us to neglect Christian meetings, warning them strongly against *"giving up meeting together, as some are in the habit of doing."* If Old Testament believers needed to gather together at the Temple, how much more do we need to gather together now that we have become God's New Covenant Temple?

Our walk with God must be characterized by *expectancy* (verse 25). The writer ends these verses by lifting our eyes above the busy pressures of the present and towards the great Day when Jesus will suddenly appear. If Old Covenant believers such as Simeon and Anna talked excitedly about the coming of God's Messiah, how can we talk less excitedly about his second coming? If they watched and prayed, how can we do anything less as we await the glorious Final Day of history?

Jesus has opened up for us a better way of knowing God. Don't take your lead from the men and women of the Old Testament. Understand that you have a far better invitation. You can come with greater confidence to greater intimacy, honesty, purity, consistency, obedience, unity and expectancy than the men and women of ancient Israel ever knew.

---

[6] See Acts 8:3; 17:5. The Greek word used for a *meeting* in 10:25 is *episunagōgē* – in other words, the Christian equivalent of a synagogue. Meeting with Christian friends is no substitute for church meetings.

[7] The Greek word used in 10:24 is *paroxusmos*, which means *provocation* or *irritation*. The only other place the word is used in the New Testament is to describe Paul's argument with Barnabas in Acts 15:39. The writer is therefore telling us that we need other Christians precisely because they tell us what we do not want to hear.

# Blood Diamond (10:26–39)

*So do not throw away your confidence; it will be richly rewarded.*

(Hebrews 10:35)

In May 1671, Colonel Thomas Blood managed to steal the Crown Jewels from the Tower of London. He bought a ticket to view the jewels with a female accomplice and, while viewing them, she feigned a stomach complaint so that the Master of the Jewel House would invite her upstairs to his apartment. Once there, she and Colonel Blood ingratiated their way in with the Master's family and called back several times in the days that followed to thank them for their kindness. Finally, during dinner with the Master's family they enquired whether a private viewing of the jewels might be possible. When the Master unlocked the grille, Colonel Blood hit him over the head and stabbed him, then quickly gagged and bound him. He put the Crown Jewels in his bag and ran.

In this second section of his letter, the writer has described a treasure far more valuable than the English Crown Jewels. He has described all that the blood of Jesus has won for us, so now he warns us to protect it far more carefully than any earthly diamond. He launches into his fourth warning passage and, since we now have a greater understanding of why the New Covenant is so valuable, this is the fiercest and most strongly worded warning passage so far.[1] The writer's language should not surprise us. We have a cunning enemy who wants to rob us

---

[1] Technically, this fourth warning passage is 10:19–39. However, the stern language only begins in 10:26.

of our treasure. The writer wants us to take this threat seriously so that we can stop him.

In verses 26–27, the writer warns us that it is time for us to choose sides.[2] These three chapters have increased our knowledge of the truth of the Gospel, using compelling logic to demonstrate that there is no escape from judgment without forgiveness and no forgiveness apart from Jesus' blood. We are therefore standing on a knife-edge. *"If we deliberately keep on sinning after we have received the knowledge of the truth, no sacrifice for sins is left, but only a fearful expectation of judgment and of raging fire that will consume the enemies of God."* It is time for us to decide once and for all whether we are followers of Jesus. The writer assumes that we are, but he warns us bluntly because there are false believers in every congregation. You may go to church, you may look like a Christian and you may have nodded your way through Hebrews so far, but have you truly surrendered your life to Jesus?[3] Without the kind of faith that results in action, you are easy pickings for the Devil. Don't let him steal this blood diamond from under your nose.

In verses 28–31, the writer helps his Jewish readers by rooting his threats in Old Testament Scripture. If the Lord decreed in Deuteronomy 17:2–7 that those who rejected the Law of Moses should be put to death, how much more severely will he judge anyone who rejects this better sacrifice and covenant? If the Lord ended the Law of Moses in Deuteronomy 32:35–36 with a promise that *"It is mine to avenge; I will repay"* and *"The Lord will judge his people"*, how much more is this

---

[2] Hebrews 10:26 is not referring to occasional sinful slip-ups. The Greek present participle refers to an unchanged lifestyle, one which *keeps on sinning* and which does so deliberately.

[3] We have already seen that the writer is not actually expecting genuine Christians to throw away their faith. However, this kind of preaching is still necessary. When Jonathan Edwards preached on Deuteronomy 32:25 and Hebrews 10:30–31 at Enfield, Connecticut, on 8th July 1741, his "Sinners in the Hands of an Angry God" sermon spread revival all across the nominally Christian communities of New England.

the case now that we have received a far better revelation of God's salvation plan?[4] If these Jewish Christians return to the synagogues, then they are trampling the Son of God underfoot, they are defiling the blood of Jesus and they are insulting the Holy Spirit whom God has graciously given them. They are in a far more dangerous place than Korah or Achan or any of the other rebels who lived in the time of Moses. They need to make a choice, for *"It is a dreadful thing to fall into the hands of the living God."*

One of the ways in which the Devil tries to steal the Crown Jewels of the Gospel from under our noses is to get us debating whether or not passages like this one are saying that we can lose our salvation. The writer is clearly addressing Christians (verse 29) and yet he warns against *eternal destruction* (verse 39).[5] The Devil wants to make us more interested in discussing how this is possible than in responding to the writer's challenge. Giving a better answer to this question than any other Bible scholar is of no use to us unless we respond to the writer's threats by laying hold of the blood sacrifice of Jesus! The cross reveals God's deep mercy towards us but it also reveals his deep commitment to judge our sin. We dare not fool ourselves that playacting as Christians can ever satisfy him. Each of us needs to take time to reflect on whether we are actually on a church-attending, Bible-reading, chorus-singing route to hell.[6]

In verses 32–36, the writer addresses those who know for sure that they are Christians. He warns the Jewish believers that they are in danger of losing their heavenly rewards. After their initial conversion, they gladly bore insults and persecution

---

[4] The second quotation in 10:30 could also come from Psalm 135:14, since it repeats Deuteronomy 32:36.

[5] This is the first time in these four warning passages that the strong word *apōleia*, or *perdition*, is used. However, note that the writer is actually saying he is confident that his Christian readers will *not* be destroyed.

[6] Paul also urges us to do this in 2 Corinthians 13:5. There is no contradiction between these warning passages and the rest of the New Testament.

for the sake of Jesus.[7] They thought nothing of becoming associated with other Christians who were being persecuted or of risking their freedom by attending Christian meetings. Even when their property was confiscated because of their faith, they considered their earthly goods as nothing in comparison with the Crown Jewels of the Gospel.[8] A great reward awaits them for this in heaven. They must not cool in their faith now by seeking an easier road. If they do, they will throw their heavenly rewards away.[9]

In verses 36–39, the writer therefore encourages Christians to keep on running hard. We must not grow lazy in our faith as we get older. The boldness with which we can enter God's presence must spur us on to persevere.[10] The writer quotes twice from Habakkuk 2:3–4 in order to remind us that Jesus will shortly return with our reward.[11] This present life is only a moment compared with the age to come. We must not miss out on the reward Jesus wants to give us in the new heavens and new earth for the way in which we have faithfully stewarded the Gospel.

Colonel Blood ran into trouble in May 1671. The Master of the Jewel House had a soldier son who happened to return

---

[7] The Greek word *athlēsis* in 10:32 means a *sporting contest* and is the root of our English word *athletics*. The writer is likening the Jewish Christians to a marathon runner who begins with a sprint and then tires. The word *theatrizō* in 10:33 means *to make a public spectacle*. They gladly became theatre for the sake of Christ.

[8] Confiscating a person's property was a common Roman punishment, and the Jews may have copied it. Perhaps this provoked Paul's frequent collections for the poverty-stricken Christians in Judea.

[9] The New Testament speaks about these rewards in some detail in passages such as Matthew 5:11–12 and 5:19, Luke 16:1–13 and 19:11–27, 1 Corinthians 3:12–15, 2 Corinthians 5:10, and Hebrews 6:10–12 and 11:35.

[10] The Greek word *parrēsia*, or *boldness*, in 10:35 is the same word which was used in 10:19.

[11] He quotes from the Greek Septuagint but changes the word order so that, instead of reading *"the righteous one will live by my faith,"* it reads *"my righteous one will live by faith."*

home from war at the very moment that his father was being robbed. He challenged Colonel Blood and alerted the guards of the Tower of London. Because of his vigilance, the Crown Jewels were saved. So don't let the Devil rob you of the treasure that is described in this second section of Hebrews. Stop the Devil's jewel heist in its tracks. Don't let him snatch away your sure reward.

Part Four:

# Better Reasons to Believe

(Hebrews 11–13)

# Better Reasons to Believe (11:1–3)

*Faith is confidence in what we hope for and assurance about what we do not see.*

(Hebrews 11:1)

We have reached the third section of Hebrews and the fourth section of this commentary. It comes as no surprise that these last three chapters are full of practical challenge about how we are to live in view of all that has gone before. This is where the rubber hits the road. We need to act on what we have read. The writer therefore reassures us that we have better reasons to believe than anybody had in ancient Israel.

Like James, the writer of Hebrews defines faith for us. James emphasized that real faith is obvious because it always leads to action. The writer of Hebrews reinforces this throughout his letter, but now he also gives it an even sharper definition. He tells us that *"Faith is confidence in what we hope for and assurance about what we do not see."*[1] In other words, faith believes that the Bible is God's Word (1:1), that God still speaks to us through it today (3:7; 4:12; 10:15) and that God can never lie (6:18). Faith believes this even when all of the evidence we see appears to contradict what God is saying (6:13–15). The writer points out in verse 2 that this faith marked everyone who

---

[1] The Greek word *hupostasis*, or *confidence*, in 11:1 is the same word which was used to describe God's *unshakeable being* in 1:3 and our firm *trust* in him in 3:14. Our faith is intrinsically linked to God's faithfulness.

experienced the power of God in the Old Testament.[2] *"This is what the ancients were commended for."*[3]

But now he points out that Jesus' coming has given us even better reasons to believe. When the invisible God became visible, it changed the nature of our faith. Unlike the ancient Israelites, God has spoken directly to us in the form of a human being (1:1–2; 2:17). He continues to speak through a new army of spokespeople, confirming that they speak his words by performing miracles for all to see (2:3–4). In short, Jesus' coming has put us in a far better position to believe God's Word than any of the Old Testament believers enjoyed. It is important that we understand this, because it is easy to assume that having faith in God is more difficult in our generation. The writer reassures us that it is easier than ever.

In order to demonstrate this, he gives us a faith overview of the Old Testament in chapter 11. He starts with creation, one of the subjects about which many of us find it hardest to believe the Bible. It is important to grasp that this difficulty did not begin with the works of Charles Darwin. The prevailing view in the Roman Empire was that the world originated through chaotic struggles involving Gaia and the Titans. The first-century Christians were just as daunted by this claim as you are by anything in modern science. The writer tells us some very good news. We will never discover the origin of the universe by endless debating, but we can discover it through Jesus.

Verse 3 reminds us that *"By faith we understand that the universe was formed at God's command."* Any belief about the origins of the universe – whether religious, scientific or otherwise – is by definition a faith statement. None of us was an

---

[2] It still does today. Hebrews 6:5 tells us that a healthy Christian diet devours the goodness of the Word of God.

[3] The Greek word *presbuteros* in 11:2 is the normal Greek word for *elders* in a church or Jewish synagogue. The writer is emphasizing that his readers' refusal to submit to the synagogue rulers does not make them any less Jewish. They are simply following the lead of the true elders of the Jewish nation.

eyewitness, so our beliefs are the result of detective work rather than observation. The ancient Israelites believed in Genesis 1–2 because they saw Moses climb Mount Sinai to meet with God, but we have something far better. Jesus was actually there. He isn't a detective or even an eyewitness. He is the Creator God (1:2). Our understanding of the origin of the universe no longer needs to be based on ancient texts or scientific treatises. It can be based on the fact that we have met the Creator personally.

Enough books have been written about creation and evolution for me not to feel any need to add another one. I don't want to win you round to my particular viewpoint. I simply want to help you to understand the writer's logic in Hebrews 11. He tells us that Jesus' coming ought to give us solid faith that at least three things are true.

First, it should convince us that God existed before anything came into being. Jesus talks to the Father in John 17:5 and 24 about what it was like for them *"before the creation of the world."* In the beginning there was God and nothing else or, in the words of verse 3, *"what is seen was not made out of what was visible."*

Second, it should convince us that God created the universe through his active command. It was not a cosmic accident or a passive observation. Jesus tells us that *"At the beginning the Creator made."*[4]

Third, it should convince us that God actively created the human race. Jesus does not tell us in Matthew 19:4–6 and Mark 10:6–9 that human beings evolved by chance from lesser species. He tells us that God created a man and a woman. To reinforce this, he talks about people such as Adam and Abel and Noah as historical individuals who played a real and specific role in God's unfolding plan.[5]

This is important. It reminds us that we will never convince

---

[4] Matthew 19:4. See also Matthew 25:34; Mark 13:19.
[5] For example, in Matthew 23:35; 24:37–38; Luke 11:51; 17:26–27.

unbelievers that God created the world by getting bogged down in discussions about evolution and dinosaurs. We must not behave like the ancient Israelites, using the fading memory of Mount Sinai to convince people that the words of Genesis are true. We don't believe in Jesus because of Genesis; we believe in Genesis because of Jesus! So let's introduce people to Jesus the Creator instead of starting lengthy conversations about black holes and Charles Darwin.

This is also important because it reminds us that we have something to add, not just to subtract, from the debate about origins. Knowing that a man's nose is bleeding because his nasal blood vessels are damaged only gets me so far. It also helps to know that his nose is bleeding because he insulted another man's girlfriend. In the same way, our questions can only truly be answered when Christians and scientists work together – revealing not just the how but also the who, not just the Big Bang but also the Big Banger.

Sir Isaac Newton was thirsty for both types of answer. He wrote about his scientific experiments that *"If I have seen further it is by standing on the shoulders of giants,"*[6] and he wrote about his adventures with God that *"This most beautiful System of the Sun, Planets and Comets, could only proceed from the counsel and dominion of an intelligent and powerful being."*[7] The writer of Hebrews invites us to see Jesus as the ultimate Giant on whose shoulders we can stand in order to see far more clearly than other men and women. God has not left us fumbling around for clues about the universe we live in. He has spoken, and Jesus' coming has given us even better reasons to believe God's Word is true.

---

[6] Sir Isaac Newton in a letter to Robert Hooke on 15th February 1676.
[7] Sir Isaac Newton in Book III of his *Principia* (1687).

# Before the Flood (11:4–7)

*Without faith it is impossible to please God.*

(Hebrews 11:6)

There is an old Country song in which Kris Kristofferson claims that "Lovin' Her Was Easier Than Anything I'll Ever Do Again". Sometimes it's tempting for us to feel the same way about Church history. Many people succumb to a strange nostalgia in which they convince themselves that having faith in God was easier in the old days than it is now. That's why the writer continues his overview of Old Testament faith by turning his attention to those who trusted in God before Noah's Flood. He continues to insist that Jesus has given us far better reasons to believe.

If you stop to think about it for any length of time, it is pretty obvious that it was harder to have faith in God during the years before the Flood. Men like Abel and Enoch and Noah did not have any Scriptures. They did not have any church. They did not have a collection of worship songs to help them put their faith in God. They had nothing but what they saw of creation and a few hand-me-down stories they were told by their parents. Faith was harder for them than it is for us, but still they trusted God.

In verse 4, the writer talks about Abel. If anybody might have felt that a previous generation of believers had things easier, it was him. His parents had walked with God in the Garden of Eden, but by the time he was born they had eaten themselves out of house and home. All that Abel had was the campfire stories his father told him about God and which inevitably revolved around what happened on the day that he first sinned. Adam told his sons about the clothes he had made from fig leaves and how they had failed to cover up his guilt when the Lord came looking for him. He explained about the first death in the Garden of Eden and how God had given him free new clothes, which cost an innocent animal its blood.

Abel's big brother Cain refused to believe in this Gospel story. Genesis 4 tells us that, while Abel brought God blood sacrifices from his flock of lambs, Cain brought him some of the crops he harvested from his fields. When God told him that the fruits of his own hard labour were dead works, Cain grew angry instead of repenting. The Lord had to warn him, *"If you do what is right, will you not be accepted?"* The writer therefore uses Abel as an example of somebody who trusted in the Gospel despite having far less evidence than we have. Even after Cain murdered him for his belief in the Lord, his blood still prophesied about the coming of a sacrifice which was better than his lambs.[1]

In verse 5, the writer turns the spotlight onto Enoch. He is another mystery man of the Old Testament whose story we might have ignored were it not highlighted here. Genesis 5:24 tells us that *"Enoch walked faithfully with God; then he was no more, because God took him away."* God took him up to heaven early before he died. If a man without a Bible, without a church and without a Christian bookshop could learn to walk so faithfully with God that he was taken up to heaven like Elijah, we have no excuse not to trust in God now that Jesus has given us better reasons to believe.

In verse 6, the writer therefore takes a pause and states the lesson of this Old Testament hall of fame: *"Without faith it is impossible to please God, because anyone who comes to him must believe that he exists and that he rewards those who earnestly seek him."* This is how to respond to the message of Hebrews. First, believe that God exists. We have far better reasons to believe this than Enoch. He merely prophesied that Jesus would come,

---

[1] Abel is mentioned again in 12:24. Cain's dead works were dead instantly, but Abel's works of faith still live on. For this reason, Jesus calls him a prophet in Luke 11:51.

but we have four gospels which tell us all about what happened when he finally came.[2] Second, believe that God can be found by those who seek him. Be like Abel and Enoch, not like Cain. Third, believe that God will reward us if we steward the Gospel well. This echoes the warning of 10:32–39 and underlines that we are without excuse. Jesus talked about these heavenly rewards in quite some detail. Believing in God has never been so easy.

In verse 7, the writer describes a final man who lived before the Flood. Noah had far less reason to trust in the Lord than we do. He was the only faithful believer in his entire generation. Even if he had had a Bible, he would not have had a single believing friend with whom to study it. If he started one of Enoch's worship songs, nobody other than his wife and sons would ever want to sing along. And yet he trusted God. He became *"a preacher of righteousness"*, attempting to convert a few other people in his generation. When nobody listened, he continued to walk with God like Enoch, enjoying friendship with the Lord even if nobody else wanted to enjoy it with him.[3]

Noah believed God even when faith required him to do something far more challenging than anybody else so far in human history. The Lord told him to build a ship over twice the length of HMS *Victory*, and he did not have any modern power tools with which to obey. He was laughed at by his landlocked neighbours for several lonely decades while he built it, but the writer points out that he was moved by something far more powerful than peer pressure. He was moved by *holy fear*.[4] He believed in the imminent arrival of the Flood, even though he

---

[2] One of Enoch's ancient prophecies survived and appears in the New Testament in Jude 14–15.

[3] Genesis 6:8–9; 2 Peter 2:5. Genesis suggests that the ark may have taken up to 70 years to build.

[4] The Greek verb *eulabeomai*, translated in 11:7 as *experiencing holy fear*, means literally *grasping well*. The more we understand God's character, the more we will be gripped by a similar holy fear ourselves. See 12:28–29.

could not see it. That's what faith means: being confident in what we hope for and assured about what we do not see. As a result of his faith, he saved his family and condemned a generation for not sharing his belief in God. How much more are we to be condemned if we ignore our own better reasons to believe?

That's precisely the point which the writer of Hebrews is trying to make in this chapter. It takes faith to believe in God today. It usually results in our being laughed at by friends, persecuted by enemies, despised by scholars and ignored by the world. But it is always worth it. By faith Noah *"became heir of the righteousness that is in keeping with faith."*[5]

So let's not sing along with Kris Kristofferson. Let's not succumb to the forgetfulness which makes us think that faith in God used to be easier in the past. Abel, Enoch and Noah walked with the Lord despite having only a fraction of our evidence that the Word of God is true. They laid hold of whatever scrappy pieces of revelation they had been given. Let's be just as diligent with the revelation which we have received through Jesus. Let's make the most of our better reasons to believe.

---

[5] The writer may be hinting here that Noah trusted in his wooden ark as a prophetic picture of Jesus' cross.

# Faith Without a Home (11:8–22)

*All these people were still living by faith when they died. They did not receive the things promised; they only saw them and welcomed them from a distance.*

(Hebrews 11:13)

Ur of the Chaldees was the kind of place you moved to and not from. Immigration was high; emigration was low. It was the largest city in the world, and the many luxury items found by archaeologists in its tombs suggest that it was also the world's richest and most civilized city. If you managed to buy a good house in Ur of the Chaldees, it was a keeper. Its citizens were the envy of the world.

That's why it was such a remarkable act of faith for Abraham to obey the call of God to leave his home in Ur. His family had traditionally worshipped the Sumerian moon god Nanna, yet he accepted God's call towards a life of faith without a home.[1]

In verses 8–10, the writer points out that it was harder for Abraham to believe God's Word than it is for us. The Lord did not tell him the whereabouts of this mysterious Promised Land. He simply asked him to trust that becoming a tent-dwelling nomad and a stranger in an undisclosed foreign land was better than continuing to be a homeowner in Ur. Abraham trusted in God's

---

[1] See Joshua 24:2. Nanna was the city's patron deity.

character and in his promises because *"He was looking forward to the city with foundations, whose architect and builder is God."*[2]

In verses 11–12, we are reminded that Abraham had an even bigger problem. The Lord's promises were all about what was going to happen to his children, but he was a childless old man. Even when she was younger his wife had been infertile, and now that she was aged a postmenopausal eighty-nine he did not need a doctor to tell him that his family prospects were *"as good as dead."* Nevertheless, Abraham and Sarah both believed in God's Word and in the fact that God can never lie.[3] As a result of their faith for a miracle, they conceived Isaac in their old age and their descendants went on to become as countless as the stars in the sky and the grains of sand on the seashore. They received the reward of trusting in God despite having far fewer reasons to do so than you or me.

Let's just pause there for a moment. Christians often say they are prepared to obey God if he guides them a bit more clearly, provides for them a bit more plentifully or fulfils his promises a bit more punctually. The writer warns us that this is not actually faith at all. The Lord will almost certainly require us to step out before we clearly see the destination, the resources or the confirmation. Hudson Taylor became convinced of this as he planted churches across China in the face of many setbacks: *"I have found that there are three stages in every great work of God: first, it is impossible, then it is difficult, then it is done... The Apostolic plan was not to raise ways and means, but to go and do the work."*[4] The writer therefore warns us to expect this to

---

[2] The Lord treated Abraham's faith in the Promised Land as if it were faith in heaven itself (12:22–23; 13:14). Since God is the builder of this city, our faith is expressed by quiet trust and not by frenzied activity.

[3] Although Sarah wobbled in her faith, the Greek text of 11:11 can just as easily be translated to mean that *she* believed as that Abraham believed. They partnered in faith together.

[4] These quotations come from two biographies of Hudson Taylor: Leslie Lyall's *A Passion for the Impossible* (1965) and A.J. Broomhall's *Hudson Taylor and China's Open Century, Volume IV* (1984).

characterize our own walk of faith too. Faith means "considering him faithful who has made the promise." It means believing that God's invisible character trumps our visible circumstances. It means believing that, however impossible our situation, it is even more impossible that God should ever lie.[5]

In verses 13–16, the writer warns us that we may not even see all of our hopes realized in our lifetime. Abraham and Sarah were still living by faith when they died. They never possessed the land of Canaan because it was not yet God's perfect timing. He simply counted their faith that they would possess the Promised Land as a primitive sort of belief in heaven. The writer tells us that the Lord loves to be associated with people who possess such patient faith. Their refusal to give up and go back to Ur earned them a great heavenly reward.

In verses 17–19, the writer tells us that Abraham's biggest faith challenge actually came after Isaac was born. This is often the case. We graduate from one battle of faith in order to fight a new and tougher one, because the Lord is passionate about developing our trust in him so that he can bless us even more. When he commanded Abraham in Genesis 22 to sacrifice his long-awaited heir, there were plenty of reasons for him to say no. It appeared to contradict God's promise. It appeared to throw God's character into question. It challenged the unchangeable character and unchanging purposes which 6:17–18 tells us were the basis of his faith in God. This warns us that our own faith is likely to be challenged in these two areas as well. Abraham obeyed because he reasoned that, if a resurrection were the only way to solve his conflicting circumstances, a resurrection it would have to be.[6]

In verses 20–22, the writer tells us that Abraham's children displayed this same radical faith in God's character and his

---

[5] Hebrews 6:18; Numbers 23:19; 1 Samuel 15:29; Romans 3:4; Titus 1:2.

[6] The quotation in 11:18 comes from Genesis 21:12, only a few verses before the command to sacrifice Isaac. God saw Abraham's faith for Isaac's resurrection as primitive faith in Jesus' death and resurrection.

purposes. They had far fewer reasons to trust him than we have, relying on occasional visions of God instead of on the perfect revelation of God's Son, yet they believed in God's Word all the same. Isaac almost destroyed his family over his conviction that the land of Canaan would belong to whichever of his two sons he blessed.[7] One of Jacob's final deathbed actions was to gather his sons together and to prophesy over each of them which areas of the Promised Land would become theirs.[8] Joseph died as one of the richest and most successful noblemen of Egypt, yet he commanded that his mummified body be put in storage and taken back to Canaan when God led his descendants to inherit the Promised Land. These men still had no Scriptures and still had to rely on campfire stories to stir their faith in God, but still they believed.

This begs the question the writer wants us to ask ourselves throughout this chapter: How are we going to respond to God's Word now that we have far better reasons to believe? Will we believe in Jesus' second coming as devotedly as Jacob believed in the day when his descendants would inherit the Promised Land? Will we believe for the growth of our churches as much as childless Abraham believed for the growth of his family? Will we believe in the power of our words to bless and curse and heal in Jesus' name as much as Isaac and Jacob, and even Esau? Will we steward God's Word as well as the patriarchs now that Jesus has given us far better reasons to believe?

---

[7] Isaac was duped over which son he blessed, but that is not the point. He displayed immense faith to bless them at all with inheriting the land and to tell Esau in Genesis 27:37 that this blessing was irrevocable.

[8] Jacob blessed his own sons along with Joseph's in Genesis 47:28–49:33, but the writer focuses on Joseph's sons in order to draw our attention to 48:17–20 – a remarkable act of faith over land which was not yet his!

# None Received (11:23–40)

*These were all commended for their faith, yet none of them received what had been promised.*

(Hebrews 11:39)

The writer of Hebrews is running out of time. He has a lot more practical application to share with us in this final section of his letter, and by now he feels that we have probably understood the main point of chapter 11. He therefore rattles through the rest of Israel's Old Testament history in just eighteen verses. Let's read them more slowly than he wrote them because they continue to reinforce the fact that we have far better reasons to believe.

In verses 24–29, the writer turns the spotlight onto Moses. His was a story of faith from start to finish. His parents believed that God had chosen him for a great destiny, so they risked their lives to hide him and to put him in a basket on the River Nile, believing that God would save him from Pharaoh's slaughter of the Hebrew baby boys.[1] When he grew up, Moses believed in God instead of in the Egyptian pantheon, knowing full well that associating himself with slaves instead of courtiers would cost him his place in Pharaoh's palace. He asked himself a faith equation: Would he choose "suffering with Christ plus its heavenly reward" or would he choose "Egyptian treasures plus nothing"? He made his choice and gladly threw in his lot with the persecuted People of God.

---

[1] The Hebrew word for his *basket* in Exodus 2:3–5 is the same word used for Noah's *ark* in Genesis. The word is used nowhere else in the Bible. They believed that God would save Moses as he had saved Noah.

At first he attempted to deliver the Hebrews from slavery through his own strength. His murder of the Egyptian slave-driver was quite literally a dead work. Nevertheless, the writer tells us that he did not flee Egypt in fear.[2] He emigrated because what he had seen of the invisible God was more real to him than his very visible failure. This faith eventually brought him back forty years later to deliver the Hebrew slaves through God's strength and through belief that the blood of the Passover lamb would redeem Israel. His faith inspired the Israelites to trust God on the shores of the Red Sea, enabling them to pass through the water as if on dry land while the Egyptian army drowned.

Moses' parents did not realize that their actions were a prophetic picture of God's deliverance of Jesus as a baby from King Herod. The Israelites did not realize that the blood of the Passover lamb on their vertical and horizontal wooden doorframes was a prophetic picture of Jesus' death on the cross. Nor did they realize that crossing the Red Sea was a prophetic picture of their participation in Jesus' death and resurrection through the waters of baptism.[3] Nevertheless, the writer tells us in verse 26 that their faith was in *Christ*, despite having far less revelation of him than we do.

In verses 30–31, the writer describes the events of the book of Joshua. The Israelites had no precedent to convince them that the walls of Jericho would fall to a shout of faith instead of to siege machines, yet when they trusted in God's Word the walls fell down.[4] Rahab had even less reason to believe that they would capture Jericho. She was a pagan prostitute who had

---

[2] Exodus 2:14–15 tells us that he was afraid of Pharaoh, but this was not the primary reason why he left Egypt. Since he could not liberate the Hebrews, he preferred to go into exile than watch them suffer any longer.

[3] See Matthew 2:13–21; 1 Corinthians 5:7; 10:1–2. Linked to this, the Greek word *katapinō* describes both the Red Sea *devouring* the Egyptians in 11:29 and Jesus *devouring* death in 1 Corinthians 15:54.

[4] Hebrews 11:30 should give us great faith to see healings when we issue commands in Jesus' name. Visible physical change occurred to the walls of Jericho as a result of Israel's faith in the Word of their invisible God.

simply heard whispered rumours about Israel's God, yet she believed and was saved.[5]

In verses 32–38, the writer speeds up and covers the rest of the Old Testament in just seven verses. Judges and kings conquered and ruled by faith. Prophets spoke by faith and escaped the swords of those they prophesied against by faith. Daniel survived the lions' den by faith. Shadrach, Meshach and Abednego survived the fiery furnace by faith.[6] Elijah and Elisha raised two boys to life by faith and handed them back to their mothers. Other Jews refused to break the Law of Moses, even under torture, because they believed that God would reward them if they earnestly sought him.[7] The writer spurs us on to follow their example by assuring us that God will give such men and women of faith *"a better resurrection."* Since being raised to life in order to spend eternity with Jesus sounds like privilege enough, how precious must these heavenly rewards be to make them so worth persevering for!

Note what the writer is doing. He has spent much of this letter trying to persuade the Jewish Christians not to go back to the synagogues in order to escape persecution from the Jews and Romans. He therefore has a clear agenda here. Who would not prefer to suffer with these men and women than to collaborate with a community that acted like their persecutors? Rebellious Jewish leaders flogged and imprisoned Jeremiah, stoned Zechariah to death for prophesying and sawed the prophet Isaiah in two. The Jewish elders conspired with Jezebel to stone Naboth to death and to put God's prophets to the

---

[5] This mention of Rahab's faith echoes James 2:25. A prostitute's obedient faith trumped her profession. The Greek word *apeitheō* in 11:31 equates lack of faith with *being disobedient.*

[6] A mountain of truth is contained in 11:34 in the simple words *"gained strength out of weakness"*. Paul unpacks what this means in 2 Corinthians 12:1–10. See also Judges 7:1–9.

[7] Hebrews 11:35 links back to 11:6. The Greek word for *others* is masculine, so it refers to a male or mixed group of people. Many Jews refused to break the Law when tortured by Antiochus IV before the Maccabean Revolt.

sword.[8] Instead of siding with the enemy, the Jewish Christians must join the host of unnamed Jews who were impoverished, ill-treated, persecuted and made homeless because of their faith in the Lord.[9] A multitude of Jewish believers suffered persecution in the BC era, and they did so without the full revelation of Jesus which gives Christians today far better reasons to believe.

Now comes the punchline: *"These were all commended for their faith, yet none of them received what had been promised."* What? Did God therefore betray their trust in him? Not at all. He gave them precisely what they hoped for, but also promised them something far better. He took all of the prophetic pictures of Jesus in which these Old Testament men and women had put their faith, and he counted it as faith in Christ himself, just as he had done for Moses in verse 26. They did not see the fullness of Jesus, like us, yet in death God has included them in the better covenant of his perfect Son. If the Jewish Christians go back to the synagogues, they will therefore not be honouring their roots. They will be betraying the historic faith of the Jews!

Hebrews 11 is therefore a wonderful chapter. Don't move on from it until you have fully grasped the depth of what the writer is trying to say. He is bringing application to what he taught us in the first two sections of the letter. He wants us to be challenged by the men and women in this hall of fame who displayed enormous faith in God despite having far less revelation than we have. Now that we have Jesus in all his fullness, we should easily exceed the exploits of their faith. We have far better reasons to believe.

---

[8] 1 Kings 19:14; 21:1–15; 2 Chronicles 24:20–21; Jeremiah 20:1–2; 26:20–23; 37:15–16. The account of Isaiah being sawn in two appears only in the Jewish Talmud, not in the Old Testament.

[9] The writer rejects any prosperity teaching that God promises to make Christians healthy and wealthy champions, free from suffering at all times.

# Keep on Running (12:1–13)

*Therefore, since we are surrounded by such a great cloud of witnesses, let us throw off everything that hinders and the sin that so easily entangles.*

(Hebrews 12:1)

A few weeks ago, I joined the crowds of spectators who lined the streets for the London Marathon. It gathers an amazing mixture of athletes and amateurs, of joggers and jokers. The race is famous for the many people who decide to run the full 26-mile course dressed in elaborate costume. This year's runners included Darth Vader, the Gingerbread Man, a rhinoceros, a camel, the Honey Monster, a gorilla, SpongeBob SquarePants, various Mr Men and Indiana Jones, dragging behind him a giant boulder.

But here's the thing I noticed. The man in the gorilla suit wasn't among the runners who sprinted over the finish line two hours after the race started. He wasn't even among the bulk of runners who completed the course within three to five hours. The sun was setting in the sky and most of the crowds had already gone home by the time the gorilla and his friends limped over the finish line outside Buckingham Palace. A marathon is seriously hard work, even without the kind of costume that makes running even harder. That's why the writer of Hebrews uses the list of people in chapter 11 to warn us that life is like a marathon. The list is over. Now it is our turn. How are we going to run?

In verse 1, he reminds us that life is not a short sprint. Anyone can start out following Jesus; what matters is whether we keep on running. We cannot eliminate the external factors that slow us down – the disappointments and discouragements that are part and parcel of running against the tide in a world that is in rebellion against Jesus – but we can deal with the internal factors. When the Holy Spirit comes to live inside us, he reveals two things lurking within our hearts: sins, which rebel against God, and false priorities, which distract us from God. The writer describes these false priorities literally as *weights*. They are the equivalent of our trying to run the London Marathon in a gorilla suit. He urges us to take them off and throw them away. This is our moment to run.

To help us with this, the writer encourages us that we are running as part of a team. When he talks about a *"great cloud of witnesses"*, he does not mean that our spiritual ancestors are cheering us on from the sky like a Christian version of *The Lion King*. He means that all of the faithful witnesses described in chapter 11 are like the cloud the Israelites followed in the desert. They have already marked out the way for us. They sacrificed everything in order to witness to the Word of God. Since we have far better reasons to believe, this should stir us to follow hard on their footsteps. It doesn't matter whether your particular struggle is with greed or pride or sexuality or sheer busyness.[1] Others have run along the same path of sacrifice ahead of you.

In verses 2–3, the writer encourages us still further by reminding us that Jesus has also run this same marathon ahead of us. He is deliberately ambiguous when he describes Jesus as the *archēgos* and *teleiōtēs* of our faith. He could mean that Jesus is the *Pioneer* and *Finished Article* of our faith (he has run the race before us so that we only have to follow in his footsteps to overcome), or he could mean that Jesus is the *Author* and *Perfecter* of our faith (he took the initiative to save us and he

[1] The Greek word *agōn* in 12:1 means an athletic *contest* or *struggle*. Paul uses the same word to describe the agony of our race in Philippians 1:30, Colossians 2:1, 1 Thessalonians 2:2, 1 Timothy 6:12 and 2 Timothy 4:7.

therefore commits himself to sustain us until we finish the entire course).[2] This double meaning is deliberate because both of these two things are true. Jesus kept running, even when his race included the agony of the cross, because he had his eyes fixed on the joy waiting for him at the finish line.[3] He will empower us to keep on running as we fix our eyes on him in heaven. Our temporary suffering is not worth comparing with the eternal reward he will confer upon us the moment we cross the finish line.

In verses 4–11, the writer encourages us not to lose heart in the face of pain and persecution. He points out that many of the Old Testament believers listed in chapter 11 laid down their lives for the sake of God's Word. Let's keep our suffering in perspective. Let's also learn from their example that suffering does not mean that God has abandoned us. Far from it. One of the major lessons of the book of Proverbs is that parents who fail to discipline their children fail to love them.[4] The writer quotes from Proverbs 3:11–12 in order to assure us that suffering is proof that God is our loving Father in heaven. *"No discipline seems pleasant at the time, but painful. Later on, however, it produces a harvest of righteousness and peace for those who have been trained by it."* We should therefore trust the Lord to know what is best for us. The men and women of chapter 11 discovered that God used the agony of their race to open their eyes to the sins and false priorities weighing them down. In the same way, we should treat our own pain as God's invitation to step out of our gorilla suit and run with the same holiness as his Son.

---

[2] Paul gives us this unequivocal promise in Philippians 1:6.

[3] Victims of crucifixion were despised by the world, yet 12:2 tells us that Jesus despised the thought of being despised. He considered it nothing compared to the joy of fulfilling his Father's plan to save a multitude of runners from every nation of the world.

[4] The Greek word *nothos* in 12:8 means a *bastard* or *illegitimate child*. It refers to a child born through an illicit sexual encounter and who, in a first-century context, was hated and disowned by an embarrassed father.

In verses 12–13, the writer therefore warns us that life is far more than a fun run. This race cost Jesus his life (12:2) and God has only given us one chance to run behind him (9:27), so we ought to train ourselves spiritually as much as any Olympic athlete trains physically. In verse 11, the writer uses the Greek word *gumnazō* to urge us to *train like athletes*,[5] and in verses 12–13 he quotes from Isaiah 35:3 and Proverbs 4:26 to convince us that following the Lord has always felt like a spiritual marathon.[6] It is a race in which the Devil hopes to wear us down through setbacks and persecution and crushing disappointments. Keep on running. We are following in the footsteps of Jesus and of the great cloud of runners who have run this way before.

The great Australian marathon runner Rob de Castella explained to his fans that *"If you feel bad at 10 miles, you're in trouble. If you feel bad at 20 miles, you're normal."* The writer of Hebrews says the same. If you are buckling under the initial pressure of following Jesus, he warns you to look at the other runners for perspective. Pain and pressure and discouragement and disappointment are the daily diet of any marathon runner. But if you are experiencing ongoing pain and persecution, be reassured that this is normal. Fix your eyes on Jesus, on the Father's love, and on the fact that you are part of a great team of runners. Take off the gorilla suit of sin and distraction. This is your moment to run.

---

[5] The writer also uses the word *gumnazō* in 5:14. It is the root of our English word *gymnasium*. Paul also uses the same word to encourage us to train ourselves to run like spiritual athletes in 1 Timothy 4:7.

[6] The writer expects us to know Isaiah 35 well enough to link the quotation in 12:12 to his description of the lame being healed (35:6) and of holiness being necessary in order to see the Lord (35:2 and 8).

# Final Warning (12:14–29)

*If they did not escape when they refused him who*
*warned them on earth, how much less will we, if we*
*turn away from him who warns us from heaven?*

(Hebrews 12:25)

God is very gracious. He did not inspire the writer of Hebrews to warn us once, twice, three times or even four times to take the message of this letter seriously. This is the fifth warning passage. It is a final, urgent plea, and it is stronger than all of the others.

This final warning passage technically began in verses 1–13.[1] There is a flipside to being encouraged that life is a marathon and that great heavenly rewards await us at the finish line. If there is a prize to lay hold of, then there is also a prize to lose. The writer warns us not to run like Paula Radcliffe, the British marathon runner who was favourite to win gold at the Athens Olympics in 2004. She broke down in a fit of vomiting before the finish line and wept in her post-race interview: *"I don't really have an explanation. I'm struggling myself to comprehend... I'm totally devastated."* Many of earth's favourites will be revealed as losers on the Final Day.

The writer steps up this warning in verses 14–17. He uses Esau's tragic example in the book of Genesis to warn us that the pages of Scripture are full of people who looked as though they were running after God until time revealed that they were truly running after themselves. Having talked about

---

[1] The five warning passages are 2:1–4, 3:7–4:13, 5:11–6:12, 10:19–39 and 12:1–29.

persecution throughout this letter, the writer uses the Greek word *diōkō*, which means *to persecute*, when he urges us in verse 14 to *pursue* holiness. We need to be more determined to run after Jesus than the Devil is to run us off the road. Nobody experiences God because they talk about it, sing about it or even pray about it. We can only experience God if we set our hearts to run after him. The writer warns us that *"without holiness no one will see the Lord."*

This is where many readers get offended. Martin Luther is not the only one to object that this sounds too much like James 2 and not enough like Ephesians 2. How does this warning that our own actions affect our relationship with God square with the Gospel command in 10:22: *"Let us draw near to God with a sincere heart and with the full assurance that faith brings"*? Well, read that verse again. It tells us that true faith in Jesus will always result in a sincere heart: a heart that doesn't crave forgiveness for continued sin but craves freedom from sin itself. Claiming that we are Christians while clinging onto the sins for which Christ died makes about as much sense as repenting of racism while remaining a member of the Ku Klux Klan. The writer is simply echoing the words of Jesus in Matthew 5:8: *"Blessed are the pure in heart, for they will see God."* How we run life's marathon reveals whether our profession of faith is real or a self-delusion.[2]

The writer steps up his warning even more in verses 18–25. He draws together all that he has taught us about the Old and New Covenants in order to warn us that better reasons to believe also carry with them greater reasons to fear if we refuse. The Lord invited every Israelite to experience his presence at Mount Sinai, but they were so terrified by the darkness, fire, thunder, lightning, angelic trumpet blast and booming voice of God that they begged Moses to go and meet the Lord without

---

[2] If we think that Hebrews is contradicting the rest of the New Testament here, then we need this letter more than we realize. See Matthew 3:8; Acts 26:20; Ephesians 5:5; 1 John 3:3,9–10.

them.³ Even Moses admitted that *"I am trembling with fear,"*⁴ but he urged them to embrace this as a good thing. He told them in Exodus 20:20 that *"The fear of God will be with you to keep you from sinning."*

People who do not understand the message of Hebrews get very confused that the New Covenant has not done away with fear entirely. That's because they think the Gospel means that God is now more lenient towards our sin. Since we have studied Hebrews together, you are unlikely to make that mistake. The New Covenant tells us that God still hates wickedness (1:9) and is still every bit as committed to judging it (6:10; 9:27). Far from sweeping sin under the carpet, the cross reveals that God will never do so. He is perfectly just, even when it costs him the life of his precious Son.⁵ The message that gives us better reasons to believe also gives us greater reasons to fear if we refuse.⁶

The writer contrasts Mount Zion with Mount Sinai in verses 22-24. Those who are part of God's New Covenant People are marked by their joy and their assurance that Jesus has borne away the wrath of God against their sin.⁷ They are full of praise that God has made them righteous and perfect through *"Jesus the mediator of a new covenant."* They rejoice that, whereas Abel's blood called out in Genesis 4:10 for vengeance upon Cain, Jesus' blood cries out for our forgiveness.⁸

---

³ The quotation in 12:20 from Exodus 19:12–13 is supposed to signpost us back to the entire passage. See Exodus 19:9–25; 20:18–21; 24:1–18.

⁴ The writer amplifies Deuteronomy 9:19 as he quotes it. The Greek Septuagint simply says *"I am afraid,"* but the writer amplifies it to *"I am trembling with fear."*

⁵ The Israelites at Mount Sinai forgot God's mercy because they experienced God's greatness. We must not forget God's greatness because we have experienced God's mercy.

⁶ The Lord prophesied in both Psalm 2:11–12 and Jeremiah 32:40 that people would fear him more, not less, after the coming of his Messiah. Our holy fear is to exceed that of Noah in Hebrews 11:7.

⁷ Paul talks just as clearly about our need to flee God's wrath into the arms of Jesus (1 Thessalonians 1:10).

⁸ See Luke 23:34. The references to Esau and Abel are meant to link the warning of Hebrews 12 back to the promise of Hebrews 11. Better reasons to

The writer is therefore asking us to search our hearts and to confirm that we have truly become part of God's New Covenant People. How are we running life's marathon?[9] If the Israelites were not spared judgment when they ignored the covenant which was given to them through Moses' intercession for them on earth, how much less will we be spared judgment if we ignore the covenant which has been given to us through Jesus' intercession for us in heaven?

The writer therefore finishes his final warning passage by reminding us in verses 26–29 that God has not changed. God is still a consuming fire, so we still need to *"worship God acceptably with reverence and awe"* (verses 28–29 and Deuteronomy 4:24).[10] The earth was shaken when God gave the Old Covenant to the Israelites through Moses, and both the heavens and the earth will be shaken through the New Covenant (verse 26 and Haggai 2:6). If the first covenant brought judgment to those who rejected it, how much more then will the New Covenant do so?[11] We ignore the mercy of the Gospel at our peril.

The writer has issued his fifth and final warning. He has assured us that we are running this marathon for far higher stakes than we imagined. Let's therefore throw off everything that hinders us from running as the holy children of God. We have far better reasons to believe, so we also have far greater reasons to fear.

---

believe mean greater reasons to fear.

[9] The Greek present participle in 12:28 emphasizes that the biggest proof we have received God's Kingdom is that *"we **are receiving"*** God's Kingdom each day. True saving faith always spills over into action.

[10] The Greek word which is used for our *reverence* in 12:28 is the same word which describes Jesus' reverence in 5:7. The writer tells us that the more we fear the Lord the more we will be grateful for our salvation.

[11] The heavens were shaken when Jesus died (Matthew 27:45–54), but they will be shaken much more when he returns (Matthew 24:29–31).

# Tragic Figure (12:15–17)

*When he wanted to inherit this blessing, he was*
*rejected. He could bring about no change of mind,*
*though he sought the blessing with tears.*

(Hebrews 12:17)

Every culture has its own tragic figures. For the Greeks, it was Cassandra of Troy. For the Romans, it was the Gracchus brothers. Nowadays the French have Cyrano de Bergerac, the Russians have Anna Karenina, the British have Othello and the Americans have the Great Gatsby. It helps if we understand when reading these verses that the Jewish Scriptures had Esau. He was the man who had everything and threw it all away.

Most readers find these three warning verses very chilling, although not necessarily for the right reasons. I have heard it argued many times that, since the word *metanoia* means *repentance*, the writer is warning in verse 17 that there may come a point when an unbeliever can no longer be forgiven. Since the writer warns people in 4:7 that they need to respond to God *today*, this argument claims that Esau was a would-be believer. He rejected the Gospel so many times that when he finally attempted to repent, he discovered that he couldn't. This view was prevalent when the main English translation of the Bible was the King James Version, since it translates verse 17 particularly unhelpfully: *"He found no place of repentance, though he sought it carefully with tears."*

The good news for non-Christians is that this interpretation can't be true.[1] All five of these warning passages are directed at churchgoers, not at pagans. The bad news is that this actually makes these warning verses far more chilling. Let's read them slowly, and you will quickly see why.

In verse 15, the writer warns us to *"See to it that no one falls short of the grace of God and that no bitter root grows up to cause trouble and defile many."* He expects us to recognize this as a reference back to Deuteronomy 29:18, where those same words are used in the Greek Septuagint to warn against any Israelite who sins and leads others astray. In case we miss it, the writer also uses the Greek word for the work of an *overseer* or *elder* when he tells us to "see to it" that no one falls short of God's grace.[2] This warning is therefore about sin within the Church. Esau is not the model of an unbeliever, but of a false believer.

In verse 16, the writer warns us that one of Esau's great sins was being *sexually immoral*. Some English translations render the verse as if only the second sin applied to Esau, but there is no reason for making this distinction in the Greek text. Esau looked as though he were part of the People of God until well into adulthood. As Abraham's grandson and Isaac's firstborn son, his pedigree could not have been more perfect. Yet while his younger brother Jacob meditated on God's covenant with his family, Esau was more interested in hunting, either for game or for local girls. Esau took several local women into his home – two Hittites, one Hivite and an Ishmaelite.[3] For all he looked

---

[1] As an example, see 2 Chronicles 33. Manasseh defiled the Temple, led Israel into idolatry, murdered his children, dabbled in the occult and laughed at several warnings from God's prophets. Nevertheless, as soon as he repented while in exile in Babylon, the Lord heard him and forgave him and restored him.

[2] The verb *episkopeō* in 12:15 is the root of the noun *episkopos*, which means *overseer* and is used to describe church leaders in Acts 20:28, 1 Timothy 3:2, Titus 1:7 and Philippians 1:1.

[3] Genesis 26:34–35; 28:8–9; 36:2–3. By way of contrast, Genesis tells us that Jacob waited for God's choice of wife, not marrying until he was in his

like a believer on the outside, his actions revealed that he was thoroughly pagan at heart.

In verse 16, the writer tells us that Esau's other great sin was that he was *ungodly*. The Greek word *bebēlos* means *profane*, so here it carries the sense of despising the promises of God. Because he never feasted his mind on God's covenant, Esau still lived on spiritual milk and thought nothing in Genesis 25:29–34 of selling his birthright to his younger brother in exchange for a chance to drink some stew. Isaac indulged his sin, never imagining that this choice was a sign that his son was in fact an unbeliever. As a result, Esau's life hurtled towards disaster.

In verse 17, the writer reminds us what happened. Isaac sent Esau off to hunt for a celebration meal so that he could officially pass on to him the covenant blessings made to Abraham. Jacob felt aggrieved – after all, he had purchased this blessing from Esau in return for a bowl of stew – so he tricked his blind father into passing the covenant blessings on to him instead. Esau was furious and wept loudly at the end of Genesis 27, but Isaac refused to reverse his blessing.[4] The word *metanoia* in verse 17 must therefore be referring to Isaac's *change of mind*. The true meaning of the verse is that *"even when he afterward desired to inherit the blessing, he was rejected; for he found no place for a change of mind in his father, though he sought it diligently with tears."*[5]

This is quite a different reading from the old assumption that the writer is telling non-Christians that they may not be able to repent unless they seize the chance today. It means that the writer is using Esau as an example of somebody who looks like a believer and yet whose actions prove otherwise. He is challenging us to test our own hearts to see that we are not like

---

eighties!

[4] Isaac is commended for this answer in 11:20, even though he had not intended to bless Jacob.

[5] The American Standard Version slightly paraphrases here, but it captures the true meaning.

him, because God will not be fooled by false professions of faith on Judgment Day. *"People are destined to die once, and after that to face judgment,"* he warned us in 9:27. Isaac shows us that a day will come when there will be no second chances.

Even if we know for sure that we are true believers, these verses are still uncomfortable. The writer has talked throughout this letter about our *"promised eternal inheritance"*.[6] We must not fail to make the link, therefore, when he warns us that Esau despised his inheritance and as a result was disinherited. The Christian marathon and its eternal prize really matter. A day is coming when it will be too late to alter how we have run.

More than that, the writer is addressing this warning to whole Christian communities. We saw in chapter 10 that he does not believe in solo Christianity. The focus of verses 15 and 16 is that we ought to look out for one another, doing what Isaac so spectacularly failed to do for Esau. We are to express our love within the Church by confronting and challenging one another. We are to express our love within our families by doing the same.[7] Be wise in how you do so, but believe the writer when he tells you that not to confront people is not wise at all. A little sin can pollute a whole person. A sinful person can pollute a whole church. *"See to it that... no bitter root grows up to cause trouble and defile many."*[8]

For it is in the little things that great rewards are lost and thrown away. Make sure you don't behave like Esau, the tragic figure of Abraham's family.

241

---

[6] Hebrews 1:14; 6:12; 9:15.

[7] It is no coincidence that this warning to parents comes in the same chapter as 12:7–11.

[8] This is the main thrust of Deuteronomy 29:18. Little sins have massive repercussions. Note the way in which Peter also refers to Deuteronomy 29:18 while modelling this for us in Acts 8:20–23.

# Zion has not Fallen
## (12:22–24)

*But you have come to Mount Zion, to the city of the living God, the heavenly Jerusalem.*

(Hebrews 12:22)

In August 70 AD, Jerusalem was captured by the Romans. After a long siege, the future Emperor Titus finally breached its walls and unleashed a tidal wave of Roman brutality across the defeated city. Soldiers torched the Temple and razed the city to the ground. The Jewish historian Josephus was there and he estimates that 1.1 million people were slaughtered: *"They killed those they overtook without mercy and set fire to the houses into which the Jews fled, burning every soul in them... They ran through everyone they met and obstructed the very lanes with their dead bodies, making the whole city run with such blood that the fire of many of the houses was quenched."*[1] Titus was so moved by the carnage that another historian tells us that he refused to accept a victory wreath because he saw *"no merit in vanquishing people forsaken by their own God."*[2]

All of this would happen only two years after the Jewish Christians received this letter. We do not know how much prophetic insight the writer of Hebrews was given into what was about to happen, but we do know that his letter proved very helpful when the disaster finally came. If you are Argentinian, think back to how you felt when Buenos Aires was wiped off the map in the movie *Starship Troopers*. If you are American, think

---

[1] Josephus in his *Wars of the Jews* (6.8.5–6.9.3).

[2] Philostratus II tells us this in his *Life of Apollonius of Tyana* (6.29).

back to how you felt when the White House was captured by North Korean terrorists in the movie *Olympus Has Fallen*. Those are pale insights into how it felt when Jerusalem fell. The writer prepares the Jewish Christians for their coming agony.

In verse 22, he argues that even if the Romans win their war against the Jews and capture the capital, it will not mean that Mount Zion has fallen. He unpacks some of what he taught us in chapter 11 when he told us that God viewed Abraham's faith in the Promised Land as if it were faith in heaven, and that God viewed Moses' faith in his plans for Israel as if it were faith in Christ. God loves the Jewish nation, so he gave them many prophetic pictures throughout the Old Testament to enable them to have faith in Jesus before he came. If an ancient Israelite expressed devotion to the Promised Land, the Temple or the People of God, the Lord considered their faith in these shadows as if it were faith in the real thing. As a result of Jesus' coming, these shadows have been done away with and the truth has been revealed in all its glory: *"You have come to Mount Zion, to the city of the living God, the heavenly Jerusalem."* Even as Jerusalem fell in 70 AD, the true Mount Zion would survive unscathed as the Church of God.[3]

This statement alone may be the reason why Hebrews is an anonymous letter. Stephen had been executed on a charge of dishonouring the Temple. Paul had almost been lynched on a similar charge. If this letter were written from Jerusalem, anyone who intercepted it would see this statement as an act of blasphemy. It says that God's plans for Herod's Temple are now over. He is building his New Covenant Temple instead.[4]

[3] The writer is not saying that Jesus was created when he calls him God's *firstborn* in 1:6 and 12:23. After all, he points out in 12:16 that Jacob became Isaac's firstborn despite having been born second. He is saying that Jesus is the true and better Israel, the one prophesied about in Exodus 4:22 and Jeremiah 31:9.

[4] Acts 6:13; 21:27-29. If the writer left his letter unsigned on purpose, he must have signified his authorship to the Jewish Christians in other ways. He clearly expects them to know his identity in 13:19.

If you have little interest in the Jewish nation or in their historic homeland, you need to hear this. I hope this letter has helped you to understand that Christianity is the true faith of the Jews. The writer has echoed the teaching of the apostles by explaining that the Gospel is the fulfilment of all God's promises to Abraham. I hope that he has made you understand why Paul says in his letters that salvation is *"first for the Jew, then for the Gentile."*[5]

But if you love the Jewish nation, you need to hear this too. I hope this letter has made you understand that Christian Zionism short-changes Jews by promising them far too little. Israel has a right to defend its borders since it was created by a UN Resolution in 1948, but the Jews also have a right to hear the Gospel. We must not think that we are loving Jews by affirming them in chasing after shadows. We must help them see those shadows fulfilled and upgraded in their Messiah. We must help them make the same spiritual journey as the Jewish apostles.

Jesus first hinted to his followers that the land of Israel was just a shadow of something better in Matthew 5:5. Quoting a famous line from Psalm 37:11, he upgraded the promise that God's People will inherit the land of Israel to *"they will inherit the earth"*.[6] The disciples were slow to grasp this, still asking him in Acts 1:6, *"Lord, are you at this time going to restore the kingdom to Israel?"* Jesus answered their question ten days later on the Day of Pentecost when he filled them with the Holy Spirit. They immediately grasped that the New Covenant had arrived. They started selling off their inheritance within the Promised Land because they saw that something far better had come.[7]

Paul explains this further in his letters. The Father promises the Messiah in Psalm 2:8, not the land of Israel, but the entire

---

[5] Romans 1:16; 2:9–10.

[6] The Greek word *gē* can mean either *the land* or *the earth*, but Jesus uses the same word elsewhere in the Sermon on the Mount to refer not just to Israel but to the whole earth (Matthew 5:18; 6:10, 19).

[7] Acts 2:45; 4:32–37. Contrast this with godly Naboth in 1 Kings 21:3.

earth. Paul therefore tells us in Romans 4:13 that God's promise to give Abraham a patch of land in the Middle East was merely an Old Covenant shadow. Through Jesus he *"would be heir of **the world"**.* Paul also spots that the prophecy about the Temple in Ezekiel 40–48 has not been fulfilled through Herod's Temple. He therefore informs us that the Jewish Temple is only a mere shadow too. The Church is God's New Covenant Temple.[8]

Although this made Paul a great many Jewish enemies, nobody loved the Jewish nation more than Paul. He tells us in Romans 9 that he would gladly be damned in hell if it would result in more of his Jewish countrymen being saved in heaven. Yet when he was attacked and almost murdered by his Jewish enemies, accused of hating his own people, he did not beat a hasty retreat and explain that they had misunderstood him. Instead, he insisted that Jesus is the true *"hope of Israel".*[9] We must not leave our Jewish friends and neighbours chasing after shadows. We must tell them that something far better has come.

The problem with many Christian Zionists is not that they carry too much hope for the Jews; it is that they carry too little. They fail to warn the Jews that Jesus is the true offspring of Abraham, the true Son of David and the founder of God's true Temple. They fail to tell the Jews that the Church is the true Mount Zion and the true Jerusalem.[10] They fail to tell the Jews that Zion has not fallen.

---

[8] 1 Corinthians 3:16–17; 2 Corinthians 6:16; Ephesians 2:21–22. See also 1 Peter 2:5.

[9] Paul says this while appealing to a group of unbelieving Jews in Acts 28:20.

[10] In case we miss this, the writer repeats it in 13:14: *"Here we do not have an enduring city, but we are looking for the city that is to come."* This city, the Church throughout the ages, is described in Galatians 4:25–26 and in Revelation 3:12, 14:1, 21:2, 21:10–27 and 22:19.

# Preaching Class (12:26–29)

*He has promised, "Once more"... The words "once more" indicate... Therefore...*

(Hebrews 12:26–28)

We do not know who wrote the letter to the Hebrews, but we know that whoever wrote it was a very skilful preacher. This letter is one of the longest and best crafted sermons in the Bible. It does more than teach us what to preach; it also demonstrates how we are to preach it. So whether you are a regular preacher or whether you simply share your faith with those around you, let's look at four verses that show us how to communicate God's Word effectively to others.

In verse 26, the writer demonstrates that we must *begin by reading Scripture*. We may need to capture people's attention first, but then we always make a beeline to the Bible. The writer quotes from Haggai 2:6 in the Greek Septuagint, amplifying a few of the words as he does so in order to thrust its message under the noses of his readers: *"Now he has promised, 'Once more I will shake not only the earth but also the heavens.'"*

This may sound obvious but it isn't. A lot of contemporary preaching consists of sharing thoughts that are largely biblical but not rooted in any particular passage of the Bible. The writer of Hebrews quotes directly from Old Testament passages thirty-five times in thirteen chapters because he truly believes what he told us in 4:12: *"The word of God is alive and active. Sharper than any double-edged sword, it penetrates even to dividing soul and spirit, joints and marrow; it judges the thoughts and attitudes of the heart."* If you want to change people's hearts through your preaching, simply unleash the Word of God upon them. The same God who spoke the Scriptures into being will speak through you whenever you read those words to people today.[1]

In verse 27, the writer demonstrates that we must *explain what the Scripture means*. He spells out for his readers what the words "once more" indicate in the passage. We do not read a passage in order to use it as a springboard for our own thoughts but in order to bring people's thinking into greater submission to the Word of God. That means showing people what the words of Scripture mean. John Piper argues that

> *We are simply pulling rank on people when we tell them, and don't show them from the text. This does not honour the Word of God or the work of the Holy Spirit. I urge you to rely on the Holy Spirit by saturating your preaching with the Word he inspired... Quote the text! Quote the text! Say the actual words of the text again and again. Show the people where your ideas are coming from. Most people do not easily follow the connections a preacher sees between his words and the text. They must be shown.*[2]

This does not mean that every sermon must be exegetical preaching, the type of sermon that takes a single passage of Scripture and explains its meaning line by line. The writer does this brilliantly in 10:5-10 and 12:26-29, but he also gives us a great example of thematic preaching in 1:5-14. What matters is that the listeners are left in no doubt that the argument they are hearing is not the preacher's idea but God's Word. Charles Spurgeon warns us that

---

[1] The writer uses present tenses in 3:7 and 10:15 in order to emphasize that God's Word still *speaks* today.

[2] John Piper in *The Supremacy of God in Preaching* (1990).

*Some brethren have done with their text as soon as they have read it. Having paid all due honour to that particular passage by announcing it, they feel no necessity further to refer to it... A sermon comes with far greater power to the consciences of the hearers when it is plainly the very word of God – not a lecture about the Scripture, but Scripture itself opened up and enforced.*[3]

In verse 28, the writer demonstrates that we must *apply the Scripture we have read to people's lives*. He does not merely read from Haggai 2:6 and explain what the passage means. He continues: *"**Therefore**, since we are receiving a kingdom that cannot be shaken, let us be thankful, and so worship God acceptably with reverence and awe."* Do not assume that your hearers can always make the mental leap between what a passage means in general and what it means specifically to their own lives. It is the preacher's job to make this leap for them, applying it to the hearts of believers and unbelievers, the young and the old, the married and the single, the backslider and the passionate leader.

In verse 29, the writer demonstrates that we must *end with a strong challenge to respond*. He is as skilful in stirring fresh passion in the hearts of his readers as he is in provoking fresh thoughts in their heads. Rather than being offended by his strong language in this final warning passage, we ought to learn from him that truth is not enough; it must be truth experienced and set on fire. Jonathan Edwards defended his own passionate pleas at the end of his sermons by explaining that *"Some talk of it as an unreasonable thing to think to fright persons to heaven, but I think it is a reasonable thing to endeavour to fright persons away from hell – 'tis a reasonable thing to fright a person out of a house on fire."*[4]

---

[3] Charles Spurgeon in *Lectures to My Students* (1890).

[4] Jonathan Edwards in *The Distinguishing Marks of a Work of the Spirit of God* (1741).

We see this throughout Hebrews. Careful logic is interspersed with tender appeals, with chilling threats, with helpful illustrations and with examples from Israel's history that dress abstract ideas in working clothes. We need to do the same. John Piper encourages us that *"Good preaching aims to stir up 'holy affections' – such emotions as hatred for sin, delight in God, hope in His promises, gratitude for His mercy, desire for holiness, and tender compassion... Therefore good preaching aims to stir up holy affections in those who hear. It targets the heart."*[5] As you do so, like the writer of Hebrews, expect your listeners to respond positively to your challenge.[6] Don't forget the promise of Jesus in Matthew 9:29: *"According to your faith will it be done to you."* Whether you believe that people will respond positively or whether you believe they won't, you are probably right!

I hope this sermon from the writer of Hebrews has excited you to follow Jesus even more devotedly. I hope it has stirred your heart to persuade others to follow him more devotedly with you. If it has, these lessons from one of the great preachers of the New Testament will help you to be more effective in your encouragement of others. If you believe that reading Scripture, explaining Scripture, applying Scripture and making strong appeals from Scripture will bring hearts into glad submission to Jesus, then you will share the same experience as the Levites in Nehemiah 8:8 and 12:

> *They read from the Book of the Law of God, making it clear and giving the meaning so that the people understood what was being read... Then all the people went away... to celebrate with great joy, because they now understood the words that had been made known to them.*

---

[5] John Piper in *The Supremacy of God in Preaching* (1990).

[6] Two good examples of this can be found 6:9 and 10:39.

# Inside-Out Love (13:1–3)

*Keep on loving one another as brothers and sisters.*
*Do not forget to show hospitality to strangers.*

(Hebrews 13:1–2)

The meaning of words matters. It therefore pays to understand a little of the language in which this letter was written. Unless we understand two Greek words at the start of chapter 13, we will make the same mistake as the Italians at the Treaty of Wuchale.

Italian diplomats thought that they had won a major victory in Africa when they signed a treaty with King Menelik II of Ethiopia in 1889. Not only did the treaty grant them rule of Eritrea, but they also believed it annexed Ethiopia too. In the Italian version of the treaty, Article 17 proclaimed that *"His Majesty the King of Kings of Ethiopia must go through the government of His Majesty the King of Italy whenever doing business with any other power or government."* Because the negotiators did not understand Amharic, the language of Ethiopia, they did not notice that the Amharic version merely stated that King Menelik *"**is permitted** to go through the government of His Majesty the King of Italy."* Misunderstanding a single Amharic word changed the entire meaning of the treaty. It led to a war in which the Italians were routed by the Ethiopians on the battlefield.[1]

The Greek word in verse 1 is easy to understand.

---

[1] Ironically, Article 19 of the treaty stated that *"This treaty is drafted in Italian and Amharic and the two versions agree with each other perfectly."* We need to take the time to understand these verses properly.

*Philadelphia* means *love for brothers and sisters*, which is why the persecuted Quakers chose it as the name of the city they founded in America. The writer begins chapter 13 with a simple exhortation for the Jewish Christians. He tells them literally to *"Let love for brothers and sisters remain."* The Jews were famous for their tight-knit community, addressing one another as brothers and sisters and living life together as one big family. The writer tells the Jewish Christians that they must not lose this in receiving Jesus as their Messiah. Now they have even better reasons to love one another as the family of God.[2]

We need this encouragement too. We live in a world that is increasingly mobile and urbanized, a world in which individualism often flourishes at the expense of community. It is not easy for Christians who have been brought up in such a world to develop the *philadelphia* the writer describes. We need to grasp that it was only after the early Christians were filled with the Holy Spirit that they *"were together and had everything in common... They broke bread in their homes and ate together with glad and sincere hearts... All the believers were one in heart and mind. No one claimed that any of their possessions was their own, but they shared everything they had."*[3] This inside-out love does not come naturally to anyone. Paul tells us that *"God's love has been poured out into our hearts through the Holy Spirit."* Only when he taught his disciples about the Holy Spirit did Jesus promise them that *"By this everyone will know that you are my disciples, if you love one another."*[4] We have better reasons to believe and better access to God's Spirit, so our churches must be marked by far greater love than the tight-knit Jewish community at its best.

Unless we understand the second Greek word, however, our churches are in danger of becoming like the Jewish community

---

[2] The Greek word *philadelphia* is also used in Romans 12:10, 1 Thessalonians 4:9, 1 Peter 1:22 and 2 Peter 1:7.

[3] Acts 2:42–47; 4:32–37.

[4] Romans 5:5; John 13:35.

at its worst. Viewing fellow believers as our brothers and sisters can easily descend into viewing non-believers as our enemies. Churches can easily hold outsiders at arm's length, treating them as *goyim*, *shgatzim* and *shiksas*, or whatever other pejorative terms the Jews have used for Gentiles over the years.[5] We must not be as foolish as the Italians who signed the Treaty of Wuchale. We need to understand the meaning of the Greek word *philoxenia*.

The writer wants us to grasp that *philadelphia* and *philoxenia* are two essential aspects of the inside-out love which the Holy Spirit works in the hearts of believers. Although the Greek word *xenizō* is sometimes used in the New Testament to refer to *lodging Christian strangers* in our homes, the writer is referring to more than this when he reminds us that Abraham, Lot and Manoah all gave food and lodging to angels unawares.[6] These two words make a deliberate parallel between *xenos* and *adelphos* in order to teach us to love *outsiders* in the same way that we love our *brothers and sisters*. The word *xenos* is used in the New Testament to describe the way in which the Jews refused to allow pagan outsiders to be buried in their graveyards or to share with them in God's covenant promises.[7] The writer is therefore telling us to do far more than entertain our fellow Christians in our homes. He is commanding us to embrace God's inside-out love by loving unbelievers as much as we love our Christian friends.

It therefore misses the point when people argue that the writer is referring to persecuted Christians in verse 3 when he urges the believers not to forget those who are in prison. Fear made the first-century believers disown their persecuted

---

[5] The writer warns us in 13:2 *"Do not forget"*, because churches can forget this as easily as synagogues.

[6] For example, in Acts 10:6; 21:16; 3 John 5. Genesis 18; 19; Judges 13.

[7] Matthew 27:7; Ephesians 2:12, 19. The only other place in the New Testament where the word *philoxenia* is used is in another deliberate contrast with *philadelphia* in Romans 12:10 and 13.

brothers and sisters in case they were imprisoned with them, but a similar fear can also make us disown many of those to whom the Lord Jesus has sent us.[8] Taken as a whole, these three verses command us to display God's inside-out love towards both Christians and non-Christians. We are to receive unbelievers into our homes and into our church meetings as beloved guests, and we are to go out and visit them wherever they may be. We are to leave them in no doubt that God's inside-out love extends towards them from the churches in their community. Jesus loved us enough to leave heaven and find us. Now he calls us to love outsiders enough to go out towards them from our churches. Jesus' inside-out love angered the Jewish leaders so much that they labelled him *"the friend of sinners"*.[9] Could that accusation be made of you and of the others in your church?

The answer to this question is so important that Paul issues a strict ruling in Titus 1:8 and 1 Timothy 3:2. He decrees that nobody should be entrusted with church leadership unless they are *philoxenos* – that is, unless they have proved that they love outsiders as much as they love their Christian brothers and sisters. They must know how to become a channel of God's inside-out love through the Holy Spirit. They must lead God's People in welcoming outsiders to their tables, to their guest bedrooms, to their families and to their church community. They must understand that this inside-out love lies at the heart of the Gospel. They must know how to demonstrate the love of Jesus to the world.

---

[8] For example, in 2 Timothy 1:15–16; 4:16.

[9] Jesus was both *"set apart from sinners"* and a *"friend of sinners"* at one and the same time (Hebrews 7:26; Matthew 11:19; Luke 7:34). So can we be through the Holy Spirit. See also Luke 6:33–38.

# Pure Sex (13:4)

> *Marriage should be honoured by all, and the marriage bed kept pure, for God will judge the adulterer and all the sexually immoral.*

> (Hebrews 13:4)

People in the Roman Empire worshipped sex. Quite literally. Not long after this letter was written, they built the largest temple in Rome to honour Venus, the goddess of sexual love. Since the Latin word for love was *amor* and the Latin word for Rome was *Roma*, they attached great significance to the fact that one word was the other word backwards. Hailing Venus as their divine ancestor, they adorned her magnificent temple with the motif *ROMA–AMOR*. They worshipped her by having sex with one another or with one of the many prostitutes who made a living at her temple.

It is helpful to remember this. Otherwise, we may be tempted to believe that widespread sexual promiscuity is a relatively modern phenomenon. The writer of Hebrews corrects this by challenging his first-century readers to see that their faith in Jesus means embracing a very different view of sex from the people around them. We are to love unbelievers, but we are not to love their deeds.

Our culture may not build temples to Venus but it still worships sex as a god. It does not view Miley Cyrus stripping naked and sitting on a wrecking ball as pornography; it simply views her video 100 million times during its first six days on Vevo. What was once seen as pornography is now seen by anyone who looks up at an advertising billboard for beer or a new pair of jeans. When Katy Perry sings that she's a lady, good for one thing, maybe, selling sex like a machine, she is telling the truth about the music industry which transformed her from church worship leader into MTV eye candy.[1] The writer of Hebrews insists that following Jesus means rejecting this worship of sex. He warns us that *"Marriage should be honoured by all, and the marriage bed kept pure, for God will judge the adulterer and all the sexually immoral."* God will judge every sin, including sexual sin.

Christians often struggle to break free from a culture that worships sex as a god. It is far easier to praise Jesus' compassion in John 8:11 when he tells a woman caught in the act of adultery, *"I do not condemn you"*, than it is to accept the rest of what he says to her: *"Go now and leave your life of sin."* Many Christians use the same excuses as unbelievers. They call pornography their addiction. They call same-sex attraction their identity. They treat sex before marriage as part of growing up and adultery part of being human. But Jesus is not fooled. The writer of Hebrews reinforces Jesus' teaching in the gospels that sex is only for a man and a woman within marriage.[2] He repeats Paul's teaching that lustful glances and sexual sin are the outward fruit of inward idolatry.[3] They are evidence that we have not fully surrendered our lives to Jesus as Lord. As such, they are a flat denial of the Gospel.

Many Christians react against worshipping sex as a god by despising sex as something gross. Pope Gregory the Great ruled at the start of the sixth century that *"Whilst we do not claim that marriage is sinful, this lawful conjugal union cannot take place without carnal pleasure, and such pleasure cannot under*

---

[1] Katy Perry in her song *Sex Sells*, recorded in 2008.

[2] For example, in Matthew 5:27–30; 15:18–20; 19:4–6. For more on this, see the chapter "Jesus on Sex" in my book *Gagging Jesus* (2013).

[3] For example, in Ephesians 5:3–7; Colossians 3:5–6.

*any circumstances be without blame."*[4] The Victorians promoted this prudish view of sex in public (despite privately managing to support 80,000 prostitutes in London alone), and this view is still prevalent in many churches today. Tony Campolo remembers being taught as a teenager that *"Sex is a dirty, filthy thing, and you should save it for the person you marry"*![5] The writer of Hebrews will have none of this. He tells us that responding to the Gospel means *keeping* the marriage bed pure (not making it pure) because sex isn't any more gross than it is godlike.

The writer tells us that sex is a pure gift from God. The Greek word he uses for *the marriage bed* is *koitus*, from which we get our English word *coitus*, meaning *the act of sex*. He therefore tells us that sex is inherently pure unless it is polluted by using God's good gift in the wrong context.[6] A bride and bridegroom arriving at the honeymoon suite on their wedding night would be outraged to discover that the bed sheets had been used by several other people before them. Knowing that sex is a good gift from God makes us care even more about the purity of our hearts and bodies when we make love than we do about the purity of the bed clothes. Virgin brides and bridegrooms and faithful husbands and wives discover what Genesis means when it tells us that sex is *"very good"*, gluing a married couple together as one flesh for the rest of their lives. Those who break God's commands sexually discover that misusing this glue causes even greater pain than misusing superglue.[7] The

---

[4] Quoted by Pierre Guichard and Jean-Pierre Cuvillier in their essay "Barbarian Europe" in André Burguière's *A History of the Family: Volume I* (1996).

[5] Tony Campolo in *Choose Love Not Power* (2009). This view dishonours marriage as much as promiscuity.

[6] The Greek word *amiantos* means literally *uncontaminated*. In its proper place, sex is good and not gross.

[7] God deems creation *"very good"* after he commands Adam and Eve to have sex (Genesis 1:28, 31). One of the main purposes of sex is to help married couples *"become one flesh"* (2:24–25), but this spiritual glue has a similar effect with unmarried couples, causing untold misery (1 Corinthians 6:16).

writer tells us that God takes sexual sin so seriously that he will judge both the *adulterer* (the married person who has sex with someone other than their spouse) and the *sexually immoral* (the unmarried person who has sex with anyone at all).[8] Sexual sin couldn't be more serious.

This teaching was just as unpopular in the first-century Roman Empire as it is today. By refusing to worship sex as a god or to despise it as something gross, the Christians offended both the promiscuous and the prudish. Yet note this: they also won the Roman Empire over to Christ when it finally grew sick of the bitter aftertaste of its sexual promiscuity. We will win our own generation to Christ in the same way if we hold firm to the Bible's teaching and proclaim that pure sex is the best sex.

While over a quarter of girls aged thirteen to seventeen admit to performing a sex act on a boy *"because I felt pressured"*, we need to show the world a better way.[9] While a quarter of the entire world's internet searches are for pornography and while 90 per cent of children aged eight to sixteen watch pornography online, we need to show the world a better way.[10] We need to show the world that sex is neither godlike nor gross; it is a pure gift from God. It is the wedding present through which he glues a man and a woman together as one flesh for an entire lifetime. A church that preaches and practises pure sex proclaims to a sex-obsessed world that, in Jesus, something far better has come.

---

[8] The two Greek words *moichoi* and *pornoi* encompass everyone who has sex outside marriage. See also 1 Corinthians 6:9–11; 2 Corinthians 12:21; Galatians 5:19–21; 1 Timothy 1:9–11; Revelation 21:8; 22:15.

[9] This data comes from a report by the UK charity the National Society for the Prevention of Cruelty to Children, entitled *Partner Exploitation and Violence in Teenage Intimate Relationships* (2009).

[10] This data comes from a report by *The Boston Globe* on 12th May 2005 entitled "The Secret Life of Boys".

# The Golden Idol (13:5–6)

*Be content with what you have, because God has said, "Never will I leave you; never will I forsake you."*

(Hebrews 13:5)

Some readers find it surprising that the writer of Hebrews places such great emphasis throughout his letter on the importance of our Christian obedience. They ask why he focuses so much on our obedience instead of assuring us that we are saved by faith and faith alone. Why does he warn us so strongly not to worship the god of self (verses 1–3), the god of sex (verse 4) or the god of money (verses 5–6)?

Enough people ask this question for it to deserve a thorough answer, although I must confess I personally find it a little strange. This final section of Hebrews is all about salvation through faith in Jesus. No chapter in the New Testament sounds a clearer call to faith than Hebrews 11. The writer does not emphasize the importance of our obedience in order to undermine the importance of our faith, but in order to demonstrate what true saving faith in Jesus looks like. The writer is simply echoing the question posed in James 2:14: *"What good is it, my brothers and sisters, if someone claims to have faith but has no deeds? Can such faith save them?"*

This isn't normally enough of an answer for those who feel that Hebrews places too much emphasis on our continued obedience and not enough on our faith and eternal security. Quoting from James does not satisfy them because they consider his letter to be guilty of the same crime. They complain that both letters focus too much on our own obedience and do not focus enough on Paul's statement in Romans 1:17 that *"In the gospel the righteousness of God is revealed – a righteousness that is by faith from first to last, just as it is written: 'The righteous will live by faith.'"*[1]

Honestly, I have to question whether those who ask this question have truly understood the writings of Paul. He emphasizes that no quantity of good works can save us and that our only hope of salvation lies therefore in placing our trust in the finished work of Jesus – but this is not his entire message. He emphasizes equally that a genuine profession of faith in Jesus will always result in a transformed lifestyle. He writes long chapters about Christian character and warns his readers that, unless they see this character in their own lives, they may not in fact be saved at all.[2] In Romans 1:5 he states that he has been given *"grace and apostleship to call all the Gentiles to the obedience that comes from faith."* In 2 Timothy 2:19 he insists that *"Everyone who confesses the name of the Lord must turn away from wickedness."* There is no contradiction, therefore, between Hebrews and James and the writings of Paul. They sound a common warning that genuine faith in Jesus will always result in genuine life change.

In verses 5–6, the writer tells us that one of the major changes to our lives will be in the way that we treat money. The default setting for a Christian is daily dependence on the God who saved them rather than dependence on their money, so the writer urges us to *"Keep your lives free from the love of money and be content with what you have."*[3] Self and sex are powerful idols, but neither is as powerful as money.

---

[1] Even if this is not your question, it is helpful to recognize that it is a question for many other readers. The irony, of course, is that Hebrews 10:38 quotes those exact same words from Habakkuk 2:4.

[2] For example, in 1 Corinthians 6:9–11; 2 Corinthians 13:5; Galatians 6:7–8; Ephesians 5:1–6.

[3] The Greek word *aphilarguros*, or *not loving money*, contains the same root word as *philadelphia* and *philoxenia* in 13:1–2. God's Spirit enables those who are truly saved to love what he loves and to hate what he hates.

Money itself is a neutral thing. It is a very helpful servant but a terrible master. It wants to become the object of our love and affection instead of God, so it tries to woo us by promising us things only God can truly give us. It promises to satisfy us, even though most of us know that the richest individuals are often the most miserable. When a reporter asked the oil billionaire J.D. Rockefeller how much money was enough to satisfy a person, he quickly replied, *"Just a few dollars more."* True satisfaction never comes through financial acquisition but only through contentment in God.

Money promises us security, even though most of us know that rich people face threats that are unknown to the poor. The writer uses two Old Testament quotations to teach that people who love money are idolaters who are seeking security through their own resources instead of through a relationship with the Lord. Deuteronomy 31:6 reminds us that God is our constant Companion: *"Never will I leave you; never will I forsake you."* Psalm 118:6 reminds us that God is our constant Protector and Sustainer: *"The Lord is my helper; I will not be afraid. What can mere mortals do to me?"* The writer expects us to know the rest of Psalm 118: *"It is better to take refuge in the Lord than to trust in humans... than to trust in princes."* He expects us to recognize that it is therefore better to take refuge in the Lord than to trust in the shifting sands of money. These two Old Testament verses are the great antidote to the love of money. They carry power to destroy the golden idol.

Since money tries to supplant God in our affections, it should not surprise us that the men and women of chapter 11 often had to forfeit their possessions before they came to true faith in the Lord. Abraham and Sarah had to leave behind Ur of the Chaldees. Jacob had to become a common shepherd. Joseph had to become a slave and then a prisoner. Moses had to turn his back on Pharaoh's palace. Rahab had to renounce her own home city. David had to become a fugitive. Daniel had to become a prisoner of war. Many others had to become destitute and homeless. This should teach us that we therefore have two options: we can either learn to trust God willingly by choosing to live frugally and to give away much of what we have, or we can learn to trust God reluctantly by forcing him to tear all of our idolatrous financial props away. Since we have far better reasons than the men and women of chapter 11 to believe, we should renounce the golden idol that much more willingly.

Jesus warned his followers that money is one of God's greatest rivals for the deep affection of our hearts. He assures us in Matthew 6:24 and Luke 16:13 that *"No one can serve two masters. Either you will hate the one and love the other, or you will be devoted to the one and despise the other. You cannot serve both God and Money."* As we draw towards the end of this letter, let's therefore formally renounce our former allegiance to our culture's golden idol. Let's replace it with complete trust in the Lord as our constant Companion, Helper and Provider. Money can never truly satisfy but God always can and always will.[4]

Let's turn our faith into action by formally renouncing all three of the idols in the first six verses of chapter 13. Let's renounce the god of self, the god of sex and the god of money, because Jesus has given us far better reasons to believe.

---

[4] This is one of the great themes of the Bible: from Genesis 21:14–19 to Psalms 34:10 and 37:25 to Philippians 4:11–19 to 1 Timothy 6:6–19.

# Jesus Hasn't Changed
## (13:7–25)

*Remember your leaders, who spoke the word of God to you... Imitate their faith. Jesus Christ is the same yesterday and today and for ever.*

(Hebrews 13:7–8)

When the fifteen-year-old Hudson Taylor paid a visit to his church minister to share his vision to plant churches across China, he did not receive much encouragement:

> *"How do you propose to go there?" he inquired. I answered that I did not at all know; that it seemed to me probable that I should need to do as the Twelve and the Seventy had done in Judea – go without purse or scrip, relying on Him who had called me to supply all my need. Kindly placing his hand upon my shoulder, the minister replied, "Ah, my boy, as you grow older you will get wiser than that. Such an idea would do very well in the days when Christ Himself was on earth, but not now."*[1]

Every new generation of believers faces this same challenge: Is Jesus still with us in the same way that he was with previous generations? The question was particularly urgent for the Jewish Christians to whom this letter was written, because their senior leaders were dropping like flies. James had been stoned to death. Peter had been crucified. Paul had been beheaded.

---

[1] This quotation and the one at the end of the chapter are taken from Hudson Taylor's autobiographical *A Retrospect* (1894).

They were expecting that Timothy would be executed too.[2] They were therefore at a turning point in the history of Christianity. Would they believe that Jesus was with them in the same way that he had been with their dying predecessors?

In verses 7–8, the writer begins to answer their question. He reminds them that they have the same Saviour as their fallen leaders. They are to reflect on the *ekbasis* of their leaders (the Greek word means *exit*, so it refers more to the manner of their dying than it does to the manner of their living),[3] and they are to pick up the baton of the Christian race from the dead fingers of their former mentors. It is time for them to imitate the previous generation of Christians by running hard for the same Saviour by the power of the same Holy Spirit.[4] *"Jesus Christ is the same yesterday and today and for ever,"* he assures them. They must not succumb to the defeatism of Hudson Taylor's minister. The death of their leaders has altered nothing, since Jesus hasn't changed.[5]

In verses 9–10, the writer emphasizes that his readers have the same Gospel as their dying leaders. They must not go back to the synagogues to snack on superseded ceremonial foods, because they can eat from a far better altar than the one at the Jewish Tabernacle or Temple. They can consume the bread and wine which signify participation in the death of Jesus on the cross. They can feast on the same Gospel of grace as James, Peter and Paul. They are as much heirs of the New Covenant as any of their martyred leaders.

---

[2] The writer informs them that Timothy has been released in 13:23. Since Paul does not mention Timothy's imprisonment in his letters to him, Hebrews must have been written in 67 AD or later.

[3] This is the same Greek word which is used to describe God giving us a *way out* in 1 Corinthians 10:13.

[4] *"Your leaders, who spoke the word of God to you"* is meant to echo 2:3–4. Jesus preached to the apostles, who preached to a new generation of believers, who must now step into their shoes.

[5] The writer denies that there is such a thing as the "apostolic age". The first generation of believers were ordinary people who were filled with God's extraordinary power (Acts 4:13; 10:26; 14:15). That power is still available today. It is business-as-usual for miracles, charismatic gifts, evangelism and church planting.

In verses 11–14, the writer says that we must also be ready to suffer in the same manner. The Law of Moses commanded the high priest to take the discarded corpses of sacrificial animals to be burned outside the Israelite camp, prophesying that Jesus would suffer for our sin outside the city walls of Jerusalem.[6] Jesus was excluded from society when he bore our shame and, as he went out, he founded a Church which is set apart as holy from the world. The writer therefore calls us to accept disgrace and exclusion for the sake of Jesus.[7] Just as Abraham left Ur of the Chaldees for the sake of God's new city, we must not compromise our faith to gain the acceptance of our own earthly cities.[8]

In verses 15–16, the writer reminds us that we still have the same call to worship God. The Greek word *thusia* in both of these verses normally refers to a *blood sacrifice,* but it is also the word which the Greek Septuagint uses to refer to the *incense* offered in the Holy Place, so the writer is telling us that when we worship in Jesus' name, pray in Jesus' name, witness about Jesus' name and serve others in Jesus' name, God breathes it in as a sweet-smelling fragrance.[9] Not a single song we sing, not a single Gospel message we share and not a single good thing we do is ever wasted. Our actions are just as precious to the Lord as the actions of the first generation of believers.

In verses 17–19, the writer reminds us that we have the same call to follow the church leaders God has appointed. He warns us not to doubt that our leaders wield the same authority as their predecessors, and he reminds church leaders that they will give the same account to Jesus for the way in which they wield it. To model this, he asks the Jewish Christians to pray for him in the same way that Paul asked churches to pray for him in

[6] Exodus 29:14 and Leviticus 4:21 prophesy his being led out of the city in Matthew 27:32 and John 19:17.

[7] The Greek word *oneidismos*, or *disgrace*, in 13:13 is the same word used to describe Moses' disgrace for the sake of Christ in 11:26. Returning to the Jewish Law and synagogues would actually be a betrayal of Moses.

[8] Hebrews 13:14 deliberately echoes 11:10 and 16. It refers to Rome as much as to Jerusalem.

[9] This is echoed by Revelation 5:8 and 8:4.

his own letters. If we respect our current leaders, we will make their task a pleasure and will benefit from their leadership at its very best.[10]

In verses 20–25, the writer ends his letter by reminding us that we have the same Senior Pastor as the first generation of Christians. Jesus is *"the great Shepherd of the sheep"*, and the New Covenant he ministers towards the Church is an eternal one.[11] He still brings us into the presence of the same Father and still fills us with the same Spirit.

Towards the end of his life, having succeeded in his goal of planting churches across China, Hudson Taylor reflected on the advice his minister had given him as a teenager:

> *I have grown older since then, but not wiser. I am more than ever convinced that if we were to take the directions of our Master and the assurances He gave to His first disciples more fully as our guide, we should find them to be just as suited to our times as to those in which they were originally given.*

Jesus is still the same in our generation. So is his Gospel. So is his call to worship and to suffer for his name. So is his commitment to act as our Senior Pastor through the church leaders he appoints for us. As we finish Hebrews, we must not side with Hudson Taylor's minister and leave the magnificent Gospel promises of this letter to a previous generation of believers. We must embrace them as our own, like Hudson Taylor, and begin to write another glorious chapter of Church history in our own generation.

---

[10] The Greek verb for *leading* in 13:7, 17 and 24 is the root of the word for a Roman *governor*. Anyone who rebelled against a governor was deemed to have rebelled against Caesar himself, so how we follow our church leaders really matters.

[11] See also Psalm 23:1; 80:1; Isaiah 40:11; John 10:11; 1 Peter 5:4. Church pastors are merely deputies.

# Conclusion: Something Far Better Has Come

*May he work in us what is pleasing to him, through*
*Jesus Christ, to whom be glory for ever and ever.*
*Amen.*

(Hebrews 13:20–21)

When Ali Pasha caught sight of the European warships on 7th October 1571, he was very pleased. This was the moment the admiral of the Ottoman fleet had long been waiting for. He outnumbered the Europeans in terms of ships, sailors and soldiers. A quick battle was all that stood between his fleet and the Muslim conquest of Europe.

But the Battle of Lepanto did not turn out the way that Ali Pasha expected. His fleet was larger, but it was armed with yesterday's weapons. He had failed to grasp that the age of gunpowder had arrived. The European galleys were bristling with cannons and sank many of the Turkish ships before their outdated weapons came into range. The European soldiers were armed with muskets, which made quick work of the long ranks of Ottoman bowmen. Five hours after he sighted the enemy, Ali Pasha's fleet was destroyed and the Turks had lost their naval supremacy forever. Ali Pasha's severed head was displayed from a pike on the bows of the European flagship. He paid a high price for relying on bowmen and catapults in a guns-and-cannons world.[12]

---

[12] In fairness to Ali Pasha, some of his ships did have cannons, but they had too few, too badly made, too poorly mounted and too badly supplied with ammunition. He had prepared for the wrong kind of battle.

We have finished reading James and Hebrews together. This is therefore our own Lepanto moment. Will we believe the news that the coming of Jesus has changed everything, or will we try to hang onto our old ways of thinking like Ali Pasha? However we decide to respond, let's be in no doubt: something far better has come.

If you are Jewish, I am very glad that you have read this commentary on James and Hebrews. These are the two New Testament letters that were written primarily for Jews, so these are your letters before they are mine. They tell you that your long-awaited Messiah has arrived. That's such fantastic news that the writer of Hebrews describes his thirteen densely argued chapters as *"only a short letter"* (13:22). His brief summary demands a wholesale change in the way you live and worship God. How will you respond to the news that, in Jesus, something far better has come?

If you are not Jewish, I am also glad that you have read this commentary on James and Hebrews. It is important that you understand that the roots of Christianity are Jewish. The Gospel is the fulfilment of God's promises to the Jewish patriarchs and of his prophecies throughout the Jewish Law and Jewish Scriptures. I hope that these two letters have helped you to understand why Paul describes the Christian Gospel as *"the hope of Israel"*, as *"the promise our twelve tribes are hoping to see fulfilled"*, and as the completion of *"what God promised our fathers"*.[1] Having understood this, you now face your own Lepanto moment. How will you respond to these two letters when they call you to surrender your life completely to Israel's God?

The majority of first-century Jews closed their ears to the message of these two letters. They greeted their Lepanto moment with the same stubbornness as Ali Pasha. They refused to believe that Jesus was their long-awaited Messiah and that he had given them a better glimpse of God, a better way of knowing

---

[1] Acts 13:32–33; 24:14–18; 26:6–7; 28:20–23.

God and a better way of living. As a result, many of them died in the fall of Jerusalem in 70 AD and most of the survivors were scattered. The Emperor Hadrian added insult to injury sixty years later by abolishing Judea as a Roman province and by building a temple to Jupiter on the former site of the Jewish Temple. Like the Ottoman navy under Ali Pasha, the majority of Jews paid a heavy price for refusing to acknowledge that something far better had come.

Nevertheless, many Jews did accept Jesus as their Messiah. It is easy to forget that Judaism was divided by the Christian Gospel and not united against it. Many priests gave up their livelihoods in the Temple to follow Jesus. Synagogue rulers resigned their positions and led an exodus of Jews to the church nearby. Even members of the Jewish Sanhedrin were converted and nailed their colours to the mast as followers of Jesus.[2] They responded wisely to their Lepanto moment. They recognized that, in Jesus, something far better than Old Covenant Judaism had come.

These Jewish Christians resisted the temptation to return to the synagogues in order to find a safe haven from persecution. Instead, they resolved to live and die to preach the Gospel message. Before he was beheaded for his testimony, Justin Martyr pleaded with the Jews to

> *Say no evil thing, my brothers, against Him who was crucified and do not treat scornfully the wounds through which everybody may be healed... Do not pour ridicule on the Son of God. Do not obey the Pharisee rabbis and do not scoff at the King of Israel, as the rulers of your synagogues teach you to do after your prayers.*[3]

Because men and women like Justin Martyr were willing to suffer in order to keep proclaiming the Gospel, large numbers

---

[2] Acts 6:7; 18:8; Luke 23:50–51; John 3:1; 19:38–39.

[3] Justin Martyr in chapter 137 of his *Dialogue with Trypho* (c.160 AD).

of Jews were converted alongside the Gentiles during the first century after these two letters were written.

So how about you? How will you respond to your own Lepanto moment? Will you put down this commentary and continue your life unchanged, or will you lay down everything to follow in the footsteps of these persecuted believers? If you are willing to live and die for the sake of Jesus' name, you will see the same advance of the Gospel in your own generation as in the century after James and Hebrews were written. The ancient Church historian Eusebius tells us that

> *The successors of the apostles... built up the foundations of the churches which had been planted everywhere by the apostles. They preached the Gospel more and more widely... They distributed their goods to the needy. Then, leaving their homes behind, they carried out the work of evangelists, filled with a desire to preach to those who had not yet heard the message of faith and to give them the written gospels inspired by God. Staying only to lay the foundations of the faith in one foreign place or another, they appointed others as pastors and entrusted them with the nurture of those who had recently been brought in. They themselves set off again for other lands and peoples with the grace and help of God, for a great many wonderful miracles were done through them by the power of God's Spirit which worked through them. As a result, at the first hearing whole multitudes eagerly embraced the worship of the Creator of the universe.*[4]

Jesus Christ is still the same today as he was when these two letters were written. Now it is your Lepanto moment. Don't put down this commentary until you have prayed to God and told him what you will do with the news that, in Jesus, something far better has come.

---

[4] Eusebius in his *Church History* (3.37.1–3).

# STRAIGHT TO THE HEART SERIES

TITLES AVAILABLE: OLD TESTAMENT

ISBN 978 0 85721 001 2

ISBN 978 0 85721 056 2

ISBN 978 0 85721 252 8

ISBN 978 0 85721 428 7

ISBN 978 0 85721 426 3

# STRAIGHT TO THE HEART SERIES

## TITLES AVAILABLE: NEW TESTAMENT

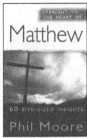

ISBN 978 1 85424 988 3

ISBN 978 0 85721 642 7

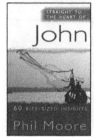

ISBN 978 0 85721 253 5

ISBN 978 1 85424 989 0

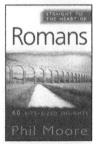

ISBN 978 0 85721 057 9

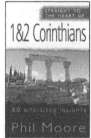

ISBN 978 0 85721 002 9

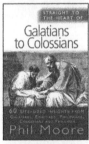

ISBN 978 0 85721 546 8

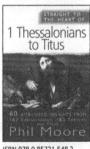

ISBN 978 0 85721 548 2

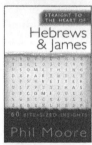

ISBN 978 0 85721 668 7

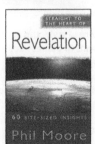

ISBN 978 1 85424 990 6

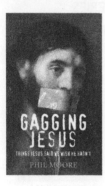

## GAGGING JESUS
**Things Jesus Said We Wish He Hadn't**
Phil Moore

If you ever suspected that Jesus wasn't crucified for acting like a polite vicar in a pair of socks and sandals, then this book is for you. Fasten your seatbelt and get ready to discover the real Jesus in all his outrageous, ungagged glory.

ISBN 978 0 85721 453 9

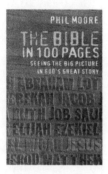

## THE BIBLE IN 100 PAGES
**Seeing the Big Picture in God's Great Story**
Phil Moore

Most people want to discover the message of the Bible but they find it hard to see the wood for the trees. That's why this book is so helpful. It will help you to see the big picture in God's great story. It will help you to read the entire Bible with fresh eyes.

ISBN 978 0 85721 551 2

## JESUS, RIGHT WHERE YOU WANT HIM
**Your biggest questions. His honest answers**
Phil Moore

Written in a punchy and easy-to-read style, this is a starting point for those who want to address key issues and get answers to the big questions, such as: Hasn't religion been the cause of appalling violence? Aren't Christians a bunch of hypocrites? And isn't the Bible full of myths and contradictions?

ISBN 978 0 85721 677 9